A DESK REFERENCE OF LEGAL TERMS FOR SCHOOL PSYCHOLOGISTS AND SPECIAL EDUCATORS

A Desk Reference of
Legal Terms for
School Psychologists
and Special Educators

By

DAVID P. HANSON, Ed.D.
James Madison University
Harrisonburg, Virginia

and

DAVID A. PENROD, J.D.
Hoover, Hoover, Penrod, and Davenport
Harrisonburg, Virginia

CHARLES C THOMAS · PUBLISHER
Springfield · Illinois · U.S.A.

Published and Distributed Throughout the World by
CHARLES C THOMAS • PUBLISHER
Bannerstone House
301-327 East Lawrence Avenue, Springfield, Illinois, U.S.A.

© *1980, by* CHARLES C THOMAS • PUBLISHER
ISBN 0-398-04015-X
Library of Congress Catalog Card Number: 79-26525

With THOMAS BOOKS *careful attention is given to all details of
manufacturing and design. It is the Publisher's desire to present books
that are satisfactory as to their physical qualities and artistic possibilities
and appropriate for their particular use.* THOMAS BOOKS *will be true
to those laws of quality that assure a good name and good will.*

Library of Congress Cataloging in Publication Data
Hanson, David P
    A desk reference of legal terms for school psychologists
and special educators.

    Bibliography: p.
    Includes index.
    1.   Handicapped children—Education—Law and legislation—
United States—Terms and phrases.   2.   Handicapped
children—Education—Law and legislation—United States.
I.   Penrod, David A., joint author.   II.   Title.
KF4210.A68H36   344'.73'0791   79-26525
ISBN 0-398-04015-X

Printed in the United States of America
W-2

To

HELEN and MARILYN
for their patience

PREFACE

IN RECENT YEARS, an avalanche of court cases and legislation has profoundly affected the rights of school children with special educational needs. School systems, and specialists working in those systems, have been the prime targets of these legally mandated changes. These changes have been quite comprehensive, and they are still taking place. They include the right to education, management of pupil records, unbiased psychological testing and assessment, mandatory special education, the use of less restrictive alternatives, and a variety of other concepts that fall under the broadening definitions of "due process" and "equal protection."

This desk reference is intended primarily as a handy guide for school psychologists and other specialists, who may be generally aware of the legal trends in their profession, but lack a convenient reference. The volume is divided into five sections. The first section provides a summary of court decisions that have had a national impact on school psychology and special education, some of which led directly to the enactment of PL 94-142. The second is a summary and description of this Act, which is described as the most comprehensive federal legislation ever enacted in this field. Third, the main section is a glossary of definitions of frequently encountered legal terms. The fourth section, the Appendix, includes The Education of All Handicapped Children Act, Part B—the final regulations that implement PL 94-142. The fifth, and final, section is a selected list of resources, which includes a bibliography of books, directories, newsletters, and periodicals and a list of organizations that serve the handicapped.

D.P.H.
D.A.P.

ACKNOWLEDGEMENT

A GREAT DEAL of time and preparation went into making this book possible. The authors would like to express deepest appreciation to the secretaries and typists and to students in the School Psychology Program at James Madison University, who contributed their time and ideas to its compilation. Without the hard work and dedicated effort of these persons this book would not have been possible.

CONTENTS

A DESK REFERENCE OF LEGAL TERMS FOR SCHOOL PSYCHOLOGISTS AND SPECIAL EDUCATORS

PART I

PRELUDE: SIGNIFICANT COURT CASES

P UBLIC LAW 94-142 (20 USC § 1401 et seq) is a major piece of legislation that deals comprehensively with the educational rights of children with special needs. That legislation did not develop in a vacuum. Rather, all of its significant individual parts were fashioned after a number of court decisions in many states. The authors of Public Law 94-142 pulled together the best aspects of litigation and used it to fashion their legislation.

Although it is difficult to cite exactly which cases had the most significant impact in the formulation of the legislation known as Public Law 94-142, scholars familiar with the area acknowledge that there are several major cases that impacted significantly upon this legislation. The most important fore-runner of the recent cases was *Brown v. Topeka Board of Education*. That landmark Supreme Court decision on civil rights struck down the previously acceptable "separate but equal" standard for education and mandated instead that blacks be integrated with whites in our nation's school systems. That same theory was applied in later special education cases by plaintiffs who urged that children with mental or physical disabilities could not be excluded from school or separated into segregated facilities if they were attending schools.

This section of the book summarizes the cases that had the most significant impact on the development of the law as it relates to the education of special children. Most of these cases were initiated in the early 1970s. Our judicial system is such that any particular case, i.e. *Mills* or *PARC*, became the law only in the particular state or jurisdiction in which the individual case was decided. Other school systems or State Departments of Education were not obligated to change their school systems or procedures to comply with these cases. The result, therefore, of the early decisions in cases like *PARC* and *Mills, Diana* and *Larry P.*, was a flurry of court activity in almost every state as groups representing special children sought to have set aside the outmoded standards that were used in their particular jurisdictions.

To some extent, the passage of Public Law 94-142 has made moot the large number of law suits which were pending or about to be brought around 1975, as for the first time the country now has a comprehensive policy dealing with the educational rights of special children. It is to be expected that most future litigation will not be of the *Mills* or *Diana* type, which sought to establish constitutional standards for the delivery of education to special children, but will be litigation that attempts to interpret or force compliance with Public Law 94-142.

Brown v. Board of Education, 347 U.S. 483, 74 S. Ct. 686 (1954)

In *Brown*, the United States Supreme Court decided the most far reaching case in the field of education during this century.

Prior to *Brown*, the racial segregation of students in public school was permitted if the racially separate facilities were approximately of equal quality. In this case the plaintiffs claimed that segregation was inherently unequal and that minority children were denied equal educational opportunities.

In noting the importance of education the court wrote, ". . . it is doubtful that any child may reasonably be expected to succeed in life if he is denied the opportunity of an education. Such an opportunity, where the state has undertaken to provide it, is a right which must be made available to all on equal terms." The court's holding was that "[s]eparate educational facilities are inherently unequal."

In the early 1970s, the Brown rationale was frequently used on behalf of children who needed special educational services. Often "special" children were segregated by classroom or school facility from the mainstream of the general student population. In its broadest sense, *Brown* mandates equal educational opportunities and prohibits this unnecessary segregation of special education children.

Hobson v. Hansen, 269 F. Supp. 401 (D.D.C. 1967)

This law suit was filed in federal court in the District of Columbia against Dr. Hansen, the Superintendent of Schools and the Board of Education. The suit sought relief from a system that discriminated not only on the basis of race, but also ability.

As part of their claim of racial discrimination, the plaintiff claimed and proved that the Board of Education used a "track system" to segregate students. The track system used aptitude tests standardized primarily on white, middle-class children to assign children to various educational tracks. Blacks and disadvantaged children were generally placed in lower tracks that perpetuated poor performance and continued assignment to the lower tracks, because of reduced curricula, the absence of remedial and compensatory education, and continuous inappropriate testing.

The court found that the inappropriate aptitude testing procedures were impermissable, and among other remedies, ordered an end to the self-perpetuating track system.

Several years later the *Hobsen* decision was frequently cited to combat similar placement systems which inappropriately used aptitude or IQ tests to justify unequal educational opportunities for special education students.

Pennsylvania Association for Retarded Children v. Commonwealth, 343 F. Supp. 279 (EDPA 1972)

This law suit, now commonly referred to as the *PARC* case, was filed as a class action in federal court in the eastern district of Pennsylvania. The plaintiffs were fourteen mentally retarded school children who sued on behalf of all similarly situated children in that Commonwealth.

The plaintiffs had been denied access to free public education under a state statutory scheme that excluded children from school who were "uneducable" or "unable to profit" from further education. The plaintiffs claimed that this denial violated their constitutional rights of due process and equal protection.

The primary defendants in *PARC* were the Commonwealth of Pennsylvania, its Departments of Education and Welfare, and several school districts. The defendants initially defended the suit on the basis that many mentally retarded children were so limited that they were indeed unable to benefit from the standard program of education offered by the school system.

During initial court hearings experts testified on behalf of the plaintiffs and supported their contention that they were capable of learning. This testimony convinced the primary defendants to change their position. As a result they reached a stipulated agreement with the plaintiffs, that was approved of and ordered into effect by the court.

The court's order in *PARC* recognized that all children are capable of "benefiting from a program of education and training." It required that all mentally retarded children in Pennsylvania between the ages of six and twenty-one be provided with a free public program of training and education appropriate to their individual capabilities. Additionally, the court set due process guidelines (a) requiring notice to parents when their child was being considered for special education placement, (b) establishing the right to a hearing on the placement decision, (c) permitting the parents to examine their child's records, and (d) providing the right to an independent educational evaluation.

The *PARC* case has had significant national impact, particularly when viewed in tandem with *Mills*. The case was the first significant challenge to school systems that systematically denied free public education to children with special education or training needs. The fact that the court's decision was based on a settlement among the parties did not significantly lessen the momentum generated by the case. *PARC* intensified an unrest among those parents whose handicapped children did not have access to public schools and it served as a model for subsequent law suits that attacked school systems that discriminated against special children.

Mills v. D.C. Board of Education, 348 F. Supp. 866
(D.D.C. 1972)

The *Mills* suit was a class action filed in federal court in the District of Columbia in the name of seven plaintiff children who sought a judicial declaration of their rights and an injunction restraining the Board of Education from infringing upon those rights.

The plaintiffs alleged that they, and the thousands of their class in the District which they represented, were denied public education because of mental, emotional, behavioral, or physical handicaps or deficiencies. They charged that the various forms of exclusion, expulsion, suspension, and reassignment used by the Board of Education denied them their constitutional rights of due process. The plaintiffs also complained that most of the children with special education needs had not even been identified by the school system.

Unlike the defendants in the *PARC* case, the D.C. Board of Education conceded they had a legal "duty to provide a publicly supported education to each resident of the District of Columbia who is capable of benefiting from such instruction." However, the defendants claimed that a lack of financial resources excused their failure to provide those educational opportunities.

Judge Waddy ordered the defendants to systematically identify all children in the District who required special education, to provide a free and suitable publicly supported education for all children regardless of their degree of mental, physcial or emotional impairment, and to refrain from using internal rules which interfered with the delivery of these mandated educational services.

With regard to the Board of Education's plea of inadequate financial resources, the judge held the following:

> . . . clearly the District of Columbia's interest in educating the excluded children clearly must outweigh its interest in preserving its financial resources. If sufficient funds are not available to finance all of the services and programs that are needed and desirable in the system, then the available funds must be expended equitably in such a manner that no child is entirely excluded from a publicly

supported education consistent with his needs and ability to benefit therefrom. The inadequacies of the District of Columbia Public School System, whether occasioned by insufficient funding or administrative inefficiency, certainly cannot be permitted to bear more heavily on the 'exceptional' child than on the normal child.

The *Mills* case had a forceful national impact, especially since it followed the *PARC* case so closely. Unlike *PARC*, which focused only upon mental retardation, *Mills* comprehensively applied to a much broader group of special children. Also, the court's opinion was the first one by a federal judge in a contested case in which the right to education for all children was based upon the application of a constitutional right. Together with *PARC*, *Mills* served as a springboard for dozens of lawsuits throughout the country that attacked the widespread practice of excluding special children from public schools. The case also provided an important impetus for corrective legislation designed to change unconstitutional educational practices directed toward special children.

Lebanks v. Spears, Civil No. 71-2897 (E.D. La. April 24, 1973)

This class action suit was brought against the the Orleans Parish School Board by several black school children classified as mentally retarded. The suit alleged that the defendants failed to provide "education or instruction" for some mentally retarded children, failed to place children beyond the age of thirteen years in special education programs, provided unequal or inadequate education for those children who had been classified as mentally retarded, and made the diagnosis of mental retardation arbitrarily, without appropriate standards, and without advising the children or their parents of their right to a hearing concerning the classification.

The case was settled without a trial with the entry of a consent order that provided for the evaluation of and placement in a free public education program all children who are mentally retarded. Also provided for was the implementation of due process standards in the evaluation and classification process, the use of individualized evaluation and development programs for each child, and periodic review of those programs, and the implementation of the philosophy of the least restrictive alternative. Perhaps one of the most innovative aspects of the court order is that the defendants obligated themselves to make education and training opportunities available to individuals "over twenty-one (21) years of age who were not provided educational services when children. . . ."

Larry P. v. Riles, Civil No. C-71-2270, 343 F. Supp. 1306 (N.D. Cal., 1972), affirmed 502 F.2d 963 (9th Cir. 1974)

Larry P. was a class action suit brought by several black school children in California. The thrust of their complaint was their inappropriate placement in special education classes.

The students claimed they were incorrectly placed in classes for the mentally retarded on the basis of inaccurate and misused IQ tests. Specifically, the plaintiffs alleged that aptitude tests were biased toward a white, middle-class culture which in turn ignored their own unique learning experiences. The result was a disproportionate number of blacks in special education classes, who were stigmatized by the inaccurate placements.

The defendants, who included local and state school officials and school board members, defended the use of IQ tests, stating that even though the tests may be racially biased, they were the best means currently available for classification of mentally retarded children.

The presiding judge found as a matter of fact that IQ tests were culturally biased, that classes for the educably mentally retarded (EMR) were racially imbalanced, and that the school system was unable to show that IQ tests were rationally related to the purpose of assigning black students to special education classes. Noting that incorrect placement in special education classes for the mentally retarded can cause irreparable injury, the court held that equal protection of the law prohibited the placement of black students in EMR classes primarily on the basis of IQ test scores.

Larry P. was a landmark case with implications for testing, classification, and placement procedures in education. It has contributed directly to the practice of unbiased, pluralistic assessment of student performance, which should be based on a comprehensive battery of measurement devices, including an evaluation of the child's adaptive behavior.

Diana v. State Board of Education, Civil No. C-70-37 (N.C. Cal. Jan. 7, 1970 and June 18, 1973)

This class action law suit was initiated by nine Mexican American school children on behalf of those who had already been placed in classes for the mentally retarded and any preschool children who might be placed in those classes in the future. The defendants were officials of both the Soledad Elementary School District and the State of California.

The thrust of the plaintiffs' claim was that the defendants used highly verbal, culturally biased and improperly standardized English IQ tests for the classification and special placement of Mexican American school children. The result was a disproportionately high number of Mexican American children who were classified and placed as mentally retarded. The plaintiffs claimed that the inappropriate use of the standardized tests perpetuated an inappropriate educational assignment for the children and led to irreparable injury because they would fall academically further and further behind their peers.

By stipulation between the parties, the Federal court entered an Order which in part provided the following:

(1) all children whose primary language was other than English would in the future be tested in both their primary language and in English;

(2) Mexican American and Chinese children already placed in classes for the mentally retarded would be retested;

(3) efforts would be made to channel previously misplaced school children into appropriate regular school program;

(4) a new intelligence quotient instrument using Mexican American children as a standard would be developed and used for future testing of Mexican American children.

Both the State Department of Education and the Court obligated itself to review for several years the progress that was made and the implementation of the consent order.

Goss v. Lopez, 419 U.S. 565, 95 S. Ct. 729 (1976)

Following a school disturbance in Columbus, Ohio, Lopez and some classmates were summarily suspended. The method in which the suspension was handled was questioned in court, and the case eventually was decided by the United States Supreme Court.

As Lopez was suspended without the benefit of a hearing, he claimed his constitutional right of due process had been violated. The court agreed and held that even for school suspensions of short duration, students are entitled to be notified of the charges against them and an opportunity to explain or rebut the charges; longer suspensions or expulsions require a more formal hearing.

The court's rationale was that education is an important benefit that cannot be removed capriciously, even for a short period of time. Even though the *Goss* decision applied to all school children, it had particular benefits for "special" children, who were frequently excluded from school by arbitrary methods of suspension and expulsion.

PART II

PL 94-142: THE EDUCATION OF ALL HANDICAPPED CHILDREN ACT 1975

INTRODUCTORY COMMENTS

The Importance of Decision-Makers

IT IS THE PERCEPTION of the public in general and parents specifically that professionals working in schools are in a pivotal position to make significant life decisions about children. For instance, school psychologists often contribute significantly to key decisions about pupils.

The awakening of parents to the importance of the role of school psychologists in the lives of their children has led to considerable preoccupation with legal-ethical matters. Hence, the functions of the psychologist, such as assessment procedures, classification, and special placements, have become a major focus of both litigation and legislation. Litigation and legislation are intended to regulate performance and also to upgrade special educational programs and related services for all handicapped children. Other professionals in the schools are increasingly coming under the same public scrutiny.

Federal Aid

The history of strong federal involvement in major legislation and funding for the handicapped is limited largely to recent years.

Direct federal support for public education was somewhat limited prior to 1958, when the advent of Sputnik, the Russian space satellite, promptly caused a change in attitude by the Congress of the United States. The National Defense Education Act (NDEA) was enacted by Congress in an effort to improve and increase quickly the nation's scientific community. Thus, the first massive federal aid to elementary and secondary education was created.

Prior to 1960, federal legislation for the handicapped was sporadic and related to specific categories of children, e.g. the deaf or the blind. Between 1960 and 1970 several important pieces of legislation were enacted by the Congress in an effort to provide more adequate programs for the handicapped.

The Elementary and Secondary Education Act of 1965 (ESEA), part of which provided funding for disadvantaged children in state operated or supported schools, helped lay the foundation for the landmark 1975 legislation, The Education of all Handicapped Children Act, PL 94-142 (EHA).

In 1966, amendments to Title VI of the ESEA provided grants to states to initiate, expand, and improve educational programs for the handicapped. The amendments later became recognized as the first version of the Education of all Handicapped Children Act, though not so named. This legislation also created the Bureau of Education for the Handicapped, and a National Advisory Committee for Handicapped Children.

In 1967, ESEA was again amended to expand programs for the handicapped, specifically providing for regional resources centers.

In 1968, the Congress specified that 10 percent of each state's allotment of funds under the Vocational Education Act would have to be used for the vocational education of handicapped persons.

Further amendments and extensions were made to the ESEA in 1974 under PL 93-380, and for the first time a specific title of the act was given as the Education of the Handicapped Amendments of 1974. Part B of the act principally dealt with changes related to appropriations, funding, state plan requirements, grants for regional programs, centers and services, personnel training, and research.

In 1975 there were additional amendments to PL 93-380 which, increasingly, has been hailed as the Bill of Rights for the Handicapped. PL 94-142, the Education of all Handicapped

Children Act of 1975, extends and amends the 1974 legislation with great precision and specificity. The 1975 Act, EHA, or PL 94-142, does not replace previous legislation. It is a revision and extension of Part B of the Education of the Handicapped Act of 1974.

With the passage of these two pieces of legislation, the Congress provided a dramatic increase in the funding of basic state grants programs for special education. The 1975 EHA legislation also included specific guidelines for the protection of the rights of exceptional children and their parents. In effect, the Act consolidated previous legislation and strengthened Part B of PL 93-380.

The Socio-Political Atmosphere

The laws enacted since 1960 did not develop in isolation, or apart from the ebb and flow of American society, or as an altruistic expression of congressional fervor to help the handicapped.

To gain greater understanding of the development of the present national stance about the handicapped, one must recall and examine three related movements spanning roughly the same recent historical period of time, and culminating in the development of this landmark federal legislation.

The Civil Rights Movement

In 1954 the landmark school integration case of *Brown v. Board of Education* (347 U.S. 483), reversed the 1896 court decision of *Plessy v. Ferguson* (163 U.S. 537), and helped uncork the dammed up backlog of civil injustice. The civil rights movement had grown out of a period of racial strife in which blacks and other disadvantaged citizens struggled for their rights over a long period of time. The contemporary civil rights movement was born with the *Brown* decision. The civil rights movement, which focused initially on racial issues, spawned an awareness among many people that the courts could be used to help change previous wrongs. One particular group that became increasingly aware of their rights were parents and advocates of the handicapped. These people learned that courts could and would redress their grievances, and they often used group action to accomplish their aims.

Lobby Groups

Secondly, and partly as a result of the civil rights issues and court actions, strong lobby groups developed for the handicapped. Parents, some professionals, school personnel, and lawyers joined to mount an attack against prejudicial school policies concerning the handicapped. Such groups as the National Association for Retarded Citizens, the Association for Children with Learning Disabilities, and the Council for Exceptional Children became influential. This early phase of the movement gained momentum in the early seventies when initial landmark court cases declared for the first time the rights of handicapped school children. The flood of court cases that followed directly contributed to the development of federal legislation in the form of PL 93-380, and PL 94-142. Thus lobby groups were paramount in the move toward litigation and legislation.

Litigation

The third contributing factor in the development of such legislation was the increasing trend of citizens, often encouraged and supported by the various lobby groups, to use the courts to correct their grievances.

In its lead article April 10, 1978, *Time* magazine stated

> These developments, litigation, legislation, and regulations have brought about a virtual revolution in American society: an all-pervasive invasion by courts, laws and administrative agencies into areas that had previously been ruled by custom, practice, or plain old-fashioned private accommodation.

The article attests to this development by citing the rise in the number of lawyers in the United States, an increase from 296,000 in 1963 to 462,000 at present. The increased tendency to go to the courts for remedy or relief of one's grievances was fanned not only by the civil rights movement and lobby groups, but also by rising general awareness of a new means of redress, by resentments about an unjust war in Vietnam, and by the whole panorama of societal unrest. The American people seemed to be demanding justice by litigation.

Three major factors—the civil rights movement, the tendency of public lobby groups to turn to the courts, and the growth in public awareness of the effectiveness of litigation—have given legislators cause to sit down and hammer out laws that address special education issues. The Education for all Handicapped Children Act of 1975 is the result.

THE EDUCATION OF ALL HANDICAPPED CHILDREN ACT, 1975

Introductory comments of the Act state:

"There are more than eight million handicapped children in the United States today"; and their needs are not being fully met.

"More than half of the handicapped children in the United States do not receive appropriate educational services that would enable them to have full equality of opportunity."

"One million" handicapped children are "excluded entirely from the public school system and will not go through the educational process with their peers."

Many others are not "having a successful educational experience because their handicaps are undetected."

State and local educational agencies have responsibility not only for the areas noted above, but also for improving teacher training and instructional methods. One aim of PL 94-142 is to provide local educational agencies (LEA) and state educational agencies (SEA) with resources necessary to manage and improve overall conditions for the handicapped in schools. The Act reinforces guarantees enacted in earlier legislation and expands on them so that virtually every handicapped child will receive special education and related services.

Perhaps the most salient feature of PL 94-142 is that it is law. Its policies and provisions *must* be carried out. The entire Act is available in the Appendix, and the reader should refer to it for elaboration on specific topics. Subpart A defines the general term *handicapped,* then defines eleven types of handicapping conditions. Other terms such as *native language, parent,* and *related services* are also defined in Subpart A.

It should be noted that *special education* is defined as ". . . specially designed instruction, at no cost to the parent, to meet the unique needs of a handicapped child, including classroom instruction, instruction in physical education, home instruction, and instruction in hospitals and institutions." Related services, vocational education and physical education are included, if these consist of specially designed instruction to meet the unique needs of handicapped children (Sec. 121 a.14).

Most professionals working in schools will be concerned with Subparts C and E, which deal with services and procedural safeguards, respectively. Other parts describe the purposes (Part A), plans and applications for state and local special education programs (Part B), private schools (Part D), state administration (Part F), and information about funding and reporting (Part G).

The major features of the Act include the following:

- The right to a free appropriate public education for all handicapped children.
- Use of the least restrictive teaching or training environment for pupils.
- Due process procedures for children and their parents.
- Non-discriminatory evaluation procedures.
- Individualized educational programs.
- Specified placement procedures.
- Confidentiality of information and record keeping.
- Related services.

Free Appropriate Public Education

The purpose of the Act is stated as follows: "To assure that all handicapped children have available to them a free appropriate public education which includes special education and related services to meet their unique needs" (Sec. 121 a.1). Special education must be provided at public expense, under public supervision and direction, and without charge. Transportation and corrective or supportive services, "including speech pathology and audiology, psychological services, physical and occupational therapy, recreation, and counseling services," must also be provided as required to assist a handicapped child to benefit from special education. Appropriate education then includes whatever is deemed necessary for an individual child to allow him or her to obtain a public education equal to that available to other students at the preschool, elementary, and secondary levels.

Annual program plans are required to show that there are policies in effect that insure that all handicapped children have these rights within the age ranges and time frame given—ages three through eighteen not later than September 1, 1978, and ages three through twenty-one not later than September 1, 1980 (Sec. 121 a.122). Each Local Educational Agency (LEA) is responsible for identifying, locating and evaluating all handicapped children who reside within the jurisdiction of that agency. The LEA is also responsible for determining which children are receiving special education and which are not.

The Least Restrictive Alternative

The concept of the least restrictive alternative, or environment, provides and insures handicapped children the same opportunities and facilities as regular children. Special children generally benefit most from services and/or placement as close to their peers as possible. The concept and process of providing the least restrictive alternative is often called "mainstreaming." It is also a concept in keeping with basic democratic principles, namely, that segregation is detrimental to equal opportunity, which should be available to all persons.

In some instances isolating a handicapped child away from regular classes, i.e. in a self-contained special classroom, may be detrimental to that child. In any event, under the concept of the least restrictive alternative, such placement of a handicapped child may not be made without providing due process safeguards for that child. In other instances, placement of a child in a self-contained classroom may be exactly what the child needs for an education most appropriate for him or her.

The "cascade" approach to special education is also reflected in the least restrictive approach to handicapped persons. First noted by Maynard Reynolds and later adopted as policy by the Council for Exceptional Children, the cascade system specifies types of service delivery for handicapped persons ranging from placement in regular classes in the neighborhood school to placement in total care settings such as residential centers or institutions. The handicapped person should be placed in the least restricted environment, which is at the same time most appropriate for his or her needs. Obviously those students with mildest handicaps will most likely be near or at the bottom of the "cascade" of available services, i.e., mostly in regular classes. Those students who are most severely handicapped will need more specialized and comprehensive services in special settings. In each case, however, the emphasis is on placing the person in the *least* restrictive setting, not the *most* restrictive, and proper attention is always devoted to due process procedures in such placements. Inherent in the cascade model of special education is the belief that the handicapped pupil should be returned as soon as possible to the next lower appropriate, or most nearly normal, level of special education.

Due Process

Under the rules and regulations of PL 94-142, the concept of due process is divided into an enormous array of significant topics. Most of these due process provisions existed previously under PL 93-380, but have been elaborated in PL 94-142. Beginning with "prior notice" and "informed consent," the guidelines lay out step-by-step procedures to be followed by school personnel working with children and their parents. The procedures are designed primarily to protect the rights of both children and their parents, but some due process safeguards may also serve to protect school personnel. The guidelines under PL 94-142 cover topics such as notice and informed consent, access to records, independent educational evaluation, evaluation procedures, individual educational programs, impartial due process hearings, hearing rights, appeals and procedures for impartial review, the least restrictive alternative, and confidentiality of information.

The concept of the least restrictive environment has already been described above; evaluations and management of confidentiality will be described in a later section.

The major portions of the due process regulations are described as follows:

(The reader may wish to refer to the Appendix for the complete text of PL 94-142.)

PRIOR NOTICE AND PARENT CONSENT. Parents must be fully informed of all information relevant to the activity for which their consent is sought, and this written information must be given in the parents' native language. Regulations about prior notice state that the notice to parents should provide full information about the purposes, procedures, and possible outcomes of any work undertaken with their child.

INDEPENDENT EDUCATIONAL EVALUATION. The parents of a handicapped child have the right to obtain an independent educational evaluation of their child from a source outside the school. The school is obligated to provide the parents with information about where to obtain such an evaluation. The independent evaluation may be at public expense, i.e. paid for by the schools, if the parent disagrees with an evaluation already obtained by the public agency. If, after a hearing, it is determined that the school's evaluation is appropriate, the parents may continue with an independent educational evaluation, but not at public expense. Evaluation findings may be submitted at their child's hearing. Hearing officers themselves may request an independent educational evaluation. Specifications about the independent examiner and the evaluation criteria are also included in the regulations.

IMPARTIAL DUE PROCESS HEARINGS. If either party, parents or school officials, refuses to agree to a request for services for the child, the dispute may be resolved by an impartial due process hearing. Thus, either the parent or the agency may initiate the hearing procedures. The PL 94-142 guidelines are explicit in regard to appropriate steps to be followed to safeguard the rights of all parties. Fairness, impartiality and objectivity are emphasized throughout the hearing regulations. Hearing rights include the following: advisement by counsel, presentation and confrontation of witnesses and evidence, cross examination, and discovery. Verbatim records are kept and (along with written findings of facts and decisions) made available to participants, after personally identifiable data is deleted.

During any hearing or complaint action the child involved in the action must remain in his or her present educational placement, unless agreement is reached otherwise.

Many states have inserted the intermediate step of mediation between school conference and the formal hearing. Mediation is an additional informal attempt at conflict resolution prior to moving to the formal hearing.

Evaluation Procedures

Evaluation procedures have come under considerable scrutiny as a result of some professionally questionable practices in the past. Some school psychologists, particularly, have found themselves the targets of much criticism and some litigation in the past. Consequently, specific and stringent regulations are included concerning testing instruments as well as practices. The law specifies that tests and evaluation materials must be selected and administered so as not to be racially or culturally discriminatory. If necessary, attempts should be made to insure that evaluation is made in the child's native language or other mode of communication, unless it is clearly not feasible to do so. Those using tests and other evaluation materials must insure that such instruments (a) are valid for the specific purpose for which they are used, (b) are given by trained persons, (c) are tailored to assess specific areas of educational need, not just general ability, (d) are administered so as to insure and reflect the best work of the child, not just deficits (unless assessment of the deficits is being sought also), and (e) include a battery of instruments, not just a single test.

The evaluation must be conducted by a multidisciplinary team that includes a teacher or specialist in the area of the child's suspected deficit. The evaluation must be comprehensive, covering all areas related to the suspected deficit. These areas for possible evaluation are specified as health, vision, hearing, social and emotional status, general intelligence, academic performance, communicative status, and motor abilities. Generally, state regulations interpret this provision to cover four broad evaluation areas: health and medical; psychological; educational; and sociocultural.

The Individualized Educational Program

The individualized educational program (IEP) is gaining increasing attention as one of the most significant requirements of PL 94-142; it is this feature that truly insures an appropriate education for the handicapped child. It is the IEP that becomes the mutually agreed upon contract among all parties for the benefit of the child. Without a clearly specified educational plan for the handicapped child, some school officials may not feel compelled to meet fully the educational needs of their pupils; in some instances, too, parents may become fully responsive to their child's special education needs. It is the IEP that attempts to hold both parents and school professionals accountable for their work.

The term IEP means a written statement for the handicapped child, developed and implemented according to the following guidelines:

a. There must be an IEP for each handicapped child at the beginning of each school year.
b. The State Education Agencies have the responsibility to insure that IEPs are available for all children placed in public agencies or private schools and facilities.
c. The IEP must be in effect before special education and related services are provided to the child, and it must be implemented as soon as possible after its need is determined. There can be no undue delays in implementation.
d. The public agency, e.g., the local education agency (LEA), is responsible for initiating and conducting meetings to develop, review, and revise an IEP for a handicapped child. Each child's IEP must be reviewed periodically, at least once a year, to revise the program if necessary.

e. Participants in each IEP meeting include the following: a representative of the public agency (other than the child's teacher) qualified in the area of special education; the child's teacher; one or both parents; the child, when appropriate; and other persons at the discretion of the parents or agency.

f. A member of the evaluation team must participate in the IEP meeting when the child has been evaluated for the first time, or alternatively, someone conversant with the evaluation procedures and results must be present.

g. Specifications for notifying parents about the IEP meeting are clear. The notice to the parents must be given in ample time for them to attend, and the meeting must be at a mutually convenient time and place. The notice must include the purpose, time, location, and those attending the meeting. If parents cannot attend, or refuse to, the school must have a record of its attempts to include the parents, e.g., letters, telephone calls, and/or home visits.

h. The public agency must make every effort to insure that parents understand the proceedings. A translator must be present if necessary, and the agency must provide the parents with a copy of the IEP, if requested.

i. The IEP must include a statement of the child's present levels of performance and of annual goals for the child, including short-term instructional objectives. It must include a statement of the specific special education and related services to be provided for the child, and the extent to which the child will be able to participate in regular programs. Moreover, projected dates for initiation of services, the expected duration of the services, and means and schedules for evaluating the services must be included. These evaluation procedures must seek objectively to determine whether the short-term goals are being achieved. This IEP review must take place at least on an annual basis. The regulations also apply to those handicapped children placed in private schools or public institutions, and the responsibility for compliance with these regulations rests with the LEA.

Placement Procedures

The concepts enunciated herein are described in PL 94-142 under the topic Least Restrictive Environment, but the principles deal with placement practices.

The placement procedures show most clearly the overlap with other sections of the Act, for this section (Sec. 121 a.533) refers to evaluations, the least restrictive environment, and the IEP. Placement procedures and the principle of the least restrictive environment are so similar in concept and content that they can be treated as one topic. The regulations for placement procedures state the following:

". . . each public agency shall: (1) Draw upon information from a variety of sources, including aptitude and achievement tests, teacher recommendations, physical conditions, social or cultural background, and adaptive behavior."

The placement decision must be made by a group of persons who are knowledgeable not only about the child, but also about the evaluation data and the placement options. If it is determined the child needs special education and related services, the decision must be made in compliance with the regulations about the least restrictive environment.

Each handicapped child's placement must be determined at least annually, and must be based on the IEP for that child. The placement of the child should be as close to the child's home as possible. To the maximum extent appropriate, handicapped children are to be educated with children who are not handicapped, and the removal of handicapped children from regular programs must occur only when the handicapping condition is such that education in the regular classroom cannot take place satisfactorily, even with the use of supplementary aids and services. However, it must be remembered that in some individual instances it may be most appropriate for the child to be placed in a self-contained special classroom.

Each public agency, such as the LEA, is responsible to insure that a continuum of alternative placements is available for handicapped children. (This continuum is the cascade model of service described in Part B, 2, The Least Restrictive Alternative.) The continuum of alternative placements include: instruction in regular classes, special classes, special schools, home instruction, and instruction in hospitals and institutions. In conjunction with regular class placement, supplementary services such as the use of resource rooms or itinerant instruction are also included. It is important to note that, in selecting the least restrictive environment for placement of the handicapped child, ". . . consideration is given to any potential harmful effect on the child or on the quality of services which he or she needs."

Two points best summarize the concepts and practices of placement and the least restrictive environment:

a. Placement decisions must be made on an individual basis, taking into consideration the needs of the individual handicapped child.

b. Each agency must have various alternative placements available to each handicapped child.

Confidentiality and Record Keeping

The rules and regulations of PL 94-142 dealing with confidentiality and records are designed chiefly to protect the interests of children and their parents. While confidentiality is not the major thrust of this law, the recommended procedures for management of records and freedom of information insure children's and parents' rights to privacy, and therefore, to confidentiality. Not only are privacy rights protected, but parents and children are also guaranteed full disclosure of pertinent personal information by providing them access to such records.

Rules and regulations pertaining to access of information are fairly explicit. Parents are allowed to see any education record relating to their children. The LEA must respond to a parental request for access to their child's record "without unnecessary delay," especially before events such as IEP meetings, placement committee meetings, or hearings. Parents may request explanations and interpretations of the records.

Parents may request the school to amend or expunge information in the child's record, if it is misleading or inaccurate or if it violates privacy rights. If the LEA refuses such a request, parents must be informed of their right to request a hearing. Pending the outcome of the hearing, the school either amends the child's record, or allows the parents to insert a statement of disagreement with the records of the agency. This parental statement must thereafter be disclosed to anyone to whom the agency grants access rights. Each agency is required to maintain a record of persons obtaining access to educational records. This record of access need not include parents of the child or authorized employees of the LEA, but, for all others, it must include the name of the person, date, and purpose of access.

Probably the most important feature of the law protecting confidentiality is the requirement that schools must obtain parental consent to allow any unauthorized person access to their child's record. There are other safeguards built into the regulations, e.g., agency designation of a person who is responsible for management of records and protection of confidentiality, rules about the proper destruction of records, and provision for training school staff about proper use of records.

Related Services

The PL 94-142 rules and regulations about related services are of special significance, particularly to school psychologists, speech pathologists and audiologists, remedial reading teachers, learning disability specialists, and others fulfilling supportive roles in schools. The term *related services* is broadly defined to include developmental, remedial, and other supportive services designed to benefit handicapped children, including transportation. It includes physical and occupational therapy, recreation, early identification, counseling, and diagnostic medical services. School health services, school social workers and parent counseling and training are also included. Each of these terms is defined in detail; for example, *psychological services* is defined as follows:

  a. Administering psychological and educational tests, and other assessment procedures.
  b. Interpreting assessment results.

   c. Obtaining, integrating, and interpreting information about child behavior and conditions relating to learning.

   d. Consulting with other staff members in planning school programs to meet the special needs of children as indicated by psychological tests, interviews, and behavioral evaluations.

   e. Planning and managing a program of psychological services, including psychological counseling for children and parents.

Comments in the rules and regulations note that the list of supportive services is not exhaustive, and that all related services noted need not apply to the case of each individual child.

The legislation has major implications for support services personnel working with handicapped students and their parents. Particularly those specialists who work most closely and frequently with handicapped children—special educators, school psychologists, social workers, guidance counselors, speech therapists, reading specialists, nurses—will be greatly affected by this legislation. By far the most significant features of PL 94-142 for these specialists deal with due process regulations, individualized educational plans for each child, early identification programs, the interrelationship of special services, and record keeping. Other features of the law—allocation of funds, application, research, and the like—will chiefly be the responsibility of administrators.

IMPLICATIONS OF PL 94-142 FOR SCHOOL SPECIALISTS

A Critique of the Law

The most important implications resulting from this comprehensive legislation are reserved for the handicapped students themselves. These individuals will benefit most from its sweeping mandates for improved special education and related services. The law not only broadens the scope of special educational activities, but it also provides national standards of quality for special education and related services.

Procedures and activities of persons involved in special education, regular education, and related services are spelled out with precision and specificity heretofore unknown in the field. In this respect it is landmark legislation. The explicit rules and regulations are a direct offshoot of years of court actions in education and special education, as well as in the several related fields of civil rights, mental health, and juvenile justice.

Many school professionals are already functioning in ways mandated by PL 94-142, and have been for years, simply because such functioning represents their best efforts and performance. For them little adjustment will be necessary.

For those school psychologists and other professionals who are accustomed to more traditional modes of casework, there are significant changes on the horizon. For example, in the past, speech therapists or learning disability teachers took cases referred by teachers through their principals. School psychologists or social workers accepted referrals of pupils via the same route. For these persons, the referral procedure will be dramatically changed to include parent conferences before proceeding with desired casework with their child because parents' informed consent and participation in all activities related to their child is mandated throughout these regulations. Specialists who have worked very nearly independently of all others will be drawn into teamwork roles in which they must communicate and interact cooperatively with each other and with parents. A few professionals are steeped in the tradition that they represent the ultimate authority in their field. They have assumed the role that they alone hold the secret key, the only answer to the child's problem. These persons will need to become more flexible in their approach or they will be at constant odds with the letter and spirit of PL 94-142, namely, that parents have a right to participate in important life decisions about their children, and that others must also make significant contributions to such decisions.

The Education of All Handicapped Children Act should bring about important specific role changes for almost all persons working with handicapped children. The single most important requisite for all will be an understanding of the importance of clear communication and cooperation on behalf of children. This communication and cooperation will be made formal by official screening and placement committees, by established procedures for parent conferences, hearings, and record keeping. The informal procedures of previous years will diminish, yet the need for all professionals, parents, teachers, and administrators to understand each other and work together will increase. School professionals will be forced to work harder to maintain positive home-school relations to enhance their work. Parents must not only be included in the referral procedure by means of informed consent, but they must also be apprised of each step taken along the way with their child. They have the right to review records and to request hearings. They may contribute to the written individualized educational plan for their child, so the need for teamwork among all those around the child is paramount. Recalcitrance and reticence on the part of school officials will diminish, but in some instances, unfortunately, only after threat of litigation or actual court action.

In instances where the professional—a school psychologist, for example—is designated as the case manager or coordinator for a team working with a handicapped child, it will be necessary for that person to operate as a child advocate in order to fulfill the rules and regulations established by PL 94-142. This may represent a significant role change as well as the potential for considerable professional conflict. Formerly, many school psychologists and others operated as advocates for their *employers,* i.e., the school district and its administrators, sometimes to the detriment of the handicapped child. In some such instances, for example, it was not uncommon for the school psychologist to recommend exclusion of a handicapped child from school, or inappropriate placement of a child in a special class—perhaps in order for the school district to receive a larger portion of categorical state aid. Such activities will diminish not only because they are recognized today as unprofessional practices, but also because PL 94-142 has built in specific safeguards against such malpractices.

Consequently, it will be to the advantage of all professionals to have their roles and functions clearly defined and understood by administrators and parents. The school social worker, for instance, is compelled to tell parents of the purpose of the data gathering interview and the possible subsequent consequences of findings that their child may be in need of special educational services. Or the remedial reading teacher may be required to open her records for parental perusal, perhaps against the wishes of the school principal. The school psychologist may have to demonstrate that the psychological evaluation was unbiased. The school administrators and support service professionals should both have a clear understanding of and agreement about this aspect of PL 94-142, namely that their primary obligation is now to the client, i.e., the pupil and parent, to serve their *best* interests. Fortunately for both school administrators and professionals working with handicapped students, there are relatively few such instances in which the interests of the child and parent are at odds with the best interests of the school.

The role of case manager, which the school psychologist and other professionals sometimes assume, will take on new dimensions. With greater frequency, the person who is assigned responsibility for integrating the various facets of casework will also be called upon to do more legwork. More communication will be required among parents, teachers, administrators, and other professionals involved in the child's case. More phone calls will be involved, more reports written, more interviews held, and more plans developed. Obviously, relatively minor cases will not be too complicated and complex to handle in terms of the data gathering and coordinating, but with youngsters who present serious problems, extensive coordinated teamwork will be essential to fulfill the requirements of PL 94-142. Such comprehensive casework will require carefully detailed professional efforts by all the persons working with handicapped children.

To implement the mandates of the Education for all Handicapped Children Act, the comprehensive case study technique will be developed more fully. Not only will it include an assessment battery of unbiased instruments covering several facets of psychological testing, but it will also include observations of children in classrooms as well as in natural settings, interviews with parents and teachers, evaluation of adaptive behaviors, and the like. Further, such comprehensive evaluations may need to be conducted in the child's native language. In each instance of such assessment, first consideration is given to placement of the child in the least restrictive alternative, the regular class if possible.

Still another important impact of PL 94-142 will be in the area of in-service education. Child study teams and support personnel in schools will be asked to conduct classes, give workshops and institutes, and hold discussion groups about handicapped children and the services they provide for them. Regular classroom teachers will need more knowledge and understanding of their handicapped students and the services available to help them. Professionals such as reading teachers and speech therapists will spend more time serving as consultants to classroom teachers, and some of this consultation will take the form of in-service education programs for teachers.

The professionals themselves will need to upgrade their expertise in areas which receive special attention under PL 94-142. The area of assessment is undergoing great change with some de-emphasis on traditional test batteries. There is a strong pressure for multicultural pluralistic assessment, and a focus on new evaluation procedures, e.g., adaptive behavior rating scales. Early identification and screening of young handicapped children and early childhood education of the handicapped child is receiving a great deal of emphasis.

The individualized educational plan is also receiving great attention, causing considerable emphasis to be placed on curriculum materials and programs in all disability categories and at all levels.

Two other features of PL 94-142 deserve specific mention because of their potential impact on professionals in the schools. The law gives attention to gathering data for research purposes. Schools, and the professionals working in them, will be held accountable for accurate record keeping and for reporting results of their casework. It appears this feature will differentiate this legislation significantly from previous laws in that this legislation requires that data shall be gathered for research.

Finally, it can be anticipated that PL 94-142 will cause a considerable increase in paper work demanded of school personnel. More record keeping of all transactions will be necessary. Individualized educational plans will require more time; minutes of committee meetings should be kept; annual reviews of cases must be completed. There must be a system for management of records. These increasing demands on professionals' time will necessitate smaller caseloads, more careful work, and more staff to do the work.

It is important to note that PL 94-142 has long-range consequences. Initial implementation of its rules and regulations will be uneven across the states with some regions already in full compliance, while others are striving to meet its initial standards. There are controversial issues about the law, i.e., financing the increase in services, the roles of specialists, noncompliance, and its management. There will be some "hardening of the arteries" by a few persons who show recalcitrance about full compliance. The "taxpayer revolt" may cause some slowdown in implementation of services. There may be some backlash or increased rigidity about existing standards for classroom learning and behavior, e.g., witness the increased emphasis on competency tests for graduation, or the apparent rise in suspension or expulsion of some pupils. But in the long run, educators and specialists *must* work through these difficulties and comply with the law.

The Education of All Handicapped Children Act is a full service mandate with significant new controls in it. It requires increased cooperation between the home and school, and more enlightened and involved parents. Over the long range, the law will vastly improve services to handicapped children in schools, provide a broad base of data for considerable research, and perhaps lead to an increase in litigation until the parameters of the act are fully defined and complied with. The law mandates change for pupils, parents, and professionals. It is a law that requires a high level of professional competency from those working with handicapped children. It is designed to help and correct those who are doing marginal work, those who are reticent to meet the new mandates, or those who function below an expected level of competency.

The years immediately following the enactment of PL 94-142 have been marked by an array of reactions from professionals as well as the public in general. Some say the law is too broad and comprehensive; others decry the impending expenses. Many persons seek further clarification of its multitude of specific regulations. Still others are "doubting Thomases" who say it will never work because of its magnitude. Regardless of these responses to it, the law is heralded by many others as the ultimate expression of democracy in action and as the true embodiment of equal rights legislation, in this case for handicapped persons.

PART III

LEGAL TERMS: A GLOSSARY

abate   to reduce, diminish, or nullify

abet   to encourage, stir up, or excite another to commit a crime

ability grouping   the school practice of assigning children of approximately equal levels of achievement to the same class for all or nearly all instruction. Assignment is often made on the basis of an IQ test, and/or achievement tests

abrogate   to annul, repeal, or destroy an order or rule issued by a subordinate authority

abstract   a condensed history or summary, a synopsis

acceleration clause   a provision in a document requiring that upon the occurrence of a stated event, the time for performance shall be advanced

accessory   one who contributes or aids, such as an accessory to a crime—**accessory before the fact**: one who, being absent at the time a crime is committed, procured, counseled, or commended another to commit it—**accessory after the fact**: one who, knowing a crime has been committed by another, receives, relieves, comforts, or assists the criminal

access to records   a privilege under due process rules and regulations entitling parents and pupils to view their school records. Each school district must have a written plan for management of pupils' records and access to them. The privilege is most broadly mandated by "The Education of Handicapped Children Act."

accident   an event that takes place without one's foresight or expectation

accommodation   an arrangement made as a favor to another; an act performed without legal obligation

accomplice   an associate in a crime who knowingly cooperates, aids, or assists in committing it

accord   an agreement, consent, or concurrence

34

accord and satisfaction the substitution of a second agreement in place of a former one

account a detailed statement of debits and credits

accountability in its general sense, refers to the concept that educators must be responsible for the success or failure of their pupils by providing specific learning goals, and methods of achieving such goals. In more precise terms, it is a regular public report by independent reviewers of demonstrated student accomplishment promised for the expenditure of resources

acknowledgment the act by which a party who has executed an instrument affirms or acknowledges its authenticity before a competent officer

acquittal a release or setting free from a criminal charge by the process of trial at law; the verdict of a judge or jury pronouncing the party not guilty

action a law suit; the formal means or method of pursuing and recovering one's rights in a court of justice

actionable that which can legally be made the ground or subject of an action or law suit

activities of daily living (ADL) used in habilitation to describe those activities that a disabled person can often learn to do for himself so that he can live independently, including self-care such as dressing and eating

act of God a violence of nature without human interference; an inevitable accident or casualty, such as lightning, tempests, perils of the sea, or earthquake

adaptive behavior the human tendency to strive for equilibrium or balance between self and environment <Children demonstrate—— when they acquire the skills and responses to cope with or adjust to a new teacher or a difficult assignment>

adequate education a due process guarantee requiring satisfactory instructional programs for every child, including the exceptional child—the definition is variable, and will change with the requirements of individual students

adequate funding according to many state mandates, special education programs must be given appropriate financial support <—— by local districts> under the federal mandate, PL 94-142, there appears to be no ceiling on expenditures for the education of handicapped children. Hence, the term may become interpreted to mean maximum funding for an adequate education, but a more precise definition of exactly what an adequate education is remains unclear and awaits further legislation or judicial interpretation

ad hoc   for this; <an—— committee meets to discuss a specific issue>

ad infinitum   indefinitely or forever

adjourn   to suspend, defer, or postpone

adjudication   a judicial or legal decision or sentence <the case was adjudicated in favor of the plaintiff>

ad litem   for the duration of the suit or litigation <a guardian —— is often appointed by a court to represent the interests of minors or disabled persons during a lawsuit>

ADM   the abbreviation refers to Average Daily Membership in a special or regular class, the basis for which allocations (usually financial) are made. The term is usually used by school administrators and supervisors dealing with special education rules and regulations

administrator   1: a person appointed by a court to manage the affairs of another, usually after his death   2: an individual responsible for carrying out state and local guidelines for a school or school system   syn superintendent, supervisor, coordinator, director, chief state school officer, commissioner

administratrix   a female administrator

admissible   that which is pertinent and proper to be considered in reaching a decision <—— evidence>

admission   1: the acknowledgement by one party to a law suit of the truth of some matter alleged by the other party   2: the voluntary placement of a person in a facility or program

admonition   a reprimand from a judge warning the offender of the consequences of his act

adoption   a taking or choosing of another's child as one's own, thereby giving him all the rights and duties of his own child

adult   one who is of full age; usually eighteen or twenty-one—the age of adulthood may vary from state to state and for different purposes within a single state

advancement   a payment of money, or a settlement of real estate, made by a parent to or for a child in advance or anticipation of the share to which such child would be entitled after the parent's death

adversary proceeding   a contested hearing or law suit with opposing parties

adversary system   the legal procedure in which each side in a lawsuit presents opposing and conflicting views in order to place guilt or responsibility on the other party

advisory opinion   a formal opinion by a court of a question of law submitted by a legislative body or government official

advocate   a person acting on behalf of another, particularly another who may be disadvantaged or handicapped <in some states ——s may be officially appointed to represent handicapped persons>

affiant   a person making an affidavit

affidavit   a written statement of fact, given voluntarily, signed and sworn to before an authority authorized to administer oaths

affirm   to assert, ratify, confirm, or establish

affirmative defense   an assertion of facts, which, if true, provides a legal defense to the claim of another

agency   a relationship in which one person is authorized to act for and represent another

aggrieved   a person suffering from an infringement or denial of legal rights <the —— complained about denial of freedom of speech>

agreement   the consent of two or more parties with respect to a set of facts and their respective rights and duties

aid and abet   see **abet**

alias [alias dictus]   otherwise called; a second or substituted name by which a person is known

alibi   elsewhere; a word used to imply defense to a criminal prosecution, in which the party accused, to prove that he could not have committed the crime with which he is charged, attempts to prove he was in another place or with another person at the time of the offense

alien   a person born in another country; not a native or natural born subject

alienate   to convey, transfer, or dispose of property

allegation   a statement, assertion, or pleading made by a party who claims it can be proved as a fact—a statement not yet proven <the newspaper alleges that the prisoner committed the crime>

allocations   in special education, funds directed for the education of handicapped children

amendment   a modification, usually for the better

amicable action   an action started and conducted according to a mutual understanding and arrangement of the contesting parties

amicus curiae   1: a friend of the court, often an attorney appointed to help the court in arriving at a decision 2: a person or group that has no legal right to be a part of a law suit, but is allowed to participate (usually on a limited basis) to protect his or its interests

ancillary services   those services of specialists who may support pupils in regular public school classes, e.g., speech therapist, guidance counselor, remedial reading teacher, school psychologist, and visiting teacher

annex   to attach or join

annul   to nullify, abolish; to make void or ineffective

answer   a defendant's response to the plaintiff's allegations

appeal   1: in court, the removal of a case from a lower court to a higher one to review the decision 2: in education, a due process right that permits a parent to challenge a school decision; i.e., a challenge of a special class placement decision to a reviewing authority

appearance   attendance at a hearing or a court session by either or both parties to the action

appellant   the party who initiates an appeal

appellate jurisdiction   the authority to review and change decisions by other courts or administrative bodies

appellee   the party against whom an appeal is taken

appropriate education   a due process right that entitles every child to educational instruction that meets his special needs

appurtenant   accessory or incident to

arbitrary decision   a decision made without regard to careful investigation or reference to established standards <special class placement of a child without proper identification would constitute an ——>

arbitration   the submission of a dispute to private or unofficial persons (often experts) for a resolution that is binding on the parties

arraign   to call an individual to court to demand that he plead not guilty or guilty to criminal charges placed against him

arrears   money unpaid at the time it is due

arrest   to stop a person and deprive him of his liberty by legal authority

assault   the intentional act of placing another person in fear of bodily harm; threatening an offensive act while having the ability to carry out the threat

assault and battery   see assault; battery

assent   agreement or compliance

assumption of risk   a legal defense that exists when a party knowingly assumes the consequences of an injury occurring; commonly used as a legal defense in personal injury law suits

at risk children   (also, at developmental risk)   infants and children who are neglected or unattended and therefore in danger of impeded (physically and psychologically) growth and development

attachment   the seizure of a debtor's property to furnish security for the debt

attest   to testify, or act as a witness to; to certify or declare

attorney at law   lawyer; an advocate who provides legal counsel or representation

attorney general   the chief law officer of a state or the United States—his function is to give legal advice on questions submitted to his office by the various government agencies

averment   a positive statement of fact

aversive stimuli   an environment of punishment or a negative reinforcer used to manipulate a child's behavior in a chosen manner

award   the judgment or decision respecting any matter in dispute <a jury ——s damages>

bail   to procure the release of one charged with a criminal offense by insuring his appearance at future court proceedings

bailiff   a court attendant who maintains the courtroom during trial

bailment   the delivery of personal property to another for a specific purpose, after which it is redelivered to the owner

bankruptcy   generally synonymous with insolvency, or inability to meet debts as they become due. More specifically, the term refers to a federal court proceeding that provides relief to debtors and their creditors by seizing a debtor's property, distributing it among his creditors, and discharging the debt.

bar   1: a railing running across the courtroom that separates the general public from the trial participants   2: members of the legal profession

barrister   an English term for lawyers who conduct trials

baseline data   the normal level of activity in a given situation used to compare with data derived from varying situations <in a thirty minute classroom observation, the number of times a child mis-behaves gives ——— as a starting point against which to measure improvement after corrective attempts have been applied>

battered child syndrome   a condition whereby a parent repeatedly beats his child excessively over an extended period of time; the parent's mental illness may be presumed

battery   1: an unlawful touching or beating of another person in a hostile manner 2: a group of tests; e.g. The battery of tests showed that the child achieves at a normal level

BEH   abbr Bureau of Education for the Handicapped, Department of Health, Education and Welfare.

behavior rating scales   a checklist of child activity patterns

bench   1: the seat occupied by judges in court 2: a collective term referring to judges

beneficiary   the individual who benefits from a trust

bequeath   to give personal property to another by will

bequest   a gift, by will, of personal property; a legacy

better functioning language   the language with which a child is best able to communicate and perform (see Diana v. Board of Education in the Court Decision section of this volume for the legal ramifications of this concept)

beyond a reasonable doubt   the standard of proof required to establish criminal guilt and thereby obtain a criminal conviction

biased testing   evaluation derived from commercialized tests normed on the white, English speaking, middle-class culture. Such tests are thought to discriminate against minority groups (see middle class test bias; native language)

bilingual homes   homes where two or more languages are used, and usually where English is not the primary language

bill   a formal written statement or declaration filed in a law suit

bill of particulars   a written statement of the details or specifications of the claims made in a law suit

blind   an individual is legally blind when having less than one-tenth of normal vision in the more efficient eye after refractive defects are fully corrected by lenses

bona fide   in good faith; honestly

bond   a certificate or evidence of a debt

breach   the breaking or violating of a law, right, or duty, either by commission or omission; e.g. **breach of the peace, breach of contract**

brief   a concise, descriptive, written statement of a case embodying a summary of facts, legal contentions, and applicable law. Most appeals are based on briefs filed by parties in appellate courts

burden of proof   the necessity to prove facts in dispute on an issue raised between the parties in a law suit

by-laws   regulations adopted by a group or association

canon   a law, rule, or ordinance

capias   an arrest warrant, usually issued by a judge; a bench warrant

case   cause; a law suit

case study   a comprehensive evaluation or assessment of a child usually involving a referral procedure, parent-teacher-pupil conferences, observations, assessment, individual educational planning, and consistent follow-up (see comprehensive case study)

catchment area   a geographic area for which a mental health facility has responsibility

categorical identification   refers to evaluation, diagnosis, and/or placement of a child in a particular educational classification according to degree of retardation, emotional disturbance, etc. (see categories of special education)

categories of special education   various areas of handicaps insofar as educational classification is concerned (see learning disability, educable mentally retarded, trainable mentally retarded). The standard categories often used by state departments of education are the following: mentally retarded, emotionally disturbed (socially-emotionally maladjusted or behavior disordered), blind, partially sighted, deaf, hard of hearing, orthopedically and chronically handicapped, learning disabled, speech defects, and gifted

cause (cause of action)   a law suit, or the right to bring a law suit

caveat emptor   let the buyer beware; a warning

CEC   (Council for Exceptional Children)   a national organization, which advocates the rights of exceptional children, especially their right of education

certify   to testify in writing; to make a declaration about a writing

certiorari   an appellate proceeding in which a superior court directs an inferior court to forward the record of a particular case for reexamination; an appellate proceeding for reexamination of a decision of an inferior court

challenge   to question the legality or legal qualifications of a decision or persons involved as legal counsel or witnesses

chancellor   the name given to a judge in a court of chancery or equity

chancery   a court of equity

change of venue   the transfer of a case from one jurisdiction to another, usually made to promote a fairer trial. A change of venue is usually discretionary with the presiding judge

charter   a legislative act creating a corporation

chattel   an article of personal property

child   one who is under full age; usually less than eighteen or twenty-one—the age may vary from state to state and for different purposes within a single state

child-find procedures   the method of identifying exceptional children through observation, testing, and other assessment techniques—usually carried out by means of a comprehensive screening procedure by community agencies and professional persons

CINS   abbr Children in Need of Supervision   J (Juvenile) INS and P (Person) INS refers to juveniles whose activities, while not criminal, bring them within the jurisdiction of juvenile courts

circuit   a jurisdictional or geographic division of a court

circuit court of appeal   see Court of Appeals

circumstantial evidence   evidence of an indirect nature, as opposed to direct or positive proof

citation   an official notice to appear in court

citizen advocacy   a one-to-one relation between a capable and trained volunteer on behalf of a handicapped person. The advocate defends the rights and interests of the handicapped or disabled protégé and provides practical assistance for that person (see advocate; class advocacy)

civil action   a case brought before a court for establishment of a right or the redress or prevention of an injury or wrong. Most special class placement and due process procedural suits involving special education are of this form—the contrast would be a criminal action

civil court   a court that decides civil actions

civil injury   an infringement of some civil right, as distinguished from a crime

civil law   revised Roman laws that became the basis of jurisprudence for most of continental Europe and subsequently affected the development of United States law

civil rights   private rights guaranteed to all citizens by the Constitution and by Acts of Congress and court decisions in pursuance thereof

class action   a law suit brought by one or more plaintiffs on behalf of a group of persons with similar legal circumstances. This form of law suit can be very effective in protecting the constitutional rights of large groups of people

class advocacy   acting on behalf of a group of people with similar interests; e.g. litigation supporting the rights of the handicapped (see advocate; class action suit)

clean hands   a maxim by which a party to a law suit has access to relief because his own conduct has been fair and equitable

clerk of court   a court officer who has charge of the clerical aspect of a court, including the maintenance of its records

client   one who employs or retains an attorney

clinical psychologist   typically a person who has received a advanced degree in psychology and is licensed to engage in the practice of evaluating and treating mental disorders

code   a collection, compilation, or revision of laws

codicil   an addition or supplement to a will

collateral   1: supplementary or auxiliary 2: security given to insure the performance of an act

collusion   an agreement between two or more persons to defraud or a conspiracy to perform some other illegal act

commercial paper   negotiable instruments, including checks, provisory notes, certificates of deposit, and bills of exchange or drafts

commitment   the process of admitting a person to a mental hospital without his consent—a court order is required to initiate and maintain such an involuntary entrance. **Voluntary commitments** are referred to as "admissions"

committee   an individual or group charged with the management of a duty 1: in the mental health field, the term is often used synonymously with that of "guardian" 2: in special education, committees often serve screening and placement functions

common carrier   1: one who as a business undertakes to transport from place to place passengers or goods   2: in special education the term may refer to those who transport the handicapped to their school destinations and home again

common law   a body of unwritten laws based on custom and habit developed in England and generally adopted in the United States. Civil law is a contrasting form of legal system

community mental health center   a community or neighborhood based facility for the prevention and treatment of mental illness—many centers have been established and regulated by Federal law since 1964

community property   property acquired by a husband and wife during their marriage and owned as a form of matrimonial partnership; a form of property ownership commonly used in several western states

compelling interest   maintaining a direct involvement in a particular suit; a legal test (principle) applied to weigh or balance various interests in a law suit

competency   1: the mental capability to be examined as a witness in a trial or to execute legal documents   2: the capability of educators, psychologists, lawyers, and other professionals

complainant   one who initiates legal proceedings against another; a plaintiff

complaint   a charge or allegation against a person <the filing of a —— formally initiates a law suit or a criminal prosecution>

compliance   to obey a court ruling or legislative requirement

compos mentis   of sound mind; having use and control of one's mental faculties

comprehensive case study   an evaluation-remediation used in schools that should include the following: (a) teacher referral; (b) observations of the child; (c) conferences with teachers, parents and pupil; (d) psycho-educational, sociological, and medical assessment of the pupil; (e) individualized educational program; and (f) planned systematic follow-up

conclusive evidence   evidence that is uncontradictable

concur   to agree or consent; in appellate court practices, a **concurring opinion** is one that agrees with the results of the other judges, but expresses a separate opinion or rationale.

confidentiality   refers to respect for and protection of individual's privileged personal communication, including the right to privacy and right to reputation

conflict of laws inconsistencies or differences between the laws of different states or jurisdictions

consanguinity a blood relationship; kinship

consent a concurrence or agreement

consent decree a decree sanctioned by the court and entered upon the recommendation of the litigating parties

conservator a guardian or protector

consign to deliver or transfer goods to an agent or factor for sale

consortium 1: mutual conjugal duties shared by husband and wife 2: in special education, an agreement of mutual duties between or among groups or school districts

conspiracy an agreement by two or more persons to accomplish an illegal act

constituent a person represented by another, as the principal in the relation of principal and agent

constitutionality the appropriateness or legality of a ruling or practice with regard to the guidelines of the United States Constitution

constitutional right a right guaranteed by the Constitution and its amendments

constructive inferred; construed by the courts to have a particular character or meaning other than what is specifically expressed

contempt a willful disobedience of rules, orders, or process of a court or a disturbance of its proceedings so that the court's authority is embarrassed, hindered, or obstructed <Those in ―――― may be fined or imprisoned>

contested placement a due process right to make a formal appeal about a school decision to assign or not to assign a child to a particular educational category or classification

continuance an adjournment of court proceedings from one period of time to another

contra opposite to; against

contract an agreement between two or more parties that is enforceable in court

contributory negligence negligence by an individual that contributed to his own injury and therefore normally prevents recovery of damages from another

conversion an unauthorized act that deprives an owner of his property. This is the civil equivalent to the criminal term theft

conveyance a transfer of real estate from one party to another

conviction finding a person guilty of an offense

cooperative educational prescriptions   instructional programs developed for exceptional children by a team of experts, teachers, and parents

corporal punishment   physical punishment, such as whipping or spanking

corporation   an artificial, legal entity, created by the authority of state law, that has a legal existence separate from its creators and officers

corpus juris   body of law

corroborate   to reinforce or strengthen; to add weight to

costs   the expenses involved in bringing or defending a law suit, with the usual exception of attorney's fees

counsel (counsellor, and counsellor at law)   a licensed attorney whose occupation and office is to give counsel or advice on the management of law suits and other legal business; may also refer to a **school guidance counsellor.**

counterclaim   a claim or action made by the defendant against the plaintiff, by which the defendant claims the plaintiff is responsible or liable for an injury or debt to the defendant

court   a tribunal established to administer justice   **syn** judge

court of appeals   an appellate tribunal with the authority to review the decisions of courts that first decide cases

court of record   a court in which a permanent record is kept of the proceedings—usually a court of original jurisdiction that decides significant civil or criminal cases.

criminal insanity   a lack of mental capacity to the extent that there is no penal culpability for criminal acts. Insanity is a legal term roughly synonymous with the term psychosis (see McNaghten Rule; Durham Rule)

criterion referenced testing   measurement designed to provide information about attainment of a specific objective (criterion) through an individual's demonstrated performance of that objective; primarily designed as instructional tools to aid in determining levels of student achievement related to specific goals for that student

cross claim   a claim or action, made by a defendant against a third party by which the defendent claims the third party is responsible or liable for the injury or debt claimed by the plaintiff

cross examination   questioning of a witness for the opposing party in order to test the accuracy of the direct examination

cruel and unusual punishment excessive, inhumane, or barbarous penalties; prohibited as criminal penalties by the Eighth Amendment to the Constitution

CSSO abbr Chief State School Officer; i.e. the state Commissioner of Education or Head of the State Department of Education

cultural discrimination unfair testing, placement, or other actions that result in unfair bias against a minority

culture fair tests tests of mental ability that attempt to ensure that the test items are perceived equally for all groups regardless of race, nationality, and social class, or any other nonintellectual factor

cultural pluralism a general term referring to integration, non-discriminatory practices <unbiased assessment should be based on ---->

custody the detention and care of property or an individual

damage a loss, hurt, injury, or hinderance sustained by a person

damages a sum allowed by courts as compensation for an injury or loss caused by another. Particular types of damages include the following: **compensatory damages** damages that replace the sustained loss and return the injured party to his pre-loss condition; **nominal damages** damages awarded for a technical loss or injury, when no real harm has occurred; and **punitive damages** damages awarded in addition to that required to compensate the injured party. Punitive damages may be awarded as a penalty to the wrong-doer when he has intentionally inflicted a loss upon another

deaf a hearing impairment that is so severe that a person is impaired in processing linguistic information through hearing, with or without amplification, which adversely affects educational performance

deaf-blind concomitant hearing and visual impairments, the combination of which causes such severe communication and other developmental and educational problems that they cannot be accommodated in special education programs solely for deaf or blind children

de bene esse conditionally or in anticipation of a future use <depositions or evidence may be taken --- so that it is preserved for trial in the absence or death of a witness>

debenture an instrument by which a corporation places part of its stock or property as collateral for a loan

debt   a sum of money due as the result of an agreement

decedent   a person who has died

decision   a judicial determination, decree, judgment, or order

declaratory judgment   a judicial decision that determines the respective legal rights of litigating parties, without actually ordering that any action or performance be taken

declaratory statute   a law, enacted by a legislative body, designed to end doubt or controversy about the interpretation or meaning of another law

decree   the judgment of a court of equity, which determines the rights of the litigating parties; it is final when it disposes of the case and temporary when it leaves some question unsettled

deed   a document that conveys an interest in real estate from one person to another

deed of trust   a document, similar to a mortgage, that conveys the legal title of real estate to trustees, who hold the real estate as collateral for a loan or other debt

de facto   in fact, actually, or in reality; in contrast to de jure <——— segregation is that which exists as a result of unofficial approval or sanction>

defamation   libel or slander against a person's reputation; injuring a person's character or reputation in writing or by spoken words

default   failure to fulfill a legal obligation

defendant   the person against whom a law suit or proceeding is brought and, therefore, defends or opposes the suit

defense   those laws or facts used by a defendant to oppose or defend a law suit

deinstitutionalization   the effort to place mentally handicapped people from large state facilities in small, community based facilities or homes

de jure   lawful, of the law, or legitimate; in contrast to de facto <——— segregation is that which results from legal sanction>

delinquent child or juvenile   a minor who has violated a law; the term also has the connotation of incorrigibility

demonstrative evidence   evidence, such as physical objects, that can be seen, heard or otherwise sensed without the aid of testimony

demurrer   a defendant's response in a law suit, which admits the truth of the plaintiff's allegations, but nonetheless claims the plaintiff's allegations are insufficient to support its requested relief

de novo   anew, a second time   <a party may be granted a trial
—— because of an error in the first trial>

depose   to give evidence in the form of a deposition; to place one's
sworn statements in the form of writing

deposition   testimony of a witness, under oath before a judicial
officer, but not in open court, that is reduced to writing

deprivation   the removal, denial, or confiscation of a legal right

descent   hereditary succession; the passing of ownership from one
person upon death to another

desegregation   the act of keeping people from being isolated or
separated from a main body. A **desegregation order** connotes more
passive action than if a court were to issue an order for integration, which is an order for more active compliance

detainer   a judicial order issued to restrain an individual's personal
liberty against his will

devise   to give real estate to another by use of a will at one's death

dicta (dictum)   an opinion expressed by a court that is not necessary
in deciding the question before the court

differential expectancies   (see self-fulfilling prophecy)

direct examination   initial testimony of a witness upon being called
to testify in court, usually followed immediately by cross examination from the opposition

directed verdict   an instruction by the trial judge to the jury to
return a verdict in favor of one of the parties in a law suit

disability   the lack of legal capacity to perform a given act. Disability may be due to such varied factors as age, mental capacity,
or imprisonment

disaffirmance   the act by which a person who has entered into a
voidable contract indicates he will not abide by the contract

discovery   pretrial procedures that enable one party to a law suit
to learn the basis of his opponent's case—methods may include
depositions, interrogatories, medical examinations, and examination
of demonstrative evidence

discrimination   special treatment or privileges arbitrarily afforded
or denied a particular group as a result of their race, nationality,
culture, sex, or handicap

dismiss   to send out of, release, or discharge from court. An **order
of dismissal** is one which disposes of a law suit

disorderly conduct   unruly behavior thought menacing to public safety

docket   a court calendar of cases ready for hearing or trial

domicile   a person's permanent home, in contrast to his temporary residence

double jeopardy   the practice (prohibited by the fifth amendment to the United States Constitution) of prosecuting a person a second time for the same offense

dower   a widow's right to use a portion of her deceased husband's estate for her lifetime

duces tecum   bring with you. A **subpoena duces tecum**   a summons that requires the summoned party to appear in court and bring specified documents with him

due process   1: constitutional guarantee of the fifth and fourteenth amendments that prohibits deprivation of life, liberty, or property without adherence to established fundamental rights and procedural fairness   2: in special education, the term refers to specific procedural rights guaranteed children and their parents with regard to a child's identification, testing, evaluation, labeling, categorization, and placement in school programs

due process hearing   a judicial or administrative review to determine whether a child and its parents have been given their procedural rights by the local or state boards of education in the decision-making process about their child

duress   coercion causing action or inaction against a person's will through fear, force, or moral persuasion

Durham rule   an infrequently used test for legal insanity, which holds that a person is not responsible for a crime if the criminal act was the product of a mental disease or defect

early identification   the implementation of a formal plan for identifying a disability as early as possible in a child's life

educable mentally retarded (EMR)   those children who reveal a rate of intellectual development and level of academic achievement significantly below that of their peer age group as evidenced by deficits in all essential learning processes—they usually are between two and three standard deviations below the mean on a normal distribution of intelligence

education   the cultivation and improvement of one's intellectual, physical, moral, and religious faculties

education for all handicapped children act of 1975 (public law 94-142) see Part II of this book for a complete summary of this Act

education 'normalization the belief that preference is to be given, whenever appropriate, to education of the exceptional child in classes with children who do not have exceptional needs, or in the most normal setting appropriate for the child

educational placement classroom assignment of a pupil based upon evaluation and categorization of that pupil; in regular classes, usually based on ability and achievement tests combined with teacher evaluation; in special education classes, usually based on a comprehensive case study conducted by a teacher and support service personnel

eleemosynary charitable; the giving of charity

eligibility in special education, deciding qualifications for inclusion or exclusion of students in special classes; e.g., **eligibility committees, eligibility hearings**

emancipation a parent's surrender of his control, care, and custody of his child

embezzlement the fraudulent appropriation of money or property that has been entrusted to one's care

eminent domain the right of the government to take private property for public use. Compensation for the property must be given to the former property owner

emotional disturbance mental disorder evidenced by one or more of the following: (a) an inability to learn which cannot be explained by intellectual, sensory or health factors; (b) an inability to build or maintain satisfactory interpersonal relationships with peers; (c) inappropriate types of behavior or feeling under normal conditions; (d) a general, pervasive mood of unhappiness or depression; (e) a tendency to develop physical symptoms, or fears associated with personal or school problems

encumbrance a lien or claim upon property that often diminishes the property's value

endowment a fund, usually in the form of a gift, bestowed upon a public institution

enforce to execute or make effective <a court order may be ——— by a sheriff or marshal>

enfranchise to set free or incorporate into a main group

enjoin a court's ordering a person to perform or abstain from an act

equal educational opportunity   child's right to appropriate instruction without regard to sex, race, religion, or handicap

equal protection   the concept that rights of all persons must rest upon the same rule under the same circumstances, both in privileges conferred and liabilities imposed. The concept is embodied in the fourteenth amendment to the United States Constitution and the court decisions that interpret the amendment

equitable   fair, just, or right. Some jurisdictions have courts of "equity" that are based upon the English tradition of judicial flexibility so that fair or ——— decisions can be made without absolute adherence to rigid rules of law

equivocal   having two or more meanings often leading to an unclear understanding

error   a mistaken judgment or incorrect belief of a trial court as to the existence of a fact or application of a law

ESEA   abbr Elementary Secondary Education Act (a federal law enacted in 1965), which promoted, among other activities, education for handicapped children

escrow   the condition of money or property that is held by a third party pending the completion of a condition between two other persons

estate   an interest in land or property

estoppel   a rule of law that prevents a person from denying a fact that his actions or words influenced others to believe was true

ethnic disproportions   unusually large numbers of blacks, Mexicans, or other minorities in special education classes, which may reflect racial discrimination in testing or placement procedures

ethnic minority   a racial or cultural group that represents a small portion of a given population; e.g., Spanish Americans, blacks, or Chinese

evaluation   the educational or psychological assessment of a child through testing, observation, parent conferences, or other valid means

evaluation and placement committee   a team of school personnel organized to meet the special educational needs of children; recent legislation provides for the parents' right to participation in the placement committee meetings

evaluation team   a team of school specialists who help to determine the appropriate educational program for a child—teams may consist of a psychologist, social worker, principal, teacher, speech therapist, nurse, reading specialist, special educator, guidance counsellor, or other specialists

evidence proof of facts presented at trial through the use of witnesses and documents

evidentiary hearing a pretrial hearing held to determine whether specific evidence may be admitted at trial

exception a formal objection made by a party during a trial to an action or ruling of the judge—by noting an objection, the objecting party preserves the right to appeal and seek reversal of the ruling

excess cost formula the economic program developed by a state to pay local districts additional funds for the education of handicapped children beyond the established state funding plan—the district determines the per pupil cost of educating a handicapped child and subtracts from this the cost of educating a nonhandicapped child, the difference being reimbursed by the state

executed completed, performed, or in full effect <an ——— document>

executive session a meeting of a governmental group that is closed to the public and news media

executor a person named in a will to handle the affairs of the deceased

executrix a female executor

ex officio by virtue of the office

ex parte on one side only; done at the request of only one party

expelled 1: ejectment or banishment 2: the permanent exclusion of a child from school (see Goss v. Lopez in the significant case section of this text for due process procedures which must be followed in expelling a student)

expert witness a person qualified in a particular matter by knowledge or experience—he may testify in a court not only to facts, but also to his opinion respecting the facts in his field of expertise

ex post facto after the act; law which takes effect retroactively

extenuating circumstances facts that tend to lessen the severity of punishment

eyewitness a person who can testify as to what he has seen

fair market value the price at which a willing buyer and seller will trade an object

family 1: a collective body of two or more persons living together in a single house and sharing household responsibilities 2: those who are related to each other by blood or marriage

felon   a person who commits a felony

felony   an offense punishable by death or imprisonment; the imprisonment is usually for a period in excess of one year—these crimes are more serious than those labeled misdemeanors

femme sole   a single woman, including those who are divorced or widowed

fiduciary   founded upon or having the quality of a trust or confidence; one who is trusted to handle the business and personal affairs of another

fine   a sum of money paid as a penalty

first priority children   handicapped children who are in the following categories: 1: in an age group for which the State must make available free appropriate public education, and 2: not receiving any education

fixture   an item of personal property that is permanently affixed to real estate or buildings; e.g. aluminum siding or wall to wall carpeting

flow-through funds   federal funds designed for distribution to local school districts, but must be controlled by the state department of education (SEA or SDOE)—hence, the funds pass through or flow through the SEA for monitoring, control, and accountability purposes

follow-up   the most important part of a child's comprehensive case study; it involves not only reassessment and program evaluation for a particular child at a particular time, but also continual review of the progress of the child

forbearance   a voluntary delay in enforcing one's rights, particularly with regard to the collection of money

force majesture   (see Act of God)

foreclosure   a proceeding in which a creditor takes possession of property, which his debtor has pledged as collateral for a loan

foreign   from another state or nation

forensic medicine   medical jurisprudence; the application of medicine to the purpose of law

forensic psychiatry   that area of psychiatry that deals with the legal aspects of mental disorders

forfeit   to lose or have taken away because of an error, fault, or crime

forgery   the fraudulent making or altering of a document

formal anonymity   a status sometimes given to persons who are involved in litigation, designed to protect the identity of such persons. Those individuals are often referred by names such as John Doe or Mary Roe

forthwith   immediately; promptly; without delay

forum   a court, tribunal, or place of litigation

fourteenth amendment   a United States Constitutional amendment that prohibits action by state government that deprives a person of life, liberty, or property without due process of law and requires equal protection of the laws

fraud   any cunning, or deception used to cheat, or deceive another; an intentional false representation of a fact intended to mislead another

free appropriate public education   special education and related services that (a) are provided at public expense, under public supervision and direction, and without charge, (b) meet the standards of the State educational agency, (c) include preschool, elementary school, or secondary school education in the State involved, and (d) are provided in conformity with an individualized education program

friend of the court   one who gives information to the court on some matter of law in respect to which the court is doubtful (see Amicus Curiae)

FTE abbr full time equivalent. Usually used in school finance to compute state aid formulas. One ——— is a student placed in an instructional delivery system for twenty-five hours per week for 180 days. Reimbursement formulas based upon this concept vary from state to state

full faith and credit clause   article 4, section 1 of the United States Constitution that requires, in some circumstances, the courts of one state to give full effect to the judgments of another state

fundamental right   rights established by the United States Constitution; e.g., the right to free speech, assembly, liberty, or freedom from unreasonable searches and seizures

garnishment   a court proceeding whereby a debtor's creditor can apply the debtor's money or property held by third parties to the payment of the debt. For example, a creditor may garnish a debtor's wages while they are still held by the debtor's employer

gift   a voluntary, gratuitous transfer of personal property

gifted   those children identified by professionally qualified persons who, by virtue of outstanding abilities, are capable of high performance $<$—— children respond best to differentiated education programs and/or services beyond those normally provided by the regular school program$>$

good faith   honest intentions

goods   personal property

grand jury   a jury of inquiry whose duty it is to receive and hear complaints or accusations in criminal cases and, if they find them supported by evidence presented by the prosecution, to indict those persons complained of

grandfather clause   an exception to new legislation that permits those who have established a practice to continue, although the new legislation forbids the practice by others in the future

grant   to transfer, convey, confer, or bestow

gratis   free; without consideration or reward

gross   1: total or all inclusive   2: flagrant, shameful, inexcusable

guaranty(ee)   a promise to be responsible for the debt or performance of another

guardian   one who is entitled to the custody of the person or property of another; e.g., a minor or a retarded person

guardian ad litem   the person who represents in court a child or an incompetent individual for the duration of a law suit $<$usually, attorneys are appointed by the court to serve as a ——$>$

habeas corpus   a writ issued by a court ordering that a prisoner be brought before the court so that the legality of his detention can be examined

habilitation   the provision of training and employment for mentally or physically handicapped persons so that they may attain their maximum individual potential

halfway house   a specialized residence for persons who do not need full time hospitalization or institutionalization, but require supportive services and protection before they return to independent community living

handicapped children   those children evaluated as being mentally retarded, hard of hearing, deaf, speech impaired, visually handicapped, seriously emotionally disturbed, orthopedically impaired, other health impaired, deaf-blind, multihandicapped, or as having specific learning disabilities, and who because of those impairments need special education and related services

hard of hearing   a hearing impairment, whether permanent or fluctuating, that adversely affects a child's educational performance, but is not included under the definition of deaf

head start (economic opportunity community partnership act of 1974): a federal child development program for preschool age children designed to increase economic and personnel services to the disadvantaged, including the handicapped

hearing   a trial; a proceeding, usually public, at which adverse parties present facts and arguments to a judge or hearing officer, who decides issues of law or fact

hearing impaired   those children whose hearing loss (after all necessary medical surgery, and/or use of hearing aids) significantly restricts benefit from or participation in the normal classroom program and necessitates a modified instructional program

hearing officer   an impartial examiner who presides in a legal hearing prior to an actual trial and who helps determine what further court action is appropriate

hearsay   evidence given by a witness based upon what others have told him and not upon his personal knowledge—because hearsay is second hand evidence, it is considered unreliable and, therefore, usually inadmissable

heir (heir at law)   one who inherits property that was not disposed of by a will; person(s) designated by law to take the property of one who dies intestate

heretofore   in time past

high risk candidate   1: those people who might be most susceptible to various categories of handicap; e.g., the culturally disadvantaged 2: in education, the term refers to children and youth who may be in danger of failure in school

holder   the person in possession of commercial paper

holding   the essence of a judicial decision in a particular case

holographic will   a will handwritten entirely by the testator

home-bound instruction   the education of handicapped children in their homes when they are unable to attend regular classes—federal or state funding usually appropriates funds for five to ten hours of such tutorial service per week for each child

homicide   the killing of a human being, either intentionally or accidentally

hung jury   a jury so irrevocably divided that it cannot reach a unanimous verdict

identification   the process by which handicapped children are sought out, screened, and evaluated

illicit   illegal; unlawful

immaterial   unnecessary, not pertinent, without consequence; e.g., immaterial evidence

imminent danger   threatened or impending danger that cannot be guarded against. This standard is used in many jurisdictions to permit the involuntary commitment or institutionalization of mentally disturbed individuals

immunity   freedom from legal obligations or consequences

impeach   1: to remove a public officer from office for misfeasance or crime 2: to contradict or question the truthfulness of a witness

inadequately served   those children who have been recipients of marginal educational programs or who have received no program at all due to exclusion from school or lack of an adequate school program (see first priority children; second priority children)

inadmissible   that which cannot be received; e.g. inadmissible evidence

in camera   in the judge's chambers; in private   <hearings which are held —— are closed to the public>

incapacity   lack of legal ability (see incompetent)

incarceration   confinement in jail or penitentiary; imprisonment

inchoate   incomplete, partial, or imperfect

incompetent   a person who, because of a mental defect, is deprived of his legal capacities, such as his right to stand trial, make a will or contract, get married, or obtain licenses

incorrigible   1: that which cannot be corrected or improved 2: an unmanageable juvenile

incriminate   to charge or involve another with a crime

indemnity   an undertaking to compensate another for loss, damage, expense or trouble incurred   <a school district may indemnify a parent for special education expenses of their child in a private school>

independent decision   the assessment made by an impartial hearing officer after hearing an appeal of a child placement decision or a parental claim of unfulfilled due process procedures

independent educational evaluation   an assessment of a child, separate from that which is conducted by school personnel, conducted by a specialist outside of and separate from the schools

indictment   a formal presentment by a grand jury charging a criminal act

individually prescribed instruction (IPI)   see individualized instruction

individualized education program (IEP)   instructional guidelines developed to meet the needs of a particular child—a specific written time-table of goals to be achieved by the child, a means for achieving the goals, and a schedule for their completion; a means of assessing the outcomes and procedures, and for revising the plan may be included

individualized instruction   the education of a child on a one-to-one basis or with materials which allow the child to progress at his own rate. This is sometimes referred to as IPI (individually pre scribed instruction), in which specific learning goals, procedures, and schedules are implemented for each child

infant   a minor; one who legally is not yet an adult

informed consent   a voluntary agreement or compliance after having received a full explanation; e.g. the parents of a child may consent to a psychological evaluation of their child, after having been informed of the need for and possible consequences of the evaluation

infraction   a violation of a law, duty, or right

infringement   an encroachment or trespass of a right or privilege <a due process right may be infringed, if a child and/or his parents are denied a hearing in some situations>

inherit   to receive property as an heir upon the death of an ancestor

injunction   a court order which restrains a party in a law suit from committing specified acts. Particular types of injunctions include the following: **mandatory injunction**   commands an act to be done or undone; **permanent injunction**   restrains a party until a final decision is reached on the merits of a case; **prohibitory injunction**   restrains the continuance of an act; **restraining order**   an injunction which may be obtained in an emergency, without giving notice to an opposing party; **temporary injunction**   restrains a party for a limited or preliminary period

injury   a wrong or damage done to a person or his property

in loco parentis   in the place of a parent; one who has the rights and responsibilities of a child's parents, for limited purposes, such as a child's teacher in school

in pari delicto   equally at fault

insanity   an outdated psychiatric term, still widely used legally, that has the approximate meaning of the term psychosis

in-service training   see training of regular educators

insolvency   the condition in which one's liabilities exceed his assets

institutional peonage   the exploitation of institutional residents by forcing them to work in nontherapeutic jobs without pay or at token wages

integrated programs   educational prescriptions designed to utilize both the special education and regular classroom; in special education, integration refers to programs in which special children are not separated from regular class children

intelligence quotient (IQ)   a numerical rating determined by psychological testing that indicates the relation between one's mental age and his chronological age

interlocutory decree   a preliminary decree that does not determine the outcome of a law suit, but directs some further proceedings before a final decree is made

intermediate educational unit (IEU)   a regional unit that pools the resources of several school divisions; common in rural areas where small school districts are individually unable to afford required services; e.g. in New York State, the Boards of Cooperative Educational Services (BOCES) cross cuts school districts' boundaries to provide regional services

international classification of diseases (ICD)   the official list of disease categories issued by the World Health Organization and subscribed to by its member nations

interrogatories   a set of written questions proposed to a witness or party that are answered under oath; frequently used as a method of pretrial discovery

intervenor   one who becomes involved in a court proceeding with permission of the court

intestate   without a will < John Doe died ----- >

in toto   in the whole; completely

intra vires   within the power or authority given by law

involuntary servitude   compulsory labor under bondage, whether paid or not—prohibited by the thirteenth amendment to the Constitution of the United States

irresistible impulse   an uncontrollable desire to commit a criminal act. Because the compulsion is believed to be based on a mental defect, the offender may not criminally be responsible for his acts. The test is accepted in approximately one-third of the states and rejected in the remainder

jeopardy   the danger of conviction that exists in a criminal trial after the jury has been sworn in

JINS   abbr juveniles in need of supervision   a juvenile delinquent or status offender

John Doe   a fictitious name commonly used in law suits as a substitute for an unknown person or a person whose identity is intended to be kept secret

joint and several   refers to a liability when two or more persons are responsible together and individually

judge   the presiding officer at a trial or hearing who has the authority to control the proceedings and make decisions involving questions of law

judgment   a judicial decision; the order or decree of a court after a hearing or trial that establishes the rights of the parties involved

jurisdiction   the authority of a court to decide cases

jury   those impartial persons (usually twelve) who hear evidence during a trial and reach a decision based upon that evidence and the instructions of law given by the judge

juvenile court   a court having special jurisdiction over delinquents or dependent minors

labelling   the identification of the handicapped into special categories

larceny   the stealing or theft of the property of another

last clear chance   a rule of law used in negligence cases which provides that the party who has the last real opportunity to avoid damage or injury is liable for subsequent losses

lawsuit   a civil court action between two or more parties in which the plaintiff seeks the authority of the court to compel the defendant to perform a specified act

lawyer   an attorney; a legal representative, or counselor

LEA   abbr local educational agency   the local school district

leading question   a question asked of a witness during trial that suggests to the witness the desired answer

learning disabled   a disorder in one or more of the basic psychological processes involved in understanding or in using language, spoken or written, which may manifest itself in an imperfect ability to listen, think, speak, read, write, spell, or to do mathematical calculations—includes such conditions as perceptual handicaps, brain injury, minimal brain disfunction, dyslexia, and developmental aphasia. The term does not include children who have learning problems that are primarily the result of visual, hearing, or motor handicaps, of mental retardation, or of environmental, cultural, or economic disadvantage

lease   an agreement whereby a landlord permits his property to be used by a tenant

least restrictive (drastic) alternative   a legal doctrine roughly equivalent to social doctrine of normalization; i.e., that handicapped persons should study, work, and live in an environment with conditions and facilities that resemble as much as possible those of a nonhandicapped person

legacy   a bequest of personal property by will

legislation   the preparation and enactment of laws by a representative group of citizens

levy   to assess, collect, or seize

liability   a debt or obligation that may be absolute or contingent, expressed or implied

libel   written, spoken, or pictured defamation against a person's reputation

lien   an obligation imposed on property by which the property secures the discharge of an obligation

life estate   the right to use designated property for one's lifetime

limitation   (see statute of limitation)

litigant   a participant in a lawsuit, either as a plaintiff or a defendant

litigation   an action or lawsuit in court

local district policy   a ruling established by a local school board, e.g. a dress code for students

local entitlements   grants given by the state or federal government to local school districts for the implementation of special education programs

magistrate   a judicial officer having the authority to issue arrest warrants

mainstream   to place the handicapped pupil in the regular classroom whenever possible and appropriate (see least restrictive alternative)

majority   the age at which a child becomes an adult

malfeasance   the performance of an act that is unlawful or wrong

malice   the intentional doing of a wrong

malpractice   professional misconduct; the negligent performance of a professional act

mandamus   a court order directing a corporation, government official, or lower court to perform a specified act

mandate   an order or authoritative command by a court

master   a referee, commissioner, examiner, or other officer appointed by the court to whom a judge may refer particular matters for a determination and report

material   significant, important, or necessary; e.g., material witness, material facts

McNaghten rule   (M'naghten, McNaughten, and McNaughton)   a legal principle that holds that an individual is not responsible for his criminal acts if he was insane; i.e., had a mental disease that prevented him from knowing what he was doing, or if he did know what he was doing, he did not know it was wrong; it is the most commonly used formula in the United States for determining criminal responsibility

medical model   the traditional method of viewing mental illness or handicapping conditions in physical and medical terms, including the physician-patient relationship, diagnosis and treatment, and the healing of sickness

mens rea   criminal intent; a guilty mind

mental age   the age level of mental ability as determined by standardized intelligence tests; in contrast to chronological age

mental capacity or competence   the ability to understand the nature and effects of one's acts

mental disorder   a psychiatric illness or disease

mental retardation   significantly subaverage general intellectual functioning existing concurrently with deficits in adaptive behavior and manifested during the developmental period, which adversely affects a child's educational performance

middle class test bias   tests unfairly normed and oriented toward middle-class culture and, therefore, have an inherent bias in favor of that population

minor   a person younger than a stated legal age; a child; an infant

Miranda rule   a United States Supreme Court decision that implemented the fifth amendment to the Constitution by holding that after a criminal suspect is arrested or deprived of his freedom, the following rights must be explained to him before he may be questioned: (a) the right to remain silent; and that statements he makes may be used as evidence against him; (b) the right to an attorney during questioning; and (c) the right to a court appointed attorney during questioning, if he cannot afford to hire his own. The failure to inform a person of these rights prior to questioning may render his statements inadmissible as evidence in his subsequent trial

misdemeanor   a criminal offense less serious than a felony, the usual punishment for which may be a fine or a jail sentence of a year or less

misfeasance   the performance of a lawful action in an improper manner

misrepresentation   an unintentional false statement of fact

mistrial   a trial that is declared invalid because of a judicial irregularity; a trial ended without a conclusion

moot case   a controversy or law suit that is hypothetical

mortgage   a lien upon real estate that secures the repayment of a debt

motion   a formal request, either written or oral, made of a judge or court

multifactored assessment   the comprehensive case study approach to evaluation of the handicapped (see case study and comprehensive case study)

multihandicapped   concomitant impairments (such as mentally retarded-blind, mentally retarded-orthopedically impaired, etc.), the combination of which causes such severe educational problems that they cannot be accommodated in special education programs solely for one of the impairments; does not include deaf-blind children

native language   "The language normally used by a person, or in the case of a child, the language normally used by the parents of the child." Test bias may occur when someone is tested in other than his native language (see biased testing; middle class test bias)

necessaries   items of need; e.g., food, clothing, shelter and medical attention

negative stereotypes   inappropriate discrimination derived from erroneous wholesale identification and categorization; e.g., to view all urban black children as mentally retarded is obviously not correct

neglect   1: to omit or fail; 2: the failure of a parent to care properly for its child

negligence   the failure to do something that an ordinarily prudent person would do; the failure to use ordinary care

negotiable instrument   a written and signed statement containing an unconditional promise to pay a certain sum of money, which can be passed freely from one person to another—checks are the most common form of negotiable instrument

need to know   the phrase refers to limitation of access to pupil's records to only those persons who have a valid need for information in the record. In some states, a written statement of why the person needs access to a pupil's record is required

nolo contendere   I will not contest it; a plea in criminal actions by which the defendant does not contest the charge against him, yet does not admit the charge

noncompliance   failure to adhere to mandates

non compos mentis   not of sound mind; without use or control of one's mental faculties

nonfeasance   the neglect or failure to do something that ought to be done

nonsuit   the abandonment or termination of a lawsuit by the plaintiff

nonsupplanting   the failure to implement a substitute for a program that has been eradicated or for a position left vacant

norm   a standard for comparison. (see test norms)

normalization   the belief that handicapped individuals ought to be accepted, treated, and served as much as possible like nonhandicapped persons

notary public   a public officer who attests or certifies various matters in writing and under an official seal

note(s)   1: an unconditional promise to pay a definite sum of money to a person or his order at a specified time   2: a condensed or informal record

notice   the expressed or implied giving of information

notice of review   a requirement that parents be notified, in writing and with reasonable time to respond, of an appeal hearing concerning special class placement of this child

notification   a requirement that parents be contacted in writing and orally of an appeal hearing concerning the school placement of their children. The written statement must be in English and in the parents' primary language; the oral communication must be in the primary language

null   invalid; without legal effect

oath   a pledge by which a person affirms the truth of a statement while bound in conscience or to a responsibility to God

objection   a formal statement that complains of an improper act during court proceedings

opinion   a statement given by a court setting forth its reasons for its decision in a law suit

option   a contract to hold open an offer for a fixed period of time

order   a written directive of a court   **syn** decree, judgment

ordinance   a legislative enactment of a municipality

orthopedically impaired   a severe orthopedic impairment that adversely affects a child's educational performance—includes impairments caused by congenital anomaly, e.g., clubfoot, absence of some member such as an arm or leg, etc., impairments caused by disease, e.g., poliomyelitis, bone tuberculosis, etc., and impairments from other causes, e.g., cerebral palsy, amputations, and fractures or burns that cause contractures

other health impaired   limited strength, vitality, or alertness, due to chronic or acute health problems such as heart condition, tuberculosis, rheumatic fever, nephritis, asthma, sickle cell anemia, hemophilia, epilepsy, lead poisoning, leukemia, or diabetes that adversely affects a child's educational performance

overrule   to annul, make void, or reverse a judicial decision

pardon   a governmental act, usually exercised by the chief executive, that relieves a criminal of the legal consequences of his crime and conviction

parent   a child's lawful father or mother

parental permission   written, informed parental consent, which allows a child's participation in an activity $<$—— is required prior to conducting a psychological evaluation of a child$>$

parity   the quality or state of being equal or equivalent

parol   oral, spoken, or verbal

parole   the conditional release of a patient from a mental treatment facility or of a prisoner from a prison—the condition is usually the successful integration of the paroled individual back into the community

partially-sighted   individuals who are not legally blind, but who have 20/70 vision or less in the better eye after best correction

particulars   the details of a legal claim or charge (see bill of particulars)

partner   a member of a partnership

partnership   a business agreement between two or more persons to pool their resources, with the understanding that individual partners will share the control and the profits or losses of their business

party   a person who is involved in a contract, conveyance, or law suit

penal   punishable; involving a penalty

peonage   see institutional peonage

per capita   by the head; share and share alike; a method of division whereby each person shares equally

per curium   by the court. A per curium opinion is one in which all judges of the court concur

per se   by itself, unconnected

percent reimbursement   a financing method whereby partial or full percentage of all costs incurred by local school districts for education of the handicapped is assumed by the state education agency

performance contract   a teaching agreement providing that students in an educational program must show achievement gains in a specified amount of time and in keeping with predetermined objectives and procedures

periodic review   the systematic follow up, or review, of children who have been evaluated and placed in special class settings. The purpose of the periodic review is to monitor the evaluation and placement decisions and to insure children's continued rights to an appropriate education

perjury   the crime of intentionally giving, under oath, false testimony as to some material matter

person   a legal entity, including men, women, children, and corporations

personal property   a right or interest in things that are moveable; all property that is not land or things permanently attached to land (in contrast see real property)

personal representative   an executor or administrator; one who administers the estate of a deceased individual; a fiduciary

petition   a written application made to a court <law suits are often initiated by the filing of a —— or complaint>

physical therapy   medically prescribed procedures and activities to relieve pain, improve circulation, promote healing, strengthen muscles, and increase mobility

PINS   abbr persons in need of supervision (see CINS)

placement process   the identification, evaluation, and decision to assign a child to a particular and appropriate educational setting

plaintiff   the party initiating a court action or proceeding

plan of implementation   the organization and design for the appropriate execution of educational objectives—usually developed by the state for the local school districts to implement according to their resources and needs

plea   the defendant's answer to the plaintiff's petition

pleadings   allegations of the respective parties in a legal action

pledge   the bailment of personal property as security for a debt

police power   that power with which any governmental body is empowered to enact laws to protect the property, life, health, and well-being of its citizens

post hoc   after the fact; hereafter

power of attorney   a written instrument in which a person authorizes another, known as an attorney in fact, to act for him

prayer   a request made of a court of equity

precedent   a court decision that sets guidelines for further court action by the same or other courts

preponderance   the greater weight or more convincing $<$the ——— (more than 50%) of the evidence$>$

preschool handicapped   a mental or physical handicap in children age zero through six—legislation requires "Child find" procedures and surveys to locate and provide appropriate evaluation and treatment of these children

presumption   a legal inference or conclusion about the truth or falsehood of a fact

presumption of innocence   a legal conclusion that a person charged with a criminal offence is innocent unless and until he is proven guilty beyond a reasonable doubt

pretrial hearing   a conference held prior to a trial during which time the court and attorneys seek to simplify the issues in controversy and eliminate matters not in dispute   to shorten and make less complicated the actual trial

prima facie evidence   evidence deemed by law to be sufficient to establish a fact, if the evidence is not disputed

prior notice   in special education, a procedure whereby parents are informed of plans to evaluate their child, told who requested the evaluation, given the right to refuse evaluation, and acquainted with other due process guarantees

private law   that body of law that regulates and enforces the rights that exist between private citizens (in contrast, see public law)

privilege   a special right or advantage

privileged communication   a communication made to an attorney, in professional confidence, that he is not permitted to divulge

privileged information   restricted or confidential records or files (see access to records)

pro bono publico   for the public good; legal services provided on a pro bono basis are donated by an attorney without charge

pro forma   as a matter of form

pro rata   proportionally; according to a given percentage

pro se   for himself; in his own behalf

probable cause hearing   a judicial hearing held to determine whether there is sufficient evidence to establish possible legal liability and therefore warrant further judicial hearings or trial

probate   the act or process of proving the validity of a will   <wills are ——d before designated judicial officers or clerks>

probation   permitting a convict to remain free of confinement during a suspended sentence, provided he is of good behavior and complies with designated restrictions of his activity

procedural displacement   the transfer of a handicapped child from one educational placement to another

promulgation   public proclamation of a law or proposed law

proof   the establishment of a fact by evidence

prosecute   to conduct a judicial procedure; most frequently used in criminal proceedings

proximate cause   an act that is the effective cause of an injury

proxy   a person who is substituted by another to represent him; an agent

psychiatrist   a physician specializing in mental, emotional, or behavioral disorders

psychological services   1: administering psychological and educational tests   2: interpreting the results   3: gathering and interpreting information about child behavior   4: working with other staff members in planning school programs to meet the special needs of children as indicated by psychological tests, interviews, and behavioral evaluations   5: planning and managing a program of psychological services, including psychological counseling for children and parents

psychologist   an individual with an advanced educational degree who specializes in the evaluation or treatment of mental disorders

public defender   one authorized or appointed to defend a person accused of crime, when the accused lacks the funds to employ private counsel

public law   that body of law that regulates and enforces the rights that exist between private citizens and the government (in contrast see private law)

punitive damages   (see damages)

pygmalion effect   (see self-fulfilling prophecy)

quash   to vacate, annul, or make void

quasi   almost, alike, or resembling

quid pro quo   an exchange of one thing for something else

quo warranto   a proceeding commenced by the government to dissolve a corporation or remove a person from public office

quorum   the minimum number of persons who must be present at a meeting before business may be lawfully transacted

ratification   the confirmation of responsibility for and obligation incurred by a previous act done by oneself or one's agent

rating scales   (see behavior rating scales)

ratio deciden   the reason or grounds used by a court for its decision in a case

rational basis   reasonable relationship or basis in the law; application of law in a just and fair manner <government may discriminate against some groups if there is a ―――― for the discrimination>

real evidence   evidence furnished by the things themselves (such as wounds, fingerprints, or weapons) as distinguished from a testimonial description of the evidence

real property   land and everything attached permanently to it (see personal property for contrast)

rebuttable presumption   a legal inference about a fact, which may be disproved by the introduction of contradictory evidence

receiver   an impartial person appointed by a court to receive and preserve the property or funds in litigation or that belong to a legally incompetent person

recess   a short suspension of court business, but without adjourning business generally

recognizance   an obligation entered into before a court to do some act, usually to appear at a later date or pay a debt

record   a written account of judicial or legislative proceedings

recovery   the collection of a debt or obtaining a thing by the use of a law suit

redirection   the examination of a witness by the party who called him, after the cross-examination of the witness by the other party

redress   compensation or satisfaction for a wrong or loss

referee   a person appointed by the court to take testimony and make a report thereof to the presiding judge

referral   the process by which a teacher or parent formally indicates the need for a child's evaluation. Most often school districts have formal written guidelines and forms that explain their referral procedures

regular program   a standard educational program in regular classes or grades; in contrast to a special class or program

rehabilitation   a program designed to help a disabled person achieve the maximum degree of self-sufficiency; the focus is on a person's strengths and assets rather than his liabilities

reimbursement for personnel   a program by which the state repays local districts all or part of costs incurred in hiring special education staff for special education pupils

release   the giving up of a right or privilege; the discharge from an obligation

relevant   when two facts are so related that the proof of one tends to prove the existence of the other

remand   to send back <an appellate court may ---- a case to the trial court for further consideration>

remedy   the means by which the violation of a right is prevented or compensated for

removal   the transfer of a case from one court or jurisdiction to another

repeal   to revoke or abrogate by legislative enactment

rescission   the annulment or cancellation of a contract entered into through fraud, misinterpretation, or excusable error

respondent   the party who answers or argues against a contract

restitution   restoration to its rightful owner

restraining order   see injunction

retainer   a down payment made by a client to his attorney to ensure future representation

return   the act of a sheriff or other officer in returning to the court a writ or notice he has served or executed

reversal   the decision of an appellate court to annul or vacate the judgment of a lower court

right   1: justice; ethical correctness   2: a privilege, power or ability; those freedoms provided and guaranteed by the Constitution

right to access   a parent's privilege to review the confidential school files of his child

right to education   this phrase refers to the relatively recent guarantee of handicapped children's ability to receive free public education that is suitable to each child's needs

right to treatment   this phrase refers to the relatively recent guarantee that mentally handicapped persons, who are involuntarily committed to mental institutions, will receive treatment as a quid pro quo for their confinement

robbery   the taking of personal property from another by the use of force or threats

sanction   legal use of force to secure obedience to law

satisfaction   the discharge of a legal obligation by paying a party what is due to him

school psychologist   a psychologist whose specific expertise is in the field of education and who is employed to help school children, their parents, and teachers

SDOE   abbr State Department of Education

SEA   abbr State Education Agency syn SDOE

seal   an impression made upon a written instrument to show that the document is authentic and executed in a formal manner

second priority children   handicapped children, within each disability, with the most severe handicaps who are receiving an inadequate education

security   assurance; collateral; indemnification; protection

segregated classes   homogeneously grouped public school classes, often self-contained—frequently based on classification of pupils; e.g. blind, deaf, mentally retarded, gifted, and others; in some public schools, pupils in regular grades are separated into homogeneous groups, or "tracks," of bright, average, and slow groups

self-fulfilling prophecy   the phenomenon that occurs when a child performs or achieves in accordance with preconceived expectations of the teacher

sentence   the formal pronouncement of the punishment given a convicted defendant in a criminal prosecution

service the formal delivery by an authorized person (such as a sheriff or marshall) of a judicial notice

set-off a counter demand that a defendant has against the plaintiff; a counterclaim or crossclaim

settlement the ending of a law suit or controversy by agreement or consensus. The settlement often involves a compromise of the parties' original demands

slander oral defamation of a person resulting in injury to his reputation

solvency the ability to pay debts as they mature

sovereign immunity the legal principle that a state government or its employees cannot be sued in court without its consent or permission

special education instruction and related services in the classroom, home, hospital, or institution designed to meet the unique needs of handicapped children

specific learning disability (see learning disability)

specific performance an equitable remedy whereby a contracting party is compelled by the court to perform as required by the terms of his contract

speech impaired a communication disorder, such as stuttering, impaired articulation, a language impairment, or a voice impairment, that adversely affects a child's educational performance

SSB abbr State School Board

stare decises the legal doctrine that judicial decisions should stand as precedents for guidance in similar cases arising in the future

status offense an activity permitted of adults, but considered a crime if committed by a juvenile; e.g., truancy, running away from home

status quo the existing state of affairs at any given time

statute a law enacted by the legislative branch of a government

statute of limitations a law that limits the time within which a law suit may be brought <jurisdictions have difference —— for different causes of action>

stay a court order that stops or restrains a judicial proceeding

stipulation an agreement made by attorneys on opposing sides in a law suit regulating matters of procedure

stockholder one who, by virtue of his ownership of stock, is an owner of a corporation

straight sum reimbursements   a financial policy whereby the state stipulates and reimburses local districts a specific amount for each handicapped child

strict liability   a legal doctrine that makes one responsible for the consequences of his actions, even though he is not negligent or has not acted in bad faith

sua sponte   voluntarily; on his own accord without prompting or suggestion

subpoena   a writ or order commanding a named person to appear and testify in a legal proceeding

subpoena duces tecum   an order commanding a named person to appear before a court and bring with him named documents he has in his possession

subrogation   the substitution of one person in another's place

substantive law   the part of the law that creates, defines, and regulates rights and duties

sue   to commence a legal proceeding to protect or enforce a civil right

sui juris   having the legal capacity to manage one's own affairs

suit   any proceeding in a court of law to recover a right or claim

summary proceeding   a form of legal proceeding in which the established procedure is disregarded, especially in the matter of trial by jury, in favor of shorter, less formal and less complicated procedures

summons   a legal notice notifying a person that an action has been brought against him and requiring him to answer the complaint within a specified time that must be personally served upon that person

supersedeas   a court order commanding a stay of legal proceedings, especially the execution of a judgment

supplemental proceeding   the procedure by which a judgment creditor has the right to force the judgment debtor to submit to an examination for the purpose of discovering any assets that may be applied to the payment of the debt

supplementary aid   additional state or federal funding allotted to local school districts for educational purposes

supplementary services   special services developed for educational needs; e.g., reading specialists, speech therapists, school psychologists, and the like

surety a person who obligates himself to be responsible for the action or debt of another; a guarantor

suspect classification the governmental grouping of individuals for the purpose of treating members of the group differently than others. When the groups contain persons who are disadvantaged or stigmatized, i.e., groupings based upon race, sex, alienage, legitimacy, their classification and separate treatment is suspect and therefore violative of the constitution right of equal protection, unless the government can demonstrate a compelling state interest for treating the group separately.

suspension 1: a temporary delay or interruption 2: temporary exclusion of a child from school attendance for disciplinary reasons (see expelled)

swear to take an oath; to verify

targeting defining and identifying those specific behaviors of a child that need correction; e.g., the recurrent temper tantrums of a behavior problem child

task-level performance an educational approach utilizing objectives specifically oriented to a child's individual needs. A reading objective might be implemented in a sequential manner, allowing the child to achieve at his own rate of learning

teacher expectancy (see self-fulfilling prophecy)

tender the act of offering money or some other performance to fulfill a legal obligation

term a period of time during which a court or school operates

test bias (see middle class test bias; biased testing; native language)

test case a single law suit selected from many similar suits embracing similar legal principals, which is decided initially and then used as a guide in deciding or setting the remaining suits

testamentary pertaining to a will

testate with a will <John Doe died ——>

testator one who dies leaving a valid will

testify to give evidence as a witness under oath in a judicial inquiry

testimony oral evidence given by a witness under oath

test norms those statistics that were derived from the population tested when the instrument was designed

testing the measurement of an individual's psychological or educational attributes through instruments designed to derive a specific type of information; i.e., achievement tests are designed to determine the amount of knowledge a child has acquired in a given subject

third party beneficiary   a person who benefits from the provisions of a contract even though he is not a party to the contract or bound by its provisions

token economy   a structured environment based on behavior modification principles in which rewards or tokens (such as poker chips or other symbols) may be exchanged for some valued activity or object at a later time. The purpose is to provide immediate positive reinforcement for desired behavior

tort   a wrongful injury to a person, his property, or his reputation

total exclusion   the refusal of a child to a school system due to a handicap for which no appropriate educational program is available; The Education of Handicapped Children Act, PL 94-142, requires that a program be developed for such a child within ten days following program request by his parents

to wit   namely; that is to say

trainable mentally retarded (TMR)   those children whose educational needs cannot be met in a program designed for the educable mentally retarded because of an inability to acquire necessary skills as determined by a substantially reduced rate of intellectual development; they usually score three standard deviations or more below the mean on the normal distribution of intelligence

training of regular educators   efforts to acquaint the regular classroom teacher with minimal knowledge in special education in order that regular classes might accommodate the handicapped child more appropriately—also known as in-service training

transcript   1: a copy of a writing 2: the printed record of a court proceeding

transition program   an educational program that enables a handicapped child to advance smoothly from one level of instruction or special class to another before being returned to a regular school program

trespass   an unlawful injury to a person, his rights, or his property

trial   a judicial examination and resolution according to established rules and procedures of a conflict between two or more parties

trier of fact   the jury, or the judge in nonjury trials, whose role it is to decide factual issues in a trial

trust   a legal mechanism by which property (the trust corpus) is held by one party (the trustee) for the benefit of another (the beneficiary)

ultra vires the act of a corporation in going beyond the powers or authority expressed or implied in its charter or by statute

undue influence the mental coercion of one person by another, particularly when the two have a fiduciary relationship

unethical not in accord with professional standards

unit financing an arrangement whereby school districts are reimbursed a fixed sum by the state for each designated unit of classroom instruction; a unit of exceptional children often refers to a classroom of sixteen students

usury the lending of money at an illegally high interest rate

vacate to cancel, rescind, annul, or set aside; e.g., a vacated judgment

vacation the period of time between terms of court

valid legally binding or effective

vendee a buyer or purchaser of property or services

vendor a seller of property or services

venireman a member of the panel of jurors

venue the geographic area, e.g., county or state, over which a court has the authority to try cases

verbatim record a complete transcription of a trial, hearing, or other official procedure

verdict the decision or finding of a jury at the conclusion of a trial

vested that which is settled and absolute; not contingent upon anything

visually impaired a visual impairment that, even with correction, adversely affects a child's educational performance—includes both partially seeing and blind children

vital statistics general information about a person, such as a date of birth, names of parents, race, and sex

void null; of no legal force or effect

voidable that which is valid, but may be voided; e.g., contracts of infants and others lacking full legal capacity are usually considered voidable

voir dire the examination under oath of prospective jurors or witnesses to assure their qualification and impartiality

waiver the surrender, either expressed or implied, of a legal right

wanton reckless or malicious

ward a person, usually a minor or one with a mental disability, who is under the care of a court

warrant a document of authority issued by a court directing an officer to perform a specific act; e.g., arrest warrant, search warrant

warranty(ee)   a guarantee; a promise that a thing is as it is represented to be

weighted formula system   a financial arrangement whereby a state reimburses a local school district for the regular per pupil expenditure multiplied by a factor that may vary by disability and from state to state

witness   one who testifies about what he has seen, heard, or otherwise knows

writ   an order issued by a court directing an officer of the law to perform an act

writ of certiorari (writ of error)   an order from an appellate court to a lower or trial court that requests that a case record be forwarded to the appellate court for review

APPENDIX

EDUCATION OF HANDICAPPED CHILDREN

Implementation of Part B of the Education of the Handicapped Act

Title 45—Public Welfare

CHAPTER 1—OFFICE OF EDUCATION, DEPARTMENT OF HEALTH, EDUCATION, AND WELFARE

EDUCATION OF HANDICAPPED CHILDREN

Implementation of Part B of the Education of the Handicapped Act

AGENCY: U.S. Office of Education, HEW.

ACTION: Final regulation.

SUMMARY: These regulations implement amendments to Part B of the Education of the Handicapped Act (as required by the Education for All Handicapped Children Act of 1975) by: (1) amending the existing regulations governing assistance to States for education of handicapped children, (2) adding a new part on incentive grants programs for handicapped children aged three through five, and (3) making certain conforming amendments to the general provisions for State-administered programs.

These regulations govern the provision of formula grant funds to State and local educational agencies to assist them in the education of handicapped children.

The regulations include provisions which are designed (1) to assure that all handicapped children have available to them a free appropriate public education; (2) to assure that the rights of handicapped children and their parents are protected; (3) to assist States and localities to provide for the education of handicapped children; and (4) to assess and assure the effectiveness of efforts to educate such children.

These regulations also include the final rules for counting and reporting handicapped children. (The child count rules were published in proposed form on September 8, 1976, and were incorporated into the December 30 proposed regulations for the convenience of the reader.)

EFFECTIVE DATE: October 1, 1977.

FOR FURTHER INFORMATION CONTACT:

Daniel Ringelheim,** Director, Division of Assistance to States, Bureau of Education for the Handicapped, 400 Maryland Ave. SW., (room 4046 Donohoe Building), Washington, D.C. 20202, telephone: 202-472-2265;

or

Thomas B. Irvin, Policy Officer, Bureau of Education for the Handicapped, 400 Maryland Ave. SW., (room 4926 Donohoe Building), Washington, D.C. 20202, telephone: 202-245-9405.

---

* Office of Education, Department of Health, Education, and Welfare. Washington, U.S. Govt. Print. Office. Reprinted from the *Federal Register*, Vol. 42, No. 163— Tuesday, August 23, 1977, pp. 42474-42518.

** Daniel Ringelheim is deceased.

SUPPLEMENTARY INFORMATION:

RULEMAKING HISTORY—PUBLIC PARTICIPATION

Because of the potential impact that Pub. L. 94-142 will have on the education of handicapped children throughout the Nation, and on the agencies that serve them, the Office of Education recognized the need for intensive public participation in the development of regulations, and took steps to insure maximum public involvement throughout the entire rulemaking process. A description of these steps is included in the following paragraphs.

Before the proposed rules were drafted, the Office of Education carried out a massive effort to obtain comments and suggestions for developing regulations from interested parties throughout the Nation. This involved participating in approximately 20 meetings about the law conducted on both a geographic and special interest basis. Approximately 2,200 people participated in these meetings and several hundred comments were received.

In June 1976, the Office of Education convened a national writing group of approximately 170 people to develop concept papers for use in writing the regulations. This group was composed of parents, representatives of special interest organizations (i.e., AFT, NEA, private schools), and administrators of State and local schools. These concept papers formed the basis for the proposed regulations.

During the months of July-November, the Office of Education prepared several redrafts of the concept papers and continued to seek inputs on these drafts from various interested parties.

On December 30, 1976, the proposed rules were published in the FEDERAL REGISTER. Written comments and recommendations on the proposed rules were invited for a 60-day comment period ending March 1, 1977; and public hearings were held in Washington, San Francisco, Denver, Chicago, Boston, and Atlanta. Over 1,600 written comments were received during that period, all of which were reviewed and considered by the Office of Education in preparing these final regulations.

The tapes of the hearings and copies of written comments are available for public inspection at the Bureau of Education for the Handicapped, room 4921, Donohoe Building, 400 6th Street SW., Washington, DC. 20202.

In addition to the above public comment activities, the Office of Education continued with other public participation efforts, including:

(1) Participating in 10 regional meetings of the American Association of School Administrators and other regional meetings with the Council of the Great City Schools;

(2) Conducting a national conference on the regulations for administrators of various State agency programs for the handicapped, and participating in meetings at other national conferences; and

(3) Participating in a special series of meetings organized by the Institute for Educational Leadership and composed of representatives of the National Governors' Conference, the National Conference of State Legislatures, the National Association of State Boards of Education, and the Education Commission of the States.

ACTION TAKEN ON PUBLIC COMMENTS PART 100b—STATE ADMINISTERED PROGRAMS

No comments were received on the proposed amendments to Part 100b, and no changes have been made.

PART 121a—ASSISTANCE TO STATES FOR EDUCATION OF HANDICAPPED CHILDREN

The Office of Education conducted a careful review of the public comments received and summarized them by subpart and topic.

A very large number of comments dealt with specific statutory requirements. These comments expressed concerns about the statute and suggested changes to be made in the statutory provisions. However, because they are statutory, the Office of Education is not able to make any changes in the regulations with respect to those points. Some of the statutory provisions on which comments were received, together with concerns about them, are included below:

(1) Free appropriate public education—problems with timelines and concerns about the cost of implementing this requirement;

(2) Priorities—concerns about Federal priorities which are not consistent with State and local priorities;

(3) Individualized education programs—suggestions that the requirement be deleted from the regulation unless more funds are available for implementing it;

(4) Prior notice and other due process procedures—concerns about the amount of detail in these requirements and the time, cost and paper work involved in their implementation;

(5) State educational agency responsibility for general supervision of all special education programs in the State—concerns about lack of authority over other State agencies and the lack of funds to efficiently implement the provision;

(6) Child count—concerns about the dates on which the count must be taken.

Another large number of commenters cited specific concerns or issues with respect to the content of the proposed rules. Because of the large number of comments received, individual comments have been consolidated.

Part 121m—Incentive Grants

Part 121m sets forth the conditions under which States may receive grants to assist in the education of handicapped children aged three through five. Congress established incentive grants in the recognition that when education begins at the earlier stages of development (1) benefits are maximized, (2) additional or more severe handicaps may be prevented, and (3) greater long-term cost effectiveness is realized.

Comment: An issue was raised concerning the possible use of incentive grant funds for children from birth through two years of age.

Response: Section 619 of the Act and the legislative history specify that the use of incentive grant funds is limited to children aged three through five years. However, the State's entitlement under section 611 of the Act may be used for children from birth through age twenty-one.

Comment: An issue was raised as to whether incentive grant funds may be used for administrative or supervisory costs.

Response: The regulation has been amended to make it clear that administrative costs are allowable.

Minimum Regulation—Future Rulemaking Plans

The preamble to the proposed rules contained the following statement regarding minimum regulations:

The Department sees the development of regulations for implementing Pub. L. 94-142 as being an evolutionary process which will continue over a period of several years. The actual impact and consequences of the statutory provision and problems which State and local educational agencies may have in implementing these provisions are not known at this time. Therefore, the Department feels that the most rational approach to follow is (1) to write minimum regulations at this point, and (2) to amend and revise such regulations in the future as need and experience dictate.

Because the Statute is very comprehensive and specific on many points, the Department has elected (1) to incorporate the basic wording or substance of the Statute directly into the regulations, and (2) to expand on the statutory provisions only where additional interpretation seems to be necessary.

Although some commenters felt that more extensive regulations were necessary, many persons who responded to the proposed rules felt that the Office of Education had already over-regulated and should cut back on the rules when they are published in final form. At this juncture, the Office of Education holds to the same position that it took in the proposed rules, and for the same reasons as set forth in that document.

The Office of Education believes that some working experience with this regulation is essential before determining whether there is a need to amend it. Once the regulation becomes effective (Oct. 1, 1977) and people gain experience in implementing it, there will likely be a series of questions raised in individual States which could result in the development of policies and interpretations that would be proposed for addition to these regulations.

OVERVIEW OF CHANGES IN THE PART 121a REGULATIONS

A substantial number of changes have been made in response to comments received on the proposed rules. However, few of these changes have resulted in adding major substantive requirements. Most of the changes are technical or have been made in an attempt to provide greater clarity or to add more explanatory material.

Extensive use has been made of explanatory comments in the text of the regulations. The purpose of these comments is to attempt, where appropriate, to clarify or further interpret a particular rule or to provide direction and assistance without imposing additional requirements. For example, an extensive explanation is included under the excess cost requirement and an example is given on how to make the computation under that requirement.

ORGANIZATION OF REGULATIONS

Three parts of Title 45 of the Code of Federal Regulations are amended by this document:

(1) Part 100b—*State Administered Programs.* This includes certain conforming amendments to the regulations under section 434(b) (1) (A) of the General Education Provisions Act.

(2) Part 121a—*Assistance to States for Education of Handicapped Children.* This is divided into seven subparts: (A) General, (B) State Annual Program Plans and Local Applications, (C) Services, (D) Private Schools, (E) Procedural Safeguards, (F) State Administration, and (G) Allocation of Funds and Reports

(3) Part 121m—*Incentive Grants.* This governs the administration of the incentive grants program for handicapped children aged three through five, authorized under section 619 of the Act.

ANALYSIS OF REGULATIONS

Appendix A of Part 121a includes an analysis of each subpart, which (1) discusses significant comments received and the action taken with respect to those comments, and (2) explains the basis for any changes made from the proposed rules published on December 30, 1976.

TOPICAL INDEX

Appendix B of Part 121a includes an index of the major topics in the regulations (e.g., free appropriate public education, priorities, and individualized education program) and the specific sections under which each term is used.

NOTE—The Department of Health,

Education, and Welfare, has determined that this document contains a major proposal requiring preparation of an Economic Impact Analysis (EIA) Statement under Executive Orders 11821 and 11949 and OMB Circular A-107, and certifies that an Economic Impact Analysis has been prepared. However, because the portion of this regulation involving major costs is virtually identical to the content of subpart D of the regulation issued on discrimination against the handicapped under section 504 of the Rehabilitation Act of 1973 (45 CFR Part 84; published May 4, 1977, at 42 FR 22675), the Department has determined that (a) this regulation involves no substantial costs not imposed by Part 84 and (b) the pertinent parts of the EIA Statement for that regulation meet the EIA requirements for this regulation. Both regulations impose the following requirements: (1) appropriate education to handicapped children; (2) identification and evaluation of handicapped children; and (3) procedural safeguards for handicapped children and their parents.

(Catalog of Federal Domestic Assistance Number 13.449, Education of Handicapped Children, Part B.) Dated: August 12, 1977.

JOHN ELLIS,

. . . .
Acting U.S. Commissioner of Education.

Approved: August 15, 1977.

HALE CHAMPION,

. . . .
Acting Secretary of Health, Education, and Welfare.

Title 45 of the Code of Federal Regulations is amended as follows:

PART 100b—STATE ADMINISTERED PROGRAMS

1. In Part 100b, § 100b.17 is revised to read as follows:

§ 100b.17 General applications.

(a) The general application of a State must meet the requirements of section 434(b) (1) (A) of the General Education Provisions Act.

(b) A State does not have to resubmit its general application.
(20 U.S.C. 1232c(b) (1) (A).)

(c) (1) The following statutes require that a State must submit certain provisions to the Commissioner which are similar to provisions in the general application.

(2) Subject to paragraph (d) of this section, if the Commissioner has approved a State's general application, the State does not have to submit the provisions required under the following statutes:

(i) *Compensatory education.* Section 142(a) (2) and (3) of Title I of the Elementary and Secondary Education Act of 1965, as amended.
(20 U.S.C. 1232c(b) (1) (A) (ii) (II), (III).)

(ii) *School library resources.* Section 203(a) (5), (6) and (7) of Title II of the Elementary and Secondary Education Act of 1965, as amended.
(20 U.S.C. 1232c(b) (1) (A) (ii) (II), (III), and (IV).)

(iii) *Supplementary educational centers and services; guidance, counseling, and testing.* Section 305(b) (9) (B), (10), and (11) of Title II of the Elementary and Secondary Education Act of 1965, as amended.
(20 U.S.C. 1232c(b) (1) (A) (ii) (II, (III) and (IV).)

(iv) *Education of the handicapped.* Section 613(a) (7) (A), (9) (B), and (10) of Part B of the Education of the Handicapped Act, as amended.
(20 U.S.C. 1232c(b) (1) (A) (ii) (II), (III) and (IV).)

(v) *Adult education.* Section 306(a) (6) and (7) of the Adult Education Act, as amended.
(20 U.S.C. 1232c(b) (1) (A) (ii) (II), (III).)

(vi) *Strengthening instruction in academic subjects.* Section 1004(a) (2) and (3) of Title X of the National Defense Education Act of 1958, as amended.
(20 U.S.C. 1232c(b) (1) (A) (ii), ((II), (III).)

(vii) *State reading improvement programs.* Section 714(a) (10) of Title VII-B of the Education Amendments of 1974.
(20 U.S.C. 1232c(b) (1) (A) (ii), (III).)

(d) (1) The general application does not change the legal substance of the provisions listed under paragraph (c) (2) of this section.

(2) If a provision listed in paragraph (c) (2) of this section is different in wording from an assurance in the general application, the provision listed in that paragraph governs any question of compliance with the assurance.
20 U.S.C. 1232c(b) (1) (B) (i), (b) (1) (B) (iii), (b) (2).)

2. In Part 100b, § 100b.35 is revised to read as follows:

§ 100b.35   Effective date of an application, plan, or amendment.

(a) Federal funds are available only for obligations incurred under:

(1) A State plan approved by the Commissioner (in the case of the programs set forth in § 100b.10 other than those referenced in § 100b.15(a); or

(2) A general application and an annual program plan approved by the Commissioner (in the case of the programs referenced in § 100b.15(a)).

(b) A State plan, general application, annual program plan, or amendment to any of them, is effective on the date the State submits it to the Federal Government in substantially approvable form. However, the effective date cannot be earlier than the first day of the fiscal period for which it is submitted.

(c) The Commissioner sends the State agency a notice of approval, in-

cluding notice of the effective date, when the application, plan, or amendment is approved.

(d) Federal funds are not available for obligation by a State or local agency before the effective date of the State plan or annual program plan (whichever is submitted under paragraph (a) of this section). If funds are expressly made available by statute for the devolopment of the State plan, general application, or annual program plan, the first sentence of this paragraph does not apply to obligations by the State for that purpose.
(20 U.S.C. 1221e-3 (a) (1).)

3. In Part 100b, § 100b.55 is revised to read as follows:

§ 100b.55   Obligation by receipts.

(a) *Period of obligation.* Federal funds which the Federal government may obligate during a fiscal period remain available for obligation by State and local recipients through the end of that fiscal period. Federal funds made available for construction of facilities remain available for obligation by State and local recipients for that purpose for a reasonable period of time as determined by the Commissioner.

(b) *Carryovers.* In accordance with section 414(b) of the General Education Provisions Act, any Federal funds which are not obligated by State and local recipients before the end of the fiscal period under paragraph (a) of this section, remain available for obligation by those agencies for one additional fiscal year.

(c) *Determinations of obligation* (1) An obligation for the acquisition of real or personal property, for the construction of facilities, or for the performance of work, is incurred by a recipient on the date it makes a binding written commitment.

(2) An obligation for personal services, for services performed by public utilities, for travel, or for the rental of real or personal property, is incurred

by a recipient on the date it receives the services, its personnel takes the travel, or it uses the rented property. (20 U.S.C. 1221c(a); 1225(b); 1232c (b) (1) (A) (ii) (II).)

4. Part 121a is revised to read as follows:

PART 121a—ASSISTANCE TO STATES FOR EDUCATION OF HANDICAPPED CHILDREN

Subpart A—General

PURPOSE, APPLICABILITY, AND GENERAL PROVISIONS REGULATIONS

AUTHORITY: Part B of the Education of the Handicapped Act, Pub. L. 91-230, Title VI, as amended, 89 Stat. 776-794 (20 U.S.C. 1411-1420), unless otherwise noted.

Subpart A—General

PURPOSE, APPLICABILITY, AND GENERAL PROVISIONS REGULATIONS

§ 121a.1 Purpose.

The purpose of this part is:
(a) To insure that all handicapped children have available to them a free appropriate public education which includes special education and related services to meet their unique needs.
(b) To insure that the rights of handicapped children and their parents are protected,
(c) To assist States and localities to provide for the education of all handicapped children, and
(d) To assess and insure the effectiveness of efforts to educate those children.
(20 U.S.C. 1401 Note.)

§ 121a.2 Applicability to State, local, and private agencies.

(a) *States.* This part applies to each State which receives payments under Part B of the Education of the Handicapped Act.
(b) *Public agencies within the State.* The annual program plan is submitted by the State educational agency on behalf of the State as a whole. Therefore, the provisions of this part apply to all political subdivisions of the State that are involved in the education of handicapped children. These would include: (1) The State educational agency, (2) local educational agencies and intermediate educational units, (3) other State agencies and schools (such as Departments of Mental Health and Welfare and State schools for the deaf or blind), and (4) State correctional facilities.
(c) *Private schools and facilities.* Each public agency in the State is responsible for insuring that the rights and protections under this part are given to children referred to or placed in private schools and facilities by that public agency.
(See §§ 121a.400-121a.403.)
(20 U.S.C. 1412(1), (6); 1413(a); 1413(a) (4) (B).)
Comment. The requirements of this part are binding on each public agency that has direct or delegated authority to provide special education and related services in a State that receives funds under Part B of the Act, regardless of

whether that agency is receiving funds under Part B.

§ 121a.3   General provisions regulations.

Assistance under Part B of the Act is subject to Parts 100, 100b, 100c, and 121 of this chapter, which include definitions and requirements relating to fiscal, administrative, property management, and other matters. (20 U.S.C. 1417(b).)

DEFINITIONS

Comment. Definitions of terms that are used throughout these regulations are included in this subpart. Other terms are defined in the specific subparts in which they are used. Below is a list of those terms and the specific sections and subparts in which they are defined:

Consent (Section 121a.500 of Subpart E)

Destruction (Section 121a.560 of Subpart E)

Direct services (Section 121a.370(b) (1) of Subpart C)

Evaluation (Section 121a.500 of Subpart E)

First priority children (Section 121a.320(a) of Subpart C)

Independent educational evaluation (Section 121a.503 of Subpart E)

Individualized education program (Section 121a.340 of Subpart C)

Participating agency (Section 121a.560 of Subpart E)

Personally identifiable (Section 121a.500 of Subpart E)

Private school handicapped children (Section 121a.450 of Subpart D)

Public expense (Section 121a.503 of Subpart E)

Second priority children (Section 121a.320(b) of Subpart C)

Special definition of "State" (Section 121a.700 of Subpart G)

Support services (Section 121a.370(b) (2) of Subpart C)

§ 121a.4   Free appropriate public education.

As used in this part, the term "free appropriate public education" means special education and related services which:

(a) Are provided at public expense, under public supervision and direction, and without charge.

(b) Meet the standards of the State educational agency, including the requirements of this part.

(c) Include preschool, elementary school, or secondary school education in the State involved, and

(d) Are provided in conformity with an individualized education program which meets the requirements under §§ 121a.340-121a.349 of Subpart C. (20 U.S.C. 1401 (18).)

§ 121a.5   Handicapped children.

(a) As used in this part, the term "handicapped children" means those children evaluated in accordance with §§ 121a.530-121a.534 as being mentally retarded, hard of hearing, deaf, speech impaired, visually handicapped, seriously emotionally disturbed, orthopedically impaired, other health impaired, deaf-blind, multi-handicapped, or as having specific learning disabilities, who because of those impairments need special education and related services.

(b) The terms used in this definition are defined as follows:

(1) "Deaf" means a hearing impairment which is so severe that the child is impaired in processing linguistic information through hearing, with or without amplification, which adversely affects educational performance.

(2) "Deaf-blind" means concomitant hearing and visual impairments, the combination of which causes such severe communication and other developmental and educational problems that they cannot be accommodated in special education programs solely for deaf or blind children.

(3) "Hard of hearing" means a hearing impairment, whether permanent or fluctuating, which adversely affects a child's educational performance but which is not included under the definition of "deaf" in this section.

(4) "Mentally retarded" means significantly subaverage general intellectual functioning existing concurrently with deficits in adaptive behavior and manifested during the developmental period, which adversely affects a child's educational performance.

(5) "Multihandicapped" means concomitant impairments (such as mentally retarded-blind, mentally retarded-orthopedically impaired, etc.), the combination of which causes such severe educational problems that they cannot be accommodated in special education programs solely for one of the impairments. The term does not include deaf-blind children.

(6) "Orthopedically impaired" means a severe orthopedic impairment which adversely affects a child's educational performance. The term includes impairments caused by congenital anomaly (e.g., clubfoot, absence of some member, etc.), impairments caused by disease (e.g. poliomyelitis, bone tuberculosis, etc.), and impairments from other causes (e.g., cerebral palsy, amputations, and fractures or burns which cause contractures).

(7) "Other health impaired" means limited strength, vitality or alertness, due to chronic or acute health problems such as a heart condition, tuberculosis, rheumatic fever, nephritis, asthma, sickle cell anemia, hemophilia, epilepsy, lead poisoning, leukemia, or diabetes, which adversely affects a child's educational performance.

(8) "Seriously emotionally disturbed" is defined as follows:

(i) The term means a condition exhibiting one or more of the following characteristics over a long period of time and to a marked degree, which adversely affects educational performance:

(A) An inability to learn which cannot be explained by intellectual, sensory or health factors;

(B) An inability to build or maintain satisfactory interpersonal relationships with peers and teachers;

(C) Inappropriate types of behavior or feelings under normal circumstances;

(D) A general pervasive mood of unhappiness or depression; or

(E) A tendency to develop physical symptoms or fears associated with personal or school problems.

(ii) The term includes children who are schizophrenic or autistic. The term does not include children who are socially maladjusted, unless it is determined that they are seriously emotionally disturbed.

(9) "Specific learning disability" means a disorder in one or more of the basic psychological processes involved in understanding or in using language, spoken or written, which may manifest itself in an imperfect ability to listen, think, speak, read, write, spell, or to do mathematical calculations. The term includes such conditions as perceptual handicaps, brain injury, minimal brain disfunction, dyslexia, and developmental aphasia. The term does not include children who have learning problems which are primarily the result of visual, hearing, or motor handicaps, of mental retardation, or of environmental, cultural, or economic disadvantage.

(10) "Speech impaired" means a communication disorder, such as stuttering, impaired articulation, a language impairment, or a voice impairment, which adversely affects a child's educational performance.

(11) "Visually handicapped" means a visual impairment which, even with correction, adversely affects a child's educational performance. The term

includes both partially seeing and blind children.
(20 U.S.C. 1401(1), (15).)

§ 121a.6 Include.

As used in this part, the term "include" means that the items named are not all of the possible items that are covered, whether like or unlike the ones named.
(20 U.S.C. 1417(b).)

§ 121a.7 Intermediate educational unit.

As used in this part, the term "intermediate educational unit" means any public authority, other than a local educational agency, which:

(a) Is under the general supervision of a State educational agency;

(b) Is established by State law for the purpose of providing free public education on a regional basis; and

(c) Provides special education and related services to handicapped children within that State.
(20 U.S.C. 1401(22).)

§ 121a.8 Local educational agency.

(a) As used in this part, the term "local educational agency" means a public board of education or other public authority legally constituted within a State for either administrative control or direction of, or to perform a service function for public elementary or secondary schools in a city, county, township, school district, or other political subdivision of a State or such combination of school districts or counties as are recognized in a State as an administrative agency for its public elementary or secondary schools. Such term also includes any other public institution or agency having administrative control and direction of a public elementary or secondary school.

(b) For the purposes of this part, the term "local educational agency" also includes intermediate educational units.

(20 U.S.C. 1401(8).)

§ 121a.9 Native language.

As used in this part, the term "native language" has the meaning given that term by section 703(a) (2) of the Bilingual Education Act, which provides as follows:

The term "native language," when used with reference to a person of limited English-speaking ability, means the language normally used by that person, or in the case of a child, the language normally used by the parents of the child.
(20 U.S.C. 880b-1(a) (2); 1401(21).)

Comment. Section 602(21) of the Education of the Handicapped Act states that the term "native language" has the same meaning as the definition from the Bilingual Educational Act. (The term is used in the prior notice and evaluation sections under §121a.-505(b) (2) and §121a.532(a) (1) of Subpart E.) In using the term, the Act does not prevent the following means of communication:

(1) In all direct contact with a child (including evaluation of the child), communication would be in the language normally used by the child and not that of the parents, if there is a difference between the two.

(2) If a person is deaf or blind, or has no written language, the mode of communication would be that normally used by the person (such as sign language, braille, or oral communication).

§ 121a.10 Parent.

As used in this part, the term "parent" means a parent, a guardian, a person acting as a parent of a child, or a surrogate parent who has been appointed in accordance with § 121a.514. The term does not include the State if the child is a ward of the State.
(20 U.S.C. 1415.)

Comment. The term "parent" is defined to include persons acting in the place of a parent, such as a grandmother or stepparent with whom a child lives, as well as persons who are legally responsible for a child's welfare.

§ 121a.11 Public agency.

As used in this part, the term "public agency" includes the State educational agency, local educational agencies, intermediate educational units, and any other political subdivisions of the State which are responsible for providing education to handicapped children. (20 U.S.C. 1412(2) (B); 1412(6); 1413(a).)

§ 121a.12 Qualified.

As used in this part, the term "qualified" means that a person has met State educational agency approved or recognized certification, licensing, registration, or other comparable requirements which apply to the area in which he or she is providing special education or related services. (20 U.S.C. 1417(b).)

§ 121a.13 Related services.

(a) As used in this part, the term "related services" means transportation and such developmental, corrective, and other supportive services as are required to assist a handicapped child to benefit from special education, and includes speech pathology and audiology, psychological services, physical and occupational therapy, recreation, early identification and assessment of disabilities in children, counseling services, and medical services for diagnostic or evaluation purposes. The term also includes school health services, social work services in schools, and parent counseling and training.

(b) The terms used in this definition are defined as follows:

(1) "Audiology" includes:

(i) Identification of children with hearing loss;

(ii) Determination of the range, nature, and degree of hearing loss, including referral for medical or other professional attention for the habilitation of hearing;

(iii) Provision of habilitative activities, such as language habilitation, auditory training, speech reading (lipreading), hearing evaluation, and speech conservation;

(iv) Creation and administration of programs for prevention of hearing loss;

(v) Counseling and guidance of pupils, parents, and teachers regarding hearing loss; and

(vi) Determination of the child's need for group and individual amplification, selecting and fitting an appropriate aid, and evaluating the effectiveness of amplification.

(2) "Counseling services" means services provided by qualified social workers, psychologists, guidance counselors, or other qualified personnel.

(3) "Early identification" means the implementation of a formal plan for identifying a disability as early as possible in a child's life.

(4) "Medical services" means services provided by a licensed physician to determine a child's medically related handicapped condition which results in the child's need for special education and related services.

(5) "Occupational therapy" includes:

(i) Improving, developing or restoring functions impaired or lost through illness, injury, or deprivation;

(ii) Improving ability to perform tasks for independent functioning when functions are impaired or lost; and

(iii) Preventing, through early intervention, initial or further impairment or loss of function.

(6) "Parent counseling and training" means assisting parents in understanding the special needs of their child and providing parents with information about child development.

(7) "Physical therapy" means services provided by a qualified physical therapist.

(8) "Psychological services" include:

(i) Administering psychological and educational tests, and other assessment procedures;

(ii) Interpreting assessment results;

(iii) Obtaining, integrating, and interpreting information about child behavior and conditions relating to learning.

(iv) Consulting with other staff members in planning school programs to meet the special needs of children as indicated by psychological tests, interviews, and behavioral evaluations; and

(v) Planning and managing a program of psychological services, including psychological counseling for children and parents.

(9) "Recreation" includes:

(i) Assessment of leisure function;

(ii) Therapeutic recreation services;

(iii) Recreation programs in schools and community agencies; and

(iv) Leisure education.

(10) "School health services" means services provided by a qualified school nurse or other qualified person.

(11) "Social work services in schools" include:

(i) Preparing a social or developmental history on a handicapped child;

(ii) Group and individual counseling with the child and family;

(iii) Working with those problems in a child's living situation (home, school, and community) that affect the child's adjustment in school; and

(iv) Mobilizing school and community resources to enable the child to receive maximum benefit from his or her educational program.

(12) "Speech pathology" includes:

(i) Identification of children with speech or language disorders;

(ii) Diagnosis and appraisal of specific speech or language disorders;

(iii) Referral for medical or other professional attention necessary for the habilitation of speech or language disorders;

(iv) Provisions of speech and language services for the habilitation or prevention of communicative disorders; and

(v) Counseling and guidance of parents, children, and teachers regarding speech and language disorders.

(13) "Transportation" includes:

(i) Travel to and from school and between schools.

(ii) Travel in and around school buildings, and

(iii) Specialized equipment (such as special or adapted buses, lifts, and ramps), if required to provide special transportation for a handicapped child. (20 U.S.C. 1401(17).)

Comment. With respect to related services, the Senate Report states:

The Committee bill provides a definition of "related services," making clear that all such related services may not be required for each individual child and that such term includes early identification and assessment of handicapping conditions and the provision of services to minimize the effects of such conditions. (Senate Report No. 94-168, p. 12 (1975).)

The list of related services is not exhaustive and may include other developmental, corrective, or supportive services (such as artistic and cultural programs, and art, music, and dance therapy), if they are required to assist a handicapped child to benefit from special education.

There are certain kinds of services which might be provided by persons from varying professional backgrounds and with a variety of operational titles, depending upon requirements in individual States. For example, counseling services might be provided by social workers, psychologists, or guidance counselors; and psychological testing might be done by qualified psychological examiners, psychometrists, or psychologists, depending upon State standards.

Each related service defined under this part may include appropriate administrative and supervisory activities that are necessary for program planning, management, and evaluation.

§ 121a.14 Special education.

(a) (1) As used in this part, the term "special education" means specially designed instruction, at no cost to the parent to meet the unique needs of a handicapped child, including classroom instruction, instruction in physical education, home instruction, and instruction in hospitals and institutions.

(2) The term includes speech pathology, or any other related service, if the service consists of specially designed instruction, at no cost to the parents, to meet the unique needs of a handicapped child, and is considered "special education" rather than a "related service" under State standards.

(3) The term also includes vocational education if it consists of specially designed instruction, at no cost to the parents, to meet the unique needs of a handicapped child.

(b) The terms in this definition are defined as follows:

(1) "At no cost" means that all specially designed instruction is provided without charge, but does not preclude incidental fees which are normally charged to non-handicapped students or their parents as a part of the regular education program.

(2) "Physical education" is defined as follows:

(i) The term means the development of:

(A) Physical and motor fitness;

(B) Fundamental motor skills and patterns; and

(C) Skills in aquatics, dance, and individual and group games and sports (including intramural and lifetime sports).

(ii) The term includes special physical education, adapted physical education, movement education, and motor development.

(20 U.S.C. 1401(16).)

(3) "Vocational education" means organized educational programs which are directly related to the preparation of individuals for paid or unpaid employment, or for additional preparation for a career requiring other than a baccalaureate or advanced degree.

(20 U.S.C. 1401(16).)

Comment. (1) The definition of "special education" is a particularly important one under these regulations, since a child is not handicapped unless he or she needs special education. (See the definition of "handicapped children" in section 121a.5.) The definition of "related services" (section 121a.13) also depends on this definition, since a related service must be necessary for a child to benefit from special education. Therefore, if a child does not need special education, there can be no "related services," and the child (because not "handicapped") is not covered under the Act.

(2) The above definition of vocational education is taken from the Vocational Education Act of 1963, as amended by Pub. L. 94-482. Under that Act, "vocational education" includes industrial arts and consumer and homemaking education programs.

§ 121a.15 State.

As used in this part, the term "State" means each of the several States, the District of Columbia, the Commonwealth of Puerto Rico, Guam, American Samoa, the Virgin Islands, and the Trust Territory of the Pacific Islands.
(20 U.S.C. 1401(6).)

Subpart B—State Annual Program Plans and Local Applications

ANNUAL PROGRAM PLANS—GENERAL

§ 121a.110 Condition of assistance.

In order to receive funds under Part B of the Act for any fiscal year, a State

must submit an annual program plan to the Commissioner through its State educational agency.
(20 U.S.C. 1232c(b), 1412, 1413.)

§ 121a.111 Contents of plan.

Each annual program plan must contain the provisions required in this subpart.
(20 U.S.C. 1412, 1413, 1232c(b).)

§ 121a.112 Certification by the State educational agency and attorney general.

Each annual program plan must include:

(a) A certification by the officer of the State educational agency authorized to submit the plan that:

(1) The plan has been adopted by the State educational agency, and

(2) The plan is the basis for the operation and administration of the activities to be carried out in that State under Part B of the Act; and

(b) A certification by the State Attorney General or other authorized State legal officer that:

(1) The State educational agency has authority under State law to submit the plan and to administer or to supervise the administration of the plan, and

(2) All plan provisions are consistent with State law.
(20 U.S.C. 1413(a).)

§ 121a.113 Approval; disapproval.

(a) The Commissioner shall approve any annual program plan which meets the requirements of this part and Subpart B of Part 100b of this chapter.

(b) The Commissioner shall disapprove any annual program plan which does not meet those requirements but may not finally disapprove a plan before giving reasonable notice and an opportunity for a hearing to the State educational agency.

(c) The Commissioner shall use the procedures set forth in §§ 121a.580-121a.583 of Subpart E for a hearing under this section.

(20 U.S.C. 1413(c).)

§ 121a.114 Effective period of annual program plan.

(a) Each annual program plan is effective for a period from the date it becomes effective under § 100b.35 of this chapter through the following June 30.

(b) The Commissioner may extend the effective period of an annual program plan, on the request of a State, if the plan meets the requirements of this part and Part B of the Act.
(20 U.S.C. 1413(a), 1222c(b).)

ANNUAL PROGRAM PLANS—CONTENTS

§ 121a.120 Public participation.

(a) Each annual program plan must include procedures which insure that the requirements in §§ 121a.280-121a.284 are met.

(b) Each annual program plan must also include the following:

(1) A statement describing the methods used by the State educational agency to provide notice of the public hearings on the annual program plan. The statement must include:

(i) A copy of each news release and advertisement used to provide notice,

(ii) A list of the newspapers and other media in which the State educational agency announced or published the notice, and

(iii) The dates on which the notice was announced or published.

(2) A list of the dates and locations of the public hearings on the annual program plan.

(3) A summary of comments received by the State educational agency and a description of the modifications that the State educational agency has made in the annual program plan as a result of the comments.

(4) A statement describing the methods by which the annual program plan will be made public after its approval by the Commissioner. This statement must include the information

required under paragraph (b) (1) of this section.
(20 U.S.C. 1412(7).)

§ 121a.121 Right to a free appropriate public education.

(a) Each annual program plan must include information which shows that the State has in effect a policy which insures that all handicapped children have the right to a free appropriate public education within the age ranges and timelines under § 121a.122.

(b) The information must include a copy of each State statute, court order, State Attorney General opinion, and other State document that shows the source of the policy.

(c) The information must show that the policy:

(1) Applies to all public agencies in the State;

(2) Applies to all handicapped children;

(3) Implements the priorities established under § 121a.127(a) (1) of this subpart; and

(4) Establishes timelines for implementing the policy, in accordance with § 121a.122.
(20 U.S.C. 1412 (1) (2) (B), (6); 1413 (a) (3).)

§ 121a.122 Timelines and ages for free appropriate public education.

(a) *General.* Each annual program plan must include in detail the policies and procedures which the State will undertake or has undertaken in order to insure that a free appropriate public education is available for all handicapped children aged three through eighteen within the State not later than September 1, 1978, and for all handicapped children aged three through twenty-one within the State not later than September 1, 1980.

(b) *Documents relating to timelines.* Each annual program plan must include a copy of each statute, court order, attorney general decision, and other State document which demonstrates that the State has established timelines in accordance with paragraph (a) of this section.

(c) *Exception.* The requirement in paragraph (a) of this section does not apply to a State with respect to handicapped children aged three, four, five, eighteen, nineteen, twenty, or twenty-one to the extent that the requirement would be inconsistent with State law or practice, or the order of any court, respecting public education for one or more of those age groups in the State.

(d) *Documents relating to exceptions.* Each annual program plan must:

(1) Describe in detail the extent to which the exception in paragraph (c) of this section applies to the State, and

(2) Include a copy of each State law, court order, and other document which provides a basis for the exception.
(20 U.S.C. 1412 (2) (B).)

§ 121a.123 Full educational opportunity goal.

Each annual program plan must include in detail the policies and procedures which the State will undertake, or has undertaken, in order to insure that the State has a goal of providing full educational opportunity to all handicapped children aged birth through twenty-one.
(20 U.S.C. 1412 (2) (A).)

§ 121a.124 Full educational opportunity goal—data requirement.

Beginning with school year 1978-1979, each annual program plan must contain the following information:

(a) The estimated number of handicapped children who need special education and related services.

(b) For the current school year:

(1) The number of handicapped children aged birth through two, who are receiving special education and related services; and

(2) The number of handicapped children:

(i) Who are receiving a free appropriate public education,

(ii) Who need, but are not receiving a free appropriate public education,

(iii) Who are enrolled in public and private institutions who are receiving a free appropriate public education, and

(iv) Who are enrolled in public and private institutions and are not receiving a free appropriate public education.

(c) The estimated numbers of handicapped children who are expected to receive special education and related services during the next school year.

(d) A description of the basis used to determine the data required under this section.

(e) The data required by paragraphs (a), (b), and (c) of this section must be provided:

(1) For each disability category (except for children aged birth through two), and

(2) For each of the following age ranges: birth through two, three through five, six through seventeen, and eighteen through twenty-one. (20 U.S.C. 1412 (2) (A).)

Comment. In Part B of the Act, the term "disability" is used interchangeably with "handicapping condition." For consistency in this regulation, a child with a "disability" means a child with one of the impairments listed in the definition of "handicapped children" in § 121a.5, if the child needs special education because of the impairment. In essence, there is a continuum of impairments. When an impairment is of such a nature that the child needs special education, it is referred to as a disability, in these regulations, and the child is a "handicapped" child.

States should note that data required under this section are not to be transmitted to the Commissioner in personally identifiable form. Generally, except for such purposes as monitoring and auditing, neither the States nor the Federal Government should have to collect data under this part in personally identifiable form.

§ 121a.125   Full educational opportunity goal—timetable.

(a) *General requirement.* Each annual program plan must contain a detailed timetable for accomplishing the goal of providing full educational opportunity for all handicapped children.

(b) *Content of timetable.* (1) The timetable must indicate what percent of the total estimated number of handicapped children the State expects to have full educational opportunity in each succeeding school year.

(2) The data required under this paragraph must be provided:

(i) For each disability category (except for children aged birth through two), and

(ii) For each of the following age ranges: birth through two, three through five, six through seventeen, and eighteen through twenty-one. (20 U.S.C. 1412 (2) (A).)

§ 121a.126—Full educational opportunity goal—facilities, personnel, and services.

(a) *General requirement.* Each annual program plan must include a description of the kind and number of facilities, personnel, and services necessary throughout the State to meet the goal of providing full educational opportunity for all handicapped children. The State educational agency shall include the data required under paragraph (b) of this section and whatever additional data are necessary to meet the requirement.

(b) *Statistical description.* Each annual program plan must include the following data:

(1) The number of additional special class teachers, resource room teachers, and itinerant or consultant teachers needed for each disability category and

the number of each of these who are currently employed in the State.

(2) The number of other additional personnel needed, and the number currently employed in the State, including school psychologists, school social workers, occupational therapists, physical therapists, home-hospital teachers, speech-language pathologists, audiologists, teacher aides, vocational education teachers, work study coordinators, physical education teachers, therapeutic recreation specialists, diagnostic personnel, supervisors, and other instructional and non-instructional staff.

(3) The total number of personnel reported under paragraph (b) (1) and (2) of this section, and the salary costs of those personnel.

(4) The number and kind of facilities needed for handicapped children and the number and kind currently in use in the State, including regular classes serving handicapped children, self-contained classes on a regular school campus, resource rooms, private special education day schools, public special education day schools, private special education residential schools, public special education residential schools, public special education residential schools, hospital programs, occupational therapy facilities, physical therapy facilities, public sheltered workshops, private sheltered workshops, and other types of facilities.

(5) The total number of transportation units needed for handicapped children, the number of transportation units designed for handicapped children which are in use in the State, and the number of handicapped children who use these units to benefit from special education.

(c) *Data categories.* The data required under paragraph (b) of this section must be provided as follows:

(1) Estimates for serving all handicapped children who require special education and related services.

(2) Current year data, based on the actual numbers of handicapped children receiving special education and related services (as reported under Subpart G), and

(3) Estimates for the next school year.

(d) *Rationale.* Each annual program plan must include a description of the means used to determine the number and salary costs of personnel. (20 U.S.C. 1412 (2) (A).)

§ 121a.127 **Priorities.**

(a) *General requirement.* Each annual program plan must include information which shows that:

(1) The State has established priorities which meet the requirements under §§ 121a.320-121a.324 of Subpart C.

(2) The State priorities meet the timelines under § 121a.122 of this subpart, and

(3) The State has made progress in meeting those timelines.

(b) *Child data.* (1) Each annual program plan must show the number of handicapped children known by the State to be in each of the first two priority groups named in §§ 121a.321 of Subpart C:

(1) By disability category, and

(2) By the age ranges in § 121a.-124 (e) (2) of this subpart.

(c) *Activities and resources.* Each annual program plan must show for each of the first two priority groups:

(1) The programs, services, and activities that are being carried out in the State,

(2) The Federal, State, and local resources that have been committed during the current school year, and

(3) The programs, services, activities, and resources that are to be provided during the next school year. (20 U.S.C. 1412 (3).)

§ 121a.128 **Identification, location, and evaluation of handicapped children.**

(a) *General requirement.* Each annual program plan must include in detail the policies and procedures which the State will undertake or has undertaken to insure that:

(1) All children who are handicapped, regardless of the severity of their handicap, and who are in need of special education and related services are identified, located, and evaluated; and

(2) A practical method is developed and implemented to determine which children are currently receiving needed special education and related services and which children are not currently receiving needed special education and related services.

(b) *Information.* Each annual program plan must:

(1) Designate the State agency (if other than the State educational agency) responsible for coordinating the planning and implementation of the policies and procedures under paragraph (a) of this section;

(2) Name each agency that participates in the planning and implementation and describe the nature and extent of its participation;

(3) Describe the extent to which:

(i) The activities described in paragraph (a) of this section have been achieved under the current annual program plan, and

(ii) The resources named for these activities in that plan have been used;

(4) Describe each type of activity to be carried out during the next school year, including the role of the agency named under pararaph (b) (1) of this section, timelines for completing those activities, resources that will be used, and expected outcomes;

(5) Describe how the policies and procedures under paragraph (a) of this section will be monitored to insure that the State educational agency obtains: children within each disability category

(i) The number of handicapped that have been identified, located, and evaluated, and

(ii) Information adequate to evaluate the effectiveness of those policies and procedures; and

(6) Describe the method the State uses to determine which children are currently receiving special education and related services and which children are not receiving special education and related services.

(20 U.S.C. 1412 (2) (C).)

Comment. The State is responsible for insuring that all handicapped children are identified, located, and evaluated, including children in all public and private agencies and institutions in the State. Collection and use of data are subject to the confidentiality requirements in §§ 121a.560-121a.576.

§ 121a.129   Confidentiality of personally identifiable information.

(a) Each annual program plan must include in detail the policies and procedures which the State will undertake or has undertaken in order to insure the protection of the confidentiality of any personally identifiable information collected, used, or maintained under this part.

(b) The Commissioner shall use the criteria in §§ 121a.560-121a.576 of Subpart E to evaluate the policies and procedures of the State under paragraph (a) of this section.

(20 U.S.C. 1412 (2) (D); 1417 (c).)

Comment. The confidentiality regulations were published in the FEDERAL REGISTER in final form on February 27, 1976 (41 FR 8603-8610), and met the requirements of Part B of the Act, as amended by Pub. L. 94-142. Those regulations are incorporated in § 121a.560-121a.576 of Subpart E.

§ 121a.130   Individualized education programs.

(a) Each annual program plan must include information which shows that each public agency in the State maintains records of the individualized education program for each handicapped child, and each public agency establishes, reviews, and revises each program as provided in Subpart C.

(b) Each annual program plan must include:

(1) A copy of each State statute, policy, and standard that regulates the manner in which individualized education programs are developed, implemented, reviewed, and revised, and

(2) The procedures which the State educational agency follows in monitoring and evaluating those programs.
(20 U.S.C. 1412 (4).)

§ 121a.131 Procedural safeguards.

Each annual program plan must include procedural safeguards which insure that the requirements in §§ 121a.-500-121a.514 of Subpart E are met.
(20 U.S.C. 1412 (5) (A).)

§ 121a.132 Least restrictive environment.

(a) Each annual program plan must include procedures which insure that the requirements in §§ 121a.550-121a.-556 of Subpart E are met.

(b) Each annual program plan must include the following information:

(1) The number of handicapped children in the State, within each disability category, who are participating in regular education programs, consistent with §§ 121a.550-121a.556 of Subpart E.

(2) The number of handicapped children who are in separate classes or separate school facilities, or who are otherwise removed from the regular education environment.
(20 U.S.C. 1412 (5) (B).)

§ 121a.133 Protection in evaluation procedures.

Each annual program plan must include procedures which insure that the requirements in §§ 121a.530-121a.534 of Subpart E are met.
(10 U.S.C. 1412 (5) (C).)

§ 121a.134 Responsibility of State educational agency for all educational programs.

(a) Each annual program plan must include information which shows that the requirements in § 121a.600 of Subpart F are met.

(b) The information under paragraph (a) of this section must include a copy of each State statute, State regulation, signed agreement between respective agency officials, and any other document that shows compliance with that paragraph.
(20 U.S.C. 1412 (6).)

§ 121a.135 Monitoring procedures.

Each annual program plan must include information which shows that the requirements in § 121a.601 and § 121a.-602 of Subpart F are met.
(20 U.S.C. 1412 (6).)

§ 121a.136 Implementation procedures —State educational agency.

Each annual program plan must describe the procedures the State educational agency follows to inform each public agency of its responsibility for insuring effective implementation of procedural safeguards for the handicapped children served by that public agency.
(20 U.S.C. 1412 (6).)

§ 121a.137 Procedures for consultation.

Each annual program plan must include an assurance that in carrying out the requirements of section 612 of the Act, procedures are established for consultation with individuals involved in or concerned with the education of handicapped children, including handicapped individuals and parents of handicapped children.
(20 U.S.C. 1412 (7) (A).)

§ 121a.138 Other Federal programs.

Each annual program plan must provide that programs and procedures are

established to insure that funds received by the State or any public agency in the State under any other Federal program, including section 121 of the Elementary and Secondary Education Act of 1965 (20 U.S.C. 241e-2), section 305 (b) (8) of that Act (20 U.S.C. 844a (b) (8)) or Title IV-C of that Act (20 U.S.C. 1831), and section 110 (a) of the Vocational Education Act of 1963, under which there is specific authority for assistance for the education of handicapped children, are used by the State, or any public agency in the State, only in a manner consistent with the goal of providing free appropriate public education for all handicapped children, except that nothing in this section limits the specific requirements of the laws governing those Federal programs.
(20 U.S.C. 1413 (a) (2).)

§ 121a.139   Comprehensive system of personnel development.

Each annual program plan must include the material required under §§ 121a.380-121a.387 of Subpart C.
(20 U.S.C. 1413 (a) (3).)

§ 121a.140   Private schools.

Each annual program plan must include policies and procedures which insure that the requirements of Subpart D are met.
(20 U.S.C. 1413 (a) (4).)

§ 121a.141   Recovery of funds for misclassified children.

Each annual program plan must include policies and procedures which insure that the State seeks to recover any funds provided under Part B of the Act for services to a child who is determined to be erroneously classified as eligible to be counted under section 611 (a) or (d) of the Act.
(20 U.S.C. 1413 (a) (5).)

§ 121a.142   Control of funds and property.

Each annual program plan must provide assurance satisfactory to the Commissioner that the control of funds provided under Part B of the Act, and title to property acquired with those funds, is in a public agency for the uses and purposes provided in this part, and that a public agency administers the funds and property.
(20 U.S.C. 1413 (a) (6).)

§ 121a.143   Records.

Each annual program plan must provide for keeping records and affording access to those records, as the Commissioner may find necessary to assure the correctness and verification of reports and of proper disbursement of funds provided under Part B of the Act.
(20 U.S.C. 1413 (a) (7) (B).)

§ 121a.144   Hearing on application.

Each annual program plan must include procedures to insure that the State educational agency does not take any final action with respect to an application submitted by a local educational agency before giving the local educational agency reasonable notice and an opportunity for a hearing.
(20 U.S.C. 1413 (a) (8).)

§ 121a.145   Prohibition of commingling.

Each annual program plan must provide assurance satisfactory to the Commissioner that funds provided under Part B of the Act are not commingled with State funds.
(20 U.S.C. 1413 (a) (9).)

Comment. This assurance is satisfied by the use of a separate accounting system that includes an "audit trail" of the expenditure of the Part B funds. Separate bank accounts are not required. (See 45 CFR 100b, Subpart F (Cash Depositories).)

§ 121a.146 Annual evaluation.

Each annual program plan must include procedures for evaluation at least annually of the effectiveness of programs in meeting the educational needs of handicapped children, including evaluation of individualized education programs.
(20 U.S.C. 1413 (a) (11).)

§ 121a.147 State advisory panel.

Each annual program plan must provide that the requirements of §§ 121a.-650-121a.653 of Subpart F are met.
(20 U.S.C. 1413 (a) (12).)

§ 121a.148 Policies and procedures for use of Part B funds.

Each annual program plan must set forth policies and procedures designed to insure that funds paid to the State under Part B of the Act are spent in accordance with the provisions of Part B, with particular attention given to sections 611 (b), 611 (c), 611 (d), 612 (2), and 612 (3) of the Act.
(20 U.S.C. 1413 (a) (1).)

§ 121a.149 Description of use of Part B funds.

(a) *State allocation.* Each annual program plan must include the following information about the State's use of funds under § 121a.370 of Subpart C and § 121a.620 of Subpart F:

(1) A list of administrative positions, and a description of duties for each person whose salary is paid in whole or in part with those funds.

(2) For each position, the percentage of salary paid with those funds.

(3) A description of each administrative activity the State educational agency will carry out during the next school year with those funds.

(4) A description of each direct service and each support service which the State educational agency will provide during the next school year with those funds, and the activities the State advisory panel will undertake during that period with those funds.

(b) *Local educational agency allocation.* Each annual program plan must include:

(1) An estimate of the number and percent of local educational agencies in the State which will receive an allocation under this part (other than local educational agencies which submit a consolidated application),

(2) An estimate of the number of local educational agencies which will receive an allocation under a consolidated application,

(3) An estimate of the number of consolidated applications and the average number of local educational agencies per application, and

(4) A description of direct services the State educational agency will provide under § 121a.360 of Subpart C.
(20 U.S.C. 1232c (b) (1) (B) (ii).)

§ 121a.150 Nondiscrimination and employment of handicapped individuals.

(a) Each annual program plan must include an assurance that the program assisted under Part B of the Act will be operated in compliance with Title 45 of the Code of Federal Regulations Part 84 (Nondiscrimination on the Basis of Handicap in Programs and Activities Receiving or Benefitting from Federal Financial Assistance). The State educational agency may incorporate this assurance by reference if it has already been filed with the Department of Health, Education, and Welfare.

(b) The assurance under paragraph (a) of this section covers, among other things, the specific requirement on employment of handicapped individuals under section 606 of the Act, which states:

The Secretary shall assure that each recipient of assistance under this Act shall make positive efforts to employ and advance in employment qualified

handicapped individuals in programs assisted under this Act.
(20 U.S.C. 1405; 29 U.S.C. 794.)

§ 121a.151 Additional information if the State educational agency provides direct services.

If a State educational agency provides free appropriate public education for handicapped children or provides them with direct services, its annual program plan must include the information required under §§ 121a.226-121a.228, 121a.231, and 121a.235.
(20 U.S.C. 1413 (b).)

LOCAL EDUCATIONAL AGENCY APPLICATIONS—GENERAL

§ 121a.180 Submission of application.

In order to receive payments under Part B of the Act for any fiscal year a local educational agency must submit an application to the State educational agency.
(20 U.S.C. 1414 (a).)

§ 121a.181 Responsibilities of State educational agency.

Each State educational agency shall establish the procedures and format which a local educational agency uses in preparing and submitting its application.
(20 U.S.C. 1414 (a).)

§ 121a.182 The excess cost requirement.

A local educational agency may only use funds under Part B of the Act for the excess costs of providing special education and related services for handicapped children.
(20 U.S.C. 1414 (a) (1), (a) (2) (B) (1).)

§ 121a.183 Meeting the excess cost requirement.

(a) A local educational agency meets the excess cost requirement if it has on the average spent at least the amount determined under § 121a.184

for the education of each of its handicapped children. This amount may not include capital outlay or debt service.

(b) Each local educational agency must keep records adequate to show that it has met the excess cost requirement.
(20 U.S.C. 1402 (20); 1414 (a) (1).)

Comment. The excess cost requirement means that the local educational agency must spend a certain minimum amount for the education of its handicapped children before Part B funds are used. This insures that children served with Part B funds have at least the same average amount spent on them, from sources other than Part B, as do the children in the school district taken as a whole.

The minimum amount that must be spent for the education of handicapped children is computed under a statutory formula. Section 121a.184 implements this formula and gives a step-by-step method to determine the minimum amount. Excess costs are those costs of special education and related services which exceed the minimum amount. Therefore, if a local educational agency can show that it has (on the average) spent the minimum amount for the education of each of its handicapped children, it has met the excess cost requirement, and all additional costs are excess costs. Part B funds can then be used to pay for these additional costs, subject to the other requirements of Part B (priorities, etc.). In the "Comment" under section 121a.184, there is an example of how the minimum amount is computed.

§ 121a.184 Excess costs—computation of minimum amount.

The minimum average amount a local educational agency must spend under § 121a.183 for the education of each of its handicapped children is computed as follows:

(a) Add all expenditures of the local educational agency in the preceding school year, except capital outlay and debt service:

(1) For elementary school students, if the handicapped child is an elementary school student.

(2) For secondary school students, if the handicapped child is a secondary school student.

(b) From this amount, subtract the total of the following amounts spent for elementary school students or for secondary school students, as the case may be:

(1) Amounts the agency spent in the preceding school year from funds awarded under Part B of the Act and Titles I and VII of the Elementary and Secondary Education Act of 1965, and

(2) Amounts from State and local funds which the agency spent in the preceding school year for:

(i) Programs for handicapped children,

(ii) Programs to meet the special educational needs of educationally deprived children, and

(iii) Programs of bilingual education for children with limited English-speaking ability.

(c) Divide the result under paragraph (b) of this section by the average number of students enrolled in the agency in the preceding school year:

(1) In its elementary schools, if the handicapped child is an elementary school student, or

(2) In its secondary schools, if the handicapped child is a secondary school student.

(20 U.S.C. 1414 (a) (1).)

Comments The following is an example of how a local educational agency might compute the average minimum amount it must spend for the education of each of its handicapped children, under § 121a.183. This example follows the formula in § 121a.-184. Under the statute and regulations, the local educational agency must make one computation for handicapped children in its elementary schools and a separate computation for handicapped children in its secondary schools. The computation for handicapped elementary school students would be done as follows:

a. First, the local educational agency must determine its total amount of expenditures for elementary school students from all sources—local, State, and Federal (including Part B)—in the preceding school year. Only capital outlay and debt service are excluded.

Example: A local educational agency spent the following amounts last year for elementary school students (including its handicapped elementary school students):

(1) From local tax funds.. $2,750,000
(2) From State funds.... 7,000,000
(3) From Federal funds.. 750,000
_____
10,500,000

Of this total, $500,000 was for capital outlay and debt service relating to the education of elementary school students. This must be subtracted from total expenditures:

$10,500,000
− 500,000
_____

Total expenditures for
elementary school students
(less capital outlay and
debt service) ....= 10,000,000

b. Next, the local educational agency must subtract amounts spent for:

(1) Programs for handicapped children;

(2) Programs to meet the special educational needs of educationally deprived children; and

(3) Programs of bilingual education for children with limited English-speaking ability.

These are funds which the local educational agency actually spent, not funds received last year but carried over for the current school year.

Example: The local educational agency spent the following amounts for elementary school students last year:

(1) From funds under Title I of the Elementary and Secondary Education Act of 1965 .... $300,000

(2) From a special State program for educationally deprived children ...   200,000

(3) From a grant under Part B   200,000

(4) From State funds for the education of handicapped children   500,000

(5) From a locally-funded program for handicapped children   250,000

(6) From a grant for a bilingual education program under Title VII of the Elementary and Secondary Education Act of 1965   150,000

Total 1,600,000

(A local educational agency would also include any other funds it spent from Federal, State, or local sources for the three basic purposes: handicapped children, educationally deprived children, and bilingual education for children with limited English-speaking ability.)

This amount is subtracted from the local educational agency's total expenditure for elementary school students computed above:

$10,000,000
− 1,600,000
—————
8,400,000

c. The local educational agency next must divide by the average number of students enrolled in the elementary schools of the agency last year (including its handicapped students).

Example: Last year, an average of 7,000 students were enrolled in the agency's elementary schools. This must be divided into the amount computed under the above paragraph:

8,400,000
—————
7,000 students
= $1,200/student

This figure is in the minimum amount the local educational agency must spend (on the average) for the education of each of its handicapped students. Funds under Part B may be used only for costs over and above this minimum. In the example, if the local educational agency has 100 handicapped elementary school students, it must keep records adequate to show that it has spent at least $120,000 for the education of those students (100 students times $1,200/student), not including capital outlay and debt service.

This $120,000 may come from any funds except funds under Part B, subject to any legal requirements that govern the use of those other funds.

If the local educational agency has handicapped secondary school students, it must do the same computation for them. However, the amounts used in the computation would be those the local educational agency spent last year for the education of secondary school students, rather than for elementary school students.

§ 121a.185 **Computation of excess costs—consolidated application.**

The minimum average amount under § 121a.183 where two or more local educational agencies submit a consolidated application, is the average of the combined minimum average amounts determined under § 121a.184 in those agencies for elementary or secondary school students, as the case may be. (20 U.S.C. 1414 (a) (1).)

§ 121a.186 **Excess costs—limitation on use of Part B funds.**

(a) The excess cost requirement prevents a local educational agency from using funds provided under Part B of the Act to pay for all of the costs directly attributable to the education of a handicapped child, subject to paragraph (b) of this section.

(b) The excess cost requirement does not prevent a local educational agency from using Part B funds to pay for all of the costs directly attributable to the education of a handicapped child in any of the age ranges three, four, five, eighteen, nineteen, twenty, or twenty-one, if no local or State funds are available for non-handicapped children in that age range. However, the local educational agency must comply with the nonsupplanting and other requirements of this part in providing the education and services.
(20 U.S.C. 1402 (20); 1414 (a) (1).)

§ 121a.190 Consolidated applications.

(a) *Voluntary applications.* Local educational agencies may submit a consolidated application for payments under Part B of the Act.

(b) *Required applications.* A State educational agency may require local educational agencies to submit a consolidated application for payments under Part B of the Act if the State educational agency determines that an individual application submitted by a local educational agency will be disapproved because:

(1) The agency's entitlement is less than the $7,500 minimum required by section 611 (c) (4) (A) (i) of the Act (§ 121a.360 (a) (1) of Subpart C); or

(2) The agency is unable to establish and maintain programs of sufficient size and scope to effectively meet the educational needs of handicapped children.

(c) *Size and scope of program.* The State educational agency shall establish standards and procedures for determinations under paragraph (b) (2) of this section.
(20 U.S.C. 1414 (c) (1).)

§ 121a.191 Payments under consolidated applications.

In any case in which a consolidated application is approved by the State educational agency, the payments to the participating local educational agencies must be equal to the sum of the entitlements of the separate local educational agencies.
(20 U.S.C. 1414 (c) (2) (A).)

§ 121a.192 State regulation of consolidated applications.

(a) The State educational agency shall issue regulations with respect to consolidated applications submitted under this part.

(b) The State educational agency's regulations must:

(1) Be consistent with section 612 (1) (7) and section 613 (a) of the Act, and

(2) Provide participating local educational agencies with joint responsibilities for implementing programs receiving payments under this part.
(20 U.S.C. 1414 (c) (2) (B).)

(c) If an intermediate educational unit is required under State law to carry out this part, the joint responsibilities given to local educational agencies under paragraph (b) (2) of this section do not apply to the administration and disbursement of any payments received by the intermediate educational unit. Those administrative responsibilities must be carried out exclusively by the intermediate educational unit.
(20 U.S.C. 1414 (c) (2) (C).)

§ 121a.193 State educational agency approval; disapproval.

(a) *Approval.* A State educational agency shall approve an application submitted by a local educational agency if the State educational agency determines that the application meets the requirements under §§ 121a.220-121a.-240. However, the State educational agency may not approve any application until the Commissioner approves its annual program plan for the school year covered by the application.

(b) *Disapproval.* The State educational agency shall disapprove an application if the State educational agency determines that the application does not meet a requirement under §§ 121a.-220-121a.240.

(20 U.S.C. 1414 (b) (1).)

(c) In carrying out its functions under this section, each State educational agency shall consider any decision resulting from a hearing under §§ 121a.506-121a.513 of Subpart E which is adverse to the local educational agency involved in the decision. (20 U.S.C. 1414 (b) (3).)

§ 121a.194 Withholding.

(a) If a State educational agency, after giving reasonable notice and an opportunity for a hearing to a local educational agency, decides that the local educational agency in the administration of an application approved by the State educational agency has failed to comply with any requirement in the application, the State educational agency, after giving notice to the local educational agency, shall:

(1) Make no further payments to the local educational agency until the State educational agency is satisfied that there is no longer any failure to comply with the requirement; or

(2) Consider its decision in its review of any application made by the local educational agency under § 121a.-180;

(3) Or both.

(b) Any local educational agency receiving a notice from a State educational agency under paragraph (a) of this section is subject to the public notice provision in § 121a.592.

(20 U.S.C. 1414 (b) (2).)

LOCAL EDUCATIONAL AGENCY
APPLICATIONS—CONTENTS

§ 121a.220 Child identification.

Each application must include pro-cedures which insure that all children residing within the jurisdiction of the local educational agency who are handicapped, regardless of the severity of their handicap, and who are in need of special education and related services are identified, located, and evaluated, including a practical method of determining which children are currently receiving needed special education and related services and which children are not currently receiving needed special education and related services.

(20 U.S.C. 1414 (a) (1) (A).)

Comment. The local educational agency is responsible for insuring that all handicapped children within its jurisdiction are identified, located, and evaluated, including children in all public and private agencies and institutions within that jurisdiction. Collection and use of data are subject to the confidentiality requirements in §§ 121a.-560-121a.576 of Subpart E.

§ 121a.221 Confidentiality of personally identifiable information.

Each application must include policies and procedures which insure that the criteria in §§ 121a.560-121a.-574 of Subpart E are met.

(20 U.S.C. 1414 (a) (1) (B).)

§ 121a.222 Full educational opportunity goal; timetable.

Each application must: (a) Include a goal of providing full educational opportunity to all handicapped children, aged birth through 21, and

(b) Include a detailed timetable for accomplishing the goal.

(20 U.S.C. 1414 (a) (1) (C), (D).)

§ 121a.223 Facilities, personnel, and services.

Each application must provide a description of the kind and number of facilities, personnel, and services necessary to meet the goal in § 121a.222.

(20 U.S.C. 1414 (a) (1) (E).)

§ 121a.224 Personnel development.

Each application must include procedures for the implementation and use of the comprehensive system of personnel development established by the State educational agency under § 121a.140.

(20 U.S.C. 1414 (a) (1) (C) (i).)

§ 121a.225 Priorities.

Each application must include priorities which meet the requirements of §§ 121a.320-121a.324.

(20 U.S.C. 1414 (a) (1) (C) (ii).)

§ 121a.226 Parent involvement.

Each application must include procedures to insure that, in meeting the goal under § 121a.222, the local educational agency makes provision for participation of and consultation with parents or guardians of handicapped children.

(20 U.S.C. 1414 (a) (1) (C) (iii).)

§ 121a.227 Participation in regular education programs.

(a) Each application must include procedures to insure that to the maximum extent practicable, and consistent with §§ 121a.550-121a.553 of Subpart E, the local educational agency provides special services to enable handicapped children to participate in regular educational programs.

(b) Each application must describe:

(1) The types of alternative placements that are available for handicapped children, and

(2) The number of handicapped children within each disability category who are served in each type of placement.

(20 U.S.C. 1414 (a) (1) (C) (iv).)

§ 121a.228 Public control of funds.

Each application must provide assurance satisfactory to the State educational agency that control of funds provided under Part B of the Act and title to property acquired with those funds, is in a public agency for the uses and

purposes under this part, and that a public agency administers the funds and property.

(20 U.S.C. 1414 (a) (2) (A).)

§ 121a.229 Excess cost.

Each application must provide assurance satisfactory to the State educational agency that the local educational agency uses funds provided under Part B of the Act only for costs which exceed the amount computed under § 121a.184 and which are directly attributable to the education of handicapped children.

(20 U.S.C. 1414 (a) (2) (B).)

§ 121a.230 Nonsupplanting.

(a) Each application must provide assurance satisfactory to the State educational agency that the local educational agency uses funds provided under Part B of the Act to supplement and, to the extent practicable, increase the level of State and local funds expended for the education of handicapped children, and in no case to supplant those State and local funds.

(b) To meet the requirement in paragraph (a) of this section:

(1) The total amount or average per capita amount of State and local school funds budgeted by the local educational agency for expenditures in the current fiscal year for the education of handicapped children must be at least equal to the total amount or average per capita amount of State and local school funds actually expended for the education of handicapped children in the most recent preceding fiscal year for which the information is available. Allowance may be made for:

(i) Decreases in enrollment of handicapped children; and

(ii) Unusually large amounts of funds expended for such long-term purposes as the acquisition of equipment and the construction of school facilities; and

(2) The local educational agency must not use Part B funds to displace State or local funds for any particular cost.

(20 U.S.C. 1414 (a) (2) (B).)

Comment. Under statutes such as Title I of the Elementary and Secondary Education Act of 1965, as amended, the requirement is to not supplant funds that "would" have been expended if the Federal funds were not available. The requirement under Part B, however, is to not supplant funds which have been "expended." This use of the past tense suggests that the funds referred to are those which the State or local agency actually spent at some time before the use of the Part B funds. Therefore, in judging compliance with this requirement, the Commissioner looks to see if Part B funds are used for any costs which were previously paid for with State or local funds.

The nonsupplanting requirement prohibits a local educational agency from supplanting State and local funds with Part B funds on either an aggregate basis or for a given expenditure. This means that if an LEA spent $100,000 for special education in FY 1977, it must budget at least $100,000 in FY 1978, unless one of the conditions in

§ 121a.230 (b) (1) applies.

Whether a local educational agency supplants with respect to a particular cost would depend on the circumstances of the expenditure. For example, if a teacher's salary has been switched from local funding to Part B funding, this would appear to be supplanting. However, if that teacher was taking over a different position (such as a resource room teacher, for example), it would not be supplanting. Moreover, it might be important to consider whether the particular action of a local educational agency led to an increase in services for handicapped children over that which previously existed. The intent of the requirement is to insure that Part B funds are used to increase State and local efforts and are not used to take their place. Compliance would be judged with this aim in mind. The supplanting requirement is not intended to inhibit better services to handicapped children.

§ 121a.231 Comparable services.

(a) Each application must provide assurance satisfactory to the State educational agency that the local educational agency meets the requirements of this section.

(b) A local educational agency may not use funds under Part B of the Act to provide services to handicapped children unless the agency uses State and local funds to provide services to those children which, taken as a whole, are at least comparable to services provided to other handicapped children in that local educational agency.

(c) Each local educational agency shall maintain records which show that the agency meets the requirement in paragraph (b) of this section.

(20 U.S.C. 1414 (a) (2) (C).)

Comment. Under the "comparability" requirement, if State and local funds are used to provide certain services, those services must be provided with State and local funds to all handicapped children in the local educational agency who need them. Part B funds may then be used to supplement existing services, or to provide additional services to meet special needs. This, of course, is subject to the other requirements of the Act, including the priorities under §§ 121a.-320-121a.324.

§ 121a.232 Information—reports.

Each application must provide that the local educational agency furnishes information (which, in the case of reports relating to performance, is in accordance with specific performance criteria developed by the local educational agency and related to program objectives) as may be necessary to

enable the State educational agency to perform its duties under this part, including information relating to the educational achievement of handicapped children participating in the local educational agency's programs for handicapped children.
(20 U.S.C. 1414 (a) (3) (A).)

§ 121a.233   Records.

Each application must provide that the local educational agency keeps such records, and affords access to those records, as the State educational agency may find necessary to insure the correctness and verification of the information that the local educational agency furnishes under § 121a.232.
(20 U.S.C. 1414 (a) (3) (B).)

§ 121a.234   Public participation.

(a) Each application must:

(1) Provide for making the application and all documents related to the application available to parents and the general public; and

(2) Provide that all evaluations and reports required under § 121a.232 are public information.

(b) In implementing the requirement in paragraph (a) (1), the local educational agency shall use methods for public participation within its jurisdiction which are comparable to those required in § 121a.280-121a.284 of this subpart. However, the local educational agency is not required to hold public hearings.
(20 U.S.C. 1414 (a) (4).)

§ 121a.235   Individualized education program.

Each application must include procedures to assure that the local educational agency complies with §§ 121a.-340-121a.349 of Subpart C.
(20 U.S.C. 1414 (a) (5).)

§ 121a.236   Local policies consistent with statute.

Each application must provide assurance satisfactory to the State educational agency that all policies and programs which the local educational agency establishes and administers are consistent with section 612 (1)-(7) and section 613 (a) of the Act.
(20 U.S.C. 1414 (a) (6).)

§ 121a.237   Procedural safeguards.

Each application must provide assurance satisfactory to the State educational agency that the local educational agency has procedural safeguards which meet the requirements of §§ 121a.500-121a.514 of Subpart E.
(20 U.S.C. 1414 (a) (7).)

§ 121a.238   Use of Part B funds.

Each application must describe how the local educational agency will use the funds under Part B of the Act during the next school year.
(20 U.S.C. 1414 (a).)

§ 121a.239   Nondiscrimination and employment of handicapped individuals.

(a) Each application must include an assurance that the program assisted under Part B of the Act will be operated in compliance with Title 45 of the Code of Federal Regulations Part 84 (Nondiscrimination the Basis of Handicap in Programs and Activities Receiving or Benefitting from Federal Financial Assistance). The local educational agency may incorporate this assurance by reference if it has already been filed with the Department of Health, Education, and Welfare.

(b) The assurance under paragraph (a) of this section covers, among other things, the specific requirement on employment of handicapped individuals under section 606 of the Act, which states:

The Secretary shall assure that each recipient of assistance under this Act shall make positive efforts to employ and advance in employment qualified handicapped individuals in programs assisted under this Act.
(20 U.S.C. 1405; 29 U.S.C. 794.)

§ 121a.240   Other requirements.

Each local application must include additional procedures and information which the State educational agency may require in order to meet the State annual program plan requirements under §§ 121a.120-121a.151.
(20 U.S.C. 1414 (a) (6).)

APPLICATION FROM SECRETARY OF INTERIOR

§ 121a.260   Submission of annual application; approval.

In order to receive payments under this part, the Secretary of Interior shall submit an annual application which:

(a) Meets applicable requirements of section 614 (a) of the Act;

(b) Includes monitoring procedures which are consistent with § 121a.601; and

(c) Includes other material as agreed to by the Commissioner and the Secretary of Interior.
(20 U.S.C. 1411 (f).)

§ 121a.261   Public participation.

In the development of the application for the Department of Interior, the Secretary of Interior shall provide for public participation consistent with §§ 121a.280-121a.284.
(20 U.S.C. 1411 (f).)

§ 121a.262   Use of Part B funds.

(a) The Department of Interior may use five percent of its payments in any fiscal year, or $200,000, whichever is greater, for administrative costs in carrying out the provisions of this Part.

(b) The remainder of the payments to the Secretary of Interior in any fiscal year must be used in accordance with the priorities under §§ 121a.320-121a.-324 of Subpart C.
(20 U.S.C. 1411 (f).)

§ 121a.263   Applicable regulations.

The Secretary of Interior shall comply with the requirements under Subparts C, E, and F.
(20 U.S.C. 1411 (f) (2).)

PUBLIC PARTICIPATION

§ 121a.280   Public hearings before adopting an annual program plan.

(a) Prior to its adoption of an annual program plan, the State educational agency shall:

(1) Make the plan available to the general public,

(2) Hold public hearings, and

(3) Provide an opportunity for comment by the general public on the plan.
(20 U.S.C. 1412 (7).)

§ 121a.281   Notice.

(a) The State educational agency shall provide notice to the general public of the public hearings.

(b) The notice must be in sufficient detail to inform the public about:

(1) The purpose and scope of the annual program plan and its relation to Part B of the Education of the Handicapped Act,

(2) The availability of the annual program plan,

(3) The date, time, and location of each public hearing,

(4) The procedures for submitting written comments about the plan, and

(5) The timetable for developing the final plan and submitting it to the Commissioner for approval.

(c) The notice must be published or announced:

(1) In newspapers or other media, or both, with circulation adequate to notify the general public about the hearings, and (2) Enough in advance of the date of the hearings to afford interested parties throughout the State a reasonable opportunity to participate.
(20 U.S.C. 1412 (7).)

§ 121a.282   Opportunity to participate; comment period.

(a) The State educational agency shall conduct the public hearings at times and places that afford interested parties throughout the State a reasonable opportunity to participate.

(b) The plan must be available for comment for a period of at least 30 days following the date of the notice under § 121a.281.

(20 U.S.C. 1412 (7).)

§ 121a.283 Review of public comments before adopting plan.

Before adopting its annual program plan, the State educational agency shall:

(a) Review and consider all public comments, and

(b) Make any necessary modifications in the plan.

(20 U.S.C. 1412 (7).)

§ 121a.284 Publication and availability of approved plan.

After the Commissioner approves an annual program plan, the State educational agency shall give notice in newspapers or other media, or both, that the plan is approved. The notice must name places throughout the State where the plan is available for access by any interested person.

(20 U.S.C. 1412 (7).)

Subpart C—Services

FREE APPROPRIATE PUBLIC EDUCATION

§ 121a.300 Timelines for free appropriate public education.

(a) *General.* Each State shall insure that free appropriate public education is available to all handicapped children aged three through eighteen within the State not later than September 1, 1978, and to all handicapped children aged three through twenty-one within the State not later than September 1, 1980.

(b) *Age ranges 3-5 and 18-21.* This paragraph provides rules for applying the requirement in paragraph (a) of this section to handicapped children aged three, four, five, eighteen, nineteen, twenty, and twenty-one:

(1) If State law or a court order requires the State to provide education for handicapped children in any disability category in any of these age groups, the State must make a free appropriate public education available to all handicapped children of the same age who have that disability.

(2) If a public agency provides education to non-handicapped children in any of these age groups, it must make a free appropriate public education available to at least a proportionate number of handicapped children of the same age.

(3) If a public agency provides education to 50 percent or more of its handicapped children in any disability category in any of these age groups, it must make a free appropriate public education available to all of its handicapped children of the same age who have that disability.

(4) If a public agency provides education to a handicapped child in any of these age groups, it must make a free appropriate public education available to that child and provide that child and his or her parents all of the rights under Part B of the Act and this part.

(5) A State is not required to make a free appropriate public education available to a handicapped child in one of these age groups if:

(i) State law expressly prohibits, or does not authorize, the expenditure of public funds to provide education to non-handicapped children in that age group; or

(ii) The requirement is inconsistent with a court order which governs the provision of free public education to handicapped children in that State.

(20 U.S.C. 1412 (2) (B); Sen. Rept. No. 94-168 p. 19 (1975).)

Comment. 1. The requirement to make free appropriate public education available applies to all handicapped children within the State who are in the age ranges required under section 121a.300 and who need special education and related services. This includes handicapped children already in school and children with less severe handicaps, who are not covered under the priorities under § 121a.321.

2. In order to be in compliance with § 121a.300, each State must insure that the requirement to identify, locate, and evaluate all handicapped children is fully implemented by public agencies throughout the State. This means that before September 1, 1978, every child who has been referred or is on a waiting list for evaluation (including children in school as well as those not receiving an education) must be evaluated in accordance with §§ 121a.530-121a.533 of Subpart E. If, as a result of the evaluation, it is determined that a child needs special education and related services, an individualized education program must be developed for the child by September 1, 1978, and all other applicable requirements of this part must be met.

3. The requirement to identify, locate, and evaluate handicapped children (commonly referred to as the "child find system") was enacted on August 21, 1974, under Pub. L. 93-380. While each State needed time to establish and implement its child find system, the four year period between August 21, 1974, and September 1, 1978, is considered to be sufficient to insure that the system is fully operational and effective on a State-wide basis.

Under the statute, the age range for the child find requirement (0-21) is greater than the mandated age range for providing free appropriate public education (FAPE). One reason for the broader age requirement under "child find" is to enable States to be aware of and plan for younger children who have that disability.

(2) If a public agency provides education to non-handicapped child in any of these age groups, it must make a free appropriate public education available to at least a proportionate number of handicapped children of the same age.

(3) If a public agency provides education to 50 percent or more of its handicapped children in any disability category in any of these age groups, it must make a free appropriate public education available to all of its handicapped children of the same age who will require special education and related services. It also ties in with the full educational opportunity goal requirement, which has the same age range as child find. Moreover, while a State is not required to provide "FAPE" to handicapped children below the age ranges mandated under § 121a.300, the State may, at its discretion, extend services to those children, subject to the requirements on priorities under §§ 121a.320-121a.324.

§ 121a.301   Free appropriate public education—methods and payments.

(a) Each State may use whatever State, local, Federal, and private sources of support are available in the State to meet the requirements of this part. For example, when it is necessary to place a handicapped child in a residential facility, a State could use joint agreements between the agencies involved for sharing the cost of that placement.

(b) Nothing in this part relieves an insurer or similar third party from an otherwise valid obligation to provide or to pay for services provided to a handicapped child.

(20 U.S.C. 1401 (18); 1412 (2) (B).)

§ 121a.302   Residential placement.

If placement in a public or private residential program is necessary to provide special education and related services to a handicapped child, the program, including non-medical care and room and board, must be at no cost to the parents of the child.

(20 U.S.C. 1412 (2) (B); 1413 (a) (4) (B).)

Comment. This requirement applies to placements which are made by public agencies for educational purposes, and includes placements in State-operated schools for the handicapped, such as a State school for the deaf or blind.

§ 121a.303 Proper functioning of hearing aids.

Each public agency shall insure that the hearing aids worn by deaf and hard of hearing children in school are functioning properly.
(20 U.S.C. 1412 (2) (B).)

Comment. The report of the House of Representatives on the 1978 appropriation bill includes the following statement regarding hearing aids:

In its report on the 1976 appropriation bill the Committee expressed concern about the condition of hearing aids worn by children in public schools. A study done at the Committee's direction by the Bureau of Education for the Handicapped reveals that up to one-third of the hearing aids are malfunctioning. Obviously, the Committee expects the Office of Education will ensure that hearing impaired school children are receiving adequate professional assessment, follow-up and services.
(House Report No. 95-381, p. 67 (1977).)

§ 121a.304 Full educational opportunity goal.

(a) Each State educational agency shall insure that each public agency establishes and implements a goal of providing full educational opportunity to all handicapped children in the area served by the public agency.

(b) Subject to the priority requirements under §§ 121a.320-121a.324, a State or local educational agency may use Part B funds to provide facilities, personnel, and services necessary to meet the full educational opportunity goal.

(20 U.S.C. 1412 (2) (A); 1414 (a) (1) (C).)

Comment. In meeting the full educational opportunity goal, the Congress also encouraged local educational agencies to include artistic and cultural activities in programs supported under this part, subject to the priority requirements under §§ 121a.320-121a.324. This point is addressed in the following statements from the Senate Report on Pub. L. 94-142:

The use of the arts as a teaching tool for the handicapped has long been recognized as a viable, effective way not only of teaching special skills, but also of reaching youngsters who had otherwise been unteachable. The Committee envisions that programs under this bill could well include an arts component and, indeed, urges that local educational agencies include the arts in programs for the handicapped funded under this Act. Such a program could cover both appreciation of the arts by the handicapped youngsters, and the utilization of the arts as a teaching tool per se.

Museum settings have often been another effective tool in the teaching of handicapped children. For example, the Brooklyn Museum has been a leader in developing exhibits utilizing the heightened tactile sensory skill of the blind. Therefore, in light of the national policy concerning the use of museums in Federally-supported education programs enunciated in the Education Amendments of 1974, the Committee also urges local educational agencies to include museums in programs for the handicapped funded under this Act.
(Senate Report No. 94-168, p. 13 (1975).)

§ 121a.305 Program options.

Each public agency shall take steps to insure that its handicapped children have available to them the variety of educational programs and services available to non-handicapped children

in the area served by the agency, including art, music, industrial arts, consumer and homemaking education, and vocational education.
(20 U.S.C. 1412 (2) (A); 1414 (a) (1) (C).)

Comment. The above list of program options is not exhaustive, and could include any program or activity in which non-handicapped students participate. Moreover, vocational education programs must be specially designed if necessary to enable a handicapped student to benefit fully from those programs; and the set-aside funds under the Vocational Education Act of 1963, as amended by Pub. L. 94-482, may be used for this purpose. Part B funds may also be used, subject to the priority requirements under §§ 121a.320-121a.-324.

§ 121a.306   Nonacademic services.

(a) Each public agency shall take steps to provide nonacademic and extracurricular services and activities in such manner as is necessary to afford handicapped children an equal opportunity for participation in those services and activities.

(b) Nonacademic and extracurricular services and activities may include counseling services, athletics, transportation, health services, recreational activities, special interest groups or clubs sponsored by the public agency, referrals to agencies which provide assistance to handicapped persons, and employment of students, including both employment by the public agency and assistance in making outside employment available.
(20 U.S.C. 1412 (2) (A); 1414 (a) (1) (C).)

§ 121a.307   Physical education.

(a) *General.* Physical education services specially designed if necessary, must be made available to every handicapped child receiving a free appropriate public education.

(b) *Regular physical education.* Each handicapped child must be afforded the opportunity to participate in the regular physical education program available to non-handicapped children unless:

(1) The child is enrolled full time in a separate facility; or

(2) The child needs specially designed physical education, as prescribed in the child's individualized education program.

(c) *Special Physical education.* If specially designed physical education is prescribed in a child's individualized education program, the public agency responsible for the education of that child shall provide the services directly, or make arrangements for it to be provided through other public or private programs.

(d) *Education in separate facilities.* The public agency responsible for the education of a handicapped child who is enrolled in a separate facility shall insure that the child receives appropriate physical education services in compliance with paragraphs (a) and (c) of this section.
(20 U.S.C. 1401 (16); 1412 (5) (B); 1414 (a) (6).)

Comment. The Report of the House of Representatives on Pub. L. 94-142 includes the following statement regarding physical education:

Special education as set forth in the Committee bill includes instruction in physical education, which is provided as a matter of course to all non-handicapped children enrolled in public elementary and secondary schools. The Committee is concerned that although these services are available to and required of all children in our school systems, they are often viewed as a luxury for handicapped children.

*   *   *   *   *

The Committee expects the Commissioner of Education to take whatever action is necessary to assure that physical education services are available to all handicapped children, and has specifically included physical education within the definition of special education to make clear that the Committee expects such services, specially designed where necessary, to be provided as an integral part of the educational program of every handicapped child. (House Report No. 94-332, p. 9 (1975).)

PRIORITIES IN THE USE OF
PART B FUNDS

§ 121a.320 Definitions of "first priority children" and "second priority children."

For the purposes of §§ 121a.321-121a.324, the term:

(a) "First priority children" means handicapped children who:

(1) Are in an age group for which the State must make available free appropriate public education under § 121a.300; and

(2) Are not receiving any education.

(b) "Second priority children" means handicapped children, within each disability, with the most severe handicaps who are receiving an inadequate education.

(20 U.S.C. 1412 (3).)

Comment. After September 1, 1978, there should be no second priority children, since States must insure, as a condition of receiving Part B funds for fiscal year 1979, that all handicapped children will have available a free appropriate public education by that date.

NOTE.—The term "free appropriate public education," as defined in § 121a.4 of Subpart A, means "special education and related services which * * * are provided in conformity with an individualized education program * * *."

New "First priority children" will continue to be found by the State after September 1, 1978 through on-going efforts to identify, locate, and evaluate all handicapped children.

§ 121a.321 Priorities.

(a) Each State and local educational agency shall use funds provided under Part B of the Act in the following order of priorities:

(1) To provide free appropriate public education to first priority children, including the identification, location, and evaluation of first priority children.

(2) To provide free appropriate public education to second priority children, including the identification, location, and evaluation of second priority children.
in this part.

(3) To meet the other requirements

(b) The requirements of paragraph (a) of this section do not apply to funds which the State uses for administration under § 121a.620.

(20 U.S.C. 1411 (b) (1) (B), (b) (2) (B), (c) (1) (B), (c) (2) (A) (ii).)

(c) State and local educational agencies may not use funds under Part B of the Act for preservice training. (20 U.S.C. 1413 (a) (3); Senate Report No. 94-168, p. 34 (1975).)

Comment. Note that a State educational agency as well as local educational agencies must use Part B funds (except the portion used for State administration) for the priorities. A State may have to set aside a portion of its Part B allotment to be able to serve newly-identified first priority children.

After September 1, 1978, Part B funds may be used:

(1) To continue supporting child identification, location, and evaluation activities;

(2) To provide free appropriate public education to newly identified first priority children;

(3) To meet the full educational opportunities goal required under section 121a.304, including employing additional personnel and providing inservice training, in order to increase the

level, intensity and quality of services provided to individual handicapped children; and

(4) To meet the other requirements of Part B.

§ 121a.322   First priority children—school year 1977-1978.

(a) In school year 1977-1978, if a major component of a first priority child's proposed educational program is not available (for example, there is no qualified teacher), the public agency responsible for the child's education shall:

(1) Provide an interim program of services for the child; and

(2) Develop an individualized education program for full implementation no later than September 1, 1978.

(b) A local educational agency may use Part B funds for training or other support services in school year 1977-1978 only if all of its first priority children have available to them at least an interim program of services.

(c) A State educational agency may use Part B funds for training or other support services in school year 1977-1978 only if all first priority children in the State have available to them at least an interim program of services. (20 U.S.C. 1411 (b), (c).)

Comment. This provision is intended to make it clear that a State or local educational agency may not delay placing a previously unserved (first priority) child until it has, for example, implemented an inservice training program. The child must be placed. After the child is in at least an interim program, the State or local educational agency may use Part B funds for training or other support services needed to provide that child with a free appropriate public education.

§ 121a.323   Services to other children.

If a State or a local educational agency is providing free appropriate public education to all of its first prior-

ity children, that State or agency may use funds provided under Part B of the Act:

(a) To provide free appropriate public education to handicapped children who are not receiving any education and who are in the age groups not covered under § 121a.300 in that State; or

(b) To provide free appropriate public education to second priority children; or

(c) Both.
(20 U.S.C. 1411 (b) (1) (B), (b) (2) (B), (c) (2) (A) (ii).)

§ 121a.324   Application of local educational agency to use funds for the second priority.

A local educational agency may use funds provided under Part B of the Act for second priority children, if it provides assurance satisfactory to the State educational agency in its application or an amendment to its application):

(a) That all first priority children have a free appropriate public education available to them;

(b) That the local educational agency has a system for the identification, location, and evaluation of handicapped children, as described in its application; and

(c) That whenever a first priority child is identified, located, and evaluated, the local educational agency makes available a free appropriate public education to the child.
(20 U.S.C. 1411 (b) (1) (B), (c) (1) (B); 1414 (a) (1) (C) (ii).)

INDIVIDUALIZED EDUCATION PROGRAMS

§ 121a.340   Definition.

As used in this part, the term "individualized education program" means a written statement for a handicapped child that is developed and implemented in accordance with §§ 121a.341-121a.349.
(20 U.S.C. 1401 (19).)

§ 121a.341 State educational agency responsibility.

(a) *Public agencies.* The State educational agency shall insure that each public agency develops and implements an individualized education program for each of its handicapped children.

(b) *Private schools and facilities.* The State educational agency shall insure that an individualized education program is developed and implemented for each handicapped child who:

(1) Is placed in or referred to a private school or facility by a public agency; or

(2) Is enrolled in a parochial or other private school and receives special education or related services from a public agency.

(20 U.S.C. 1412 (4), (6); 1413 (a) (4).)

Comment: This section applies to all public agencies, including other State agencies (e.g., departments of mental health and welfare), which provide special education to a handicapped child either directly, by contract or through other arrangements. Thus, if a State welfare agency contracts with a private school or facility to provide special education to a handicapped child, that agency would be responsible for insuring that an individualized education program is developed for the child.

§ 121a.342 When individualized education programs must be in effect.

(a) On October 1, 1977, and at the beginning of each school year thereafter, each public agency shall have in effect an individualized education program for every handicapped child who is receiving special education from that agency.

(b) An individualized education program must:

(1) Be in effect before special education and related services are provided to a child; and

(2) Be implemented as soon as possible following the meetings under § 121a.343.

(20 U.S.C. 1412 (2) (B), (4), (6); 1414 (a) (5); Pub. L. 94-142, Sec. 8 (c) (1975).)

Comment. Under paragraph (b) (2), it is expected that a handicapped child's individualized education program (IEP) will be implemented immediately following the meetings under § 121a.343. An exception to this would be (1) when the meetings occur during the summer or a vacation period, or (2) where there are circumstances which require a short delay (e.g., working out transportation arrangements). However, there can be no undue delay in providing special education and related services to the child.

§ 121a.343 Meetings.

(a) *General.* Each public agency is responsible for initiating and conducting meetings for the purpose of developing, reviewing, and revising a handicapped child's individualized education program.

(b) *Handicapped children currently served.* If the public agency has determined that a handicapped child will receive special education during school year 1977-1978, a meeting must be held early enough to insure that an individualized education program is developed by October 1, 1977.

(c) *Other handicapped children.* For a handicapped child who is not included under paragraph (b) of this action, a meeting must be held within thirty calendar days of a determination that the child needs special education and related services.

(d) *Review.* Each public agency shall initiate and conduct meetings to periodically review each child's individualized education program and if appropriate revise its provisions. A meeting must be held for this purpose at least once a year.

(20 U.S.C. 1412 (2) (B), (4), (6); 1414 (a) (5).)

Comment. The dates on which agencies must have individualized education programs (IEPs) in effect are specified in § 121a.342 (October 1, 1977, and the beginning of each school year thereafter). However, except for new handicapped children (i.e., those evaluated and determined to need special education after October 1, 1977), the timing of meetings to develop, review, and revise IEPs is left to the discretion of each agency.

In order to have IEPs in effect by the dates in § 121a.342, agencies could hold meetings at the end of the school year or during the summer preceding those dates. In meeting the October 1, 1977 timeline, meetings could be conducted up through the October 1 date. Thereafter, meetings may be held any time throughout the year, as long as IEPs are in effect at the beginning of each school year.

The statute requires agencies to hold a meeting at least once each year in order to review, and if appropriate revise, each child's IEP. The timing of those meetings could be on the anniversary date of the last IEP meeting on the child, but this is left to the discretion of the agency.

§ 121a.344 Participants in meetings.

(a) *General.* The public agency shall insure that each meeting includes the following participants:

(1) A representative of the public agency, other than the child's teacher, who is qualified to provide, or supervise the provision of, special education.

(2) The child's teacher.

(3) One or both of the child's parents, subject to § 121a.345.

(4) The child, where appropriate.

(5) Other individuals at the discretion of the parent or agency.

(b) *Evaluation personnel.* For a handicapped child who has been evaluated for the first time, the public agency shall insure:

(1) That a member of the evaluation team participates in the meeting; or

(2) That the representative of the public agency, the child's teacher, or some other person is present at the meeting, who is knowledgeable about the evaluation procedures used with the child and is familiar with the results of the evaluation.

(20 U.S.C. 1401 (19); 1412 (2) (B), (4), (6); 1414 (a) (5).)

Comment. 1. In deciding which a child's individualized education program, the agency may wish to consider the following possibilities:

(a) For a handicapped child who is receiving special education, the "teacher" could be the child's special education teacher. If the child's handicap is a speech impairment, the "teacher" could be the speech-language pathologist.

(b) For a handicapped child who is being considered for placement in special education, the "teacher" could be the child's regular teacher, or a teacher qualified to provide education in the type of program in which the child may be placed, or both.

(c) If the child is not in school or has more than one teacher, the agency may designate which teacher will participate in the meeting.

2. Either the teacher or the agency representative should be qualified in the area of the child's suspected disability.

3. For a child whose primary handicap is a speech impairment, the evaluation personnel participating under paragraph (b) (1) of this section would normally be the speech-language pathologist.

§ 121a.345 Parent participation.

(a) Each public agency shall take steps to insure that one or both of the parents of the handicapped child are present at each meeting or are afforded the opportunity to participate, including:

(1) Notifying parents of the meeting early enough to insure that they will have an opportunity to attend; and

(2) Scheduling the meeting at a mutually agreed on time and place.

(b) The notice under paragraph (a) (1) of this section must indicate the purpose, time, and location of the meeting, and who will be in attendance.

(c) If neither parent can attend, the public agency shall use other methods to insure parent participation, including individual or conference telephone calls.

(d) A meeting may be conducted without a parent in attendance if the public agency is unable to convince the parents that they should attend. In this case the public agency must have a record of its attempts to arrange a mutually agreed on time and place such as:

(1) Detailed records of telephone calls made or attempted and the results of those calls.

(2) Copies of correspondence sent to the parents and any responses received, and

(3) Detailed records of visits made to the parent's home or place of employment and the results of those visits.

(e) The public agency shall take whatever action is necessary to insure that the parent understands the proceedings at a meeting, including arranging for an interpreter for parents who are deaf or whose native language is other than English.

(f) The public agency shall give the parent, on request, a copy of the individualized education program.
(20 U.S.C. 1401 (19); 1412 (2) (B), (4), (6); 1414 (a) (5).)

Comment. The notice in paragraph (a) could also inform parents that they may bring other people to the meeting. As indicated in paragraph (c), the procedure used to notify parents (whether oral or written or both) is left to the discretion of the agency, but the agency must keep a record of its efforts to contact parents.

§ 121a.346 Content of individualized education program.

The individualized education program for each child must include:

(a) A statement of the child's present levels of educational performance;

(b) A statement of annual goals, including short term instructional objectives;

(c) A statement of the specific special education and related services to be provided to the child, and the extent to which the child will be able to participate in regular educational programs;

(d) The projected dates for initiation of services and the anticipated duration of the services; and

(e) Appropriate objective criteria and evaluation procedures and schedules for determining, on at least an annual basis, whether the short term instructional objectives are being achieved.
(20 U.S.C. 1401 (19); 1412 (2) (B), (4), (6), 1414 (a) (5); Senate Report No. 94-168, p. 11 (1975).)

§ 121a.347 Private school placements.

(a) *Developing individualized education programs.* (1) Before a public agency places a handicapped child in, or refers a child to, a private school or facility, the agency shall initiate and conduct a meeting to develop an individualized education program for the child in accordance with § 121a.343.

(2) The agency shall insure that a representative of the private school facility attends the meeting. If the representative cannot attend, the agency shall use other methods to insure participation by the private school or facility, including individual or conference telephone calls.

(3) The public agency shall also

develop an indiviualized educational program for each handicapped child who was placed in a private school or facility by the agency before the effective date of these regulations.

(b) *Reviewing and revising individualized education programs.* (1) After a handicapped child enters a private school or facility, any meetings to review and revise the child's individualized education program may be initiated and conducted by the private school or facility at the discretion of the public agency.

(2) If the private school or facility initiates and conducts these meetings, the public agency shall insure that the parents and an agency representative:

(i) Are involved in any decision about the child's individualized education program; and

(ii) Agree to any proposed changes in the program before those changes are implemented.

(c) *Responsibility.* Even if a private school or facility implements a child's individualized education program, responsibility for compliance with this part remains with the public agency and the State educational agency. (20 U.S.C. 1413 (a) (4) (B).)

§ 121a.348   Handicapped children in parochial or other private schools.

If a handicapped child is enrolled in a parochial or other private school and receives special education or related services from a public agency, the public agency shall:

(a) Initiate and conduct meetings to develop, review, and revise an individualized education program for the child, in accordance with § 121a.343; and

(b) Insure that a representative of the parochial or other private school attends each meeting. If the representative cannot attend, the agency shall use other methods to insure participation by the private school, including individual or conference telephone calls. (20 U.S.C. 1413 (a) (4) (A).)

§ 121a.349   Individualized education program—accountability.

Each public agency must provide special education and related services to a handicapped child in accordance with an individualized education program. However, Part B of the Act does not require that any agency, teacher, or other person be held accountable if a child does not achieve the growth projected in the annual goals and objectives. (20 U.S.C. 1412 (2) (B); 1414 (a) (5), (6); Cong. Rec. at H 7152 (daily ed., July 21, 1975).)

Comment. This section is intended to relieve concerns that the individualized education program constitutes a guarantee by the public agency and the teacher that a child will progress at a specified rate. However, this section does not relieve agencies and teachers from making good faith efforts to assist the child in achieving the objectives and goals listed in the individualized education program. Further, the section does not limit a parent's right to complain and ask for revisions of the child's program, or to invoke due process procedures, if the parent feels that these efforts are not being made.

DIRECT SERVICE BY THE STATE EDUCATIONAL AGENCY

§ 121a.360   Use of local educational agency allocation for direct services.

(a) A State educational agency may not distribute funds to a local educational agency, and shall use those funds to insure the provision of a free appropriate public education to handicapped children residing in the area served by the local educational agency, if the local educational agency, in any fiscal year:

(1) Is entitled to less than $7,500 for that fiscal year (beginning with fiscal year 1979);

(2) Does not submit an application

that meets the requirements of §§ 121a.220-121a.240;

(3) Is unable or unwilling to establish and maintain programs of free appropriate public education;

(4) Is unable or unwilling to be consolidated with other local educational agencies in order to establish and maintain those programs; or

(5) Has one or more handicapped children who can best be served by a regional or State center designed to meet the needs of those children.

(b) In meeting the requirements of paragraph (a) of this section, the State educational agency may provide special education and related services directly, by contract, or through other arrangements.

(c) The excess cost requirements under §§ 121a.182-121a.186 do not apply to the State educational agency.
(20 U.S.C. 1411 (c) (4); 1413 (b); 1414(d).)

Comment. Section 121a.360 is a combination of three provisions in the statute (Section 611 (c) (4), 613 (b), and 614 (d)). This section focuses mainly on the State's administration and use of local entitlements under Part B.

The State educational agency, as a recipient of Part B funds is responsible for insuring that all public agencies in the State comply with the provisions of the Act, regardless of whether they receive Part B funds. If a local educational agency elects not to apply for its Part B entitlement, the State would be required to use those funds to insure that a free appropriate public education (FAPE) is made available to children residing in the area served by that local agency. However, if the local entitlement is not sufficient for this purpose, additional State or local funds would have to be expended in order to insure that "FAPE" and the other requirements of the Act are met.

Moreover, if the local educational agency is the recipient of any other Federal funds, it would have to be in compliance with Subpart D of the regulations for section 504 of the Rehabilitation Act of 1973 (45 CFR Part 84). It should be noted that the term "FAPE" has different meanings under Part B and section 504. For example, under Part B, "FAPE" is a statutory term which requires special education and related services to be provided in accordance with an individualized education program (IEP). However, under section 504, each recipient must provide an education which includes services that are "designed to meet individual educational needs of handicapped persons as adequately as the needs of nonhandicapped persons are met * * *" Those regulations state that implementation of an IEP, in accordance with Part B, is one means of meeting the "FAPE" requirement.

§ 121a.361 Nature and location of services.

The State educational agency may provide special education and related services under § 121a.360 (a) in the manner and at the location it considers appropriate. However, the manner in which the education and services are provided must be consistent with the requirements of this part (including the least restrictive environment provisions in §§ 121a.550-121a.556 of Subpart E).
(20 U.S.C. 1414 (d).)

§ 121.370 Use of State educational agency allocation for direct and support services.

(a) The State shall use the portion of its allocation it does not use for administration to provide support services and direct services in accordance with the priority requirements under §§ 121a.320-121a.324.

(b) For the purposes of paragraph (a) of this section:

(1) "Direct services" means services provided to a handicapped child by the

State directly, by contract, or through other arrangements.

(2) "Support services" includes implementing the comprehensive system of personnel development under §§ 121a.380-121a.388, recruitment and training of hearing officers and surrogate parents, and public information and parent training activities relating to a free appropriate public education for handicapped children.

(20 U.S.C. 1411 (b) (2), (c) (2).)

§ 121a.371 State matching.

Beginning with the period July 1, 1978-June 30, 1979, and for each following year, the funds that a State uses for direct and support services under § 121a.370 must be matched on a program basis by the State from funds other than Federal funds. This requirement does not apply to funds that the State uses under § 121a.360.

(20 U.S.C. 1411 (c) (2) (B), (c) (4) (B).)

Comment. The requirement in § 121a.371 would be satisfied if the State can document that the amount of State funds expended for each major program area (e.g., the comprehensive system of personnel development) is at least equal to the expenditure of Federal funds in that program area.

§ 121a.372 Applicability of nonsupplanting requirements.

Beginning with funds appropriated for Fiscal Year 1979 and for each following Fiscal Year, the requirement in section 613 (a) (9) of the Act, which prohibits supplanting with Federal funds, does not apply to funds that the State uses from its allocation under § 121a.706 (a) of Subpart G for administration, direct services, or support services.

(20 U.S.C. 1411 (c) (3).)

COMPREHENSIVE SYSTEM OF PERSONNEL DEVELOPMENT

§ 121a.380 Scope of system.

Each annual program plan must include a description of programs and procedures for the development and implementation of a comprehensive system of personnel development which includes:

(a) The inservice training of general and special educational instructional, related services, and support personnel;

(b) Procedures to insure that all personnel necessary to carry out the purposes of the Act are qualified (as defined in § 121a.12 of Subpart A) and that activities sufficient to carry out this personnel development plan are scheduled; and

(c) Effective procedures for acquiring and disseminating to teachers and administrators of programs for handicapped children significant information derived from educational research, demonstration, and similar projects, and for adopting, where appropriate, promising educational practices and materials developed through those projects.

(20 U.S.C. 1413 (a) (3).)

§ 121a.381 Participation of other agencies and institutions.

(a) The State educational agency must insure that all public and private institutions of higher education, and other agencies and organizations (including representatives of handicapped, parent, and other advocacy organizations) in the State which have an interest in the preparation of personnel for the education of handicapped children, have an opportunity to participate fully in the development, review, and annual updating of the comprehensive system of personnel development.

(b) The annual program plan must describe the nature and extent of participation under paragraph (a) of this section and must describe responsibilities of the State educational agency, local educational agencies, public and private institutions of higher education, and other agencies:

(1) With respect to the comprehensive system as a whole, and

(2) With respect to the personnel development plan under § 121a.383.

(20 U.S.C. 1412 (7) (A); 1413 (a) (3).)

§ 121a.382 Inservice training.

(a) As used in this section, "inservice training" means any training other than that received by an individual in a full-time program which leads to a degree.

(b) Each annual program plan must provide that the State educational agency:

(1) Conducts an annual needs assessment to determine if a sufficient number of qualified personnel are available in the State; and

(2) Initiates inservice personnel development programs based on the assessed needs of State-wide significance related to the implementation of the Act.

(c) Each annual program plan must include the results of the needs assessment under paragraph (b) (1) of this section, broken out by need for new personnel and need for retrained personnel.

(d) The State educational agency may enter into contracts with institutions of higher education, local educational agencies or other agencies, institutions, or organizations (which may include parent, handicapped, or other advocacy organizations), to carry out:

(1) Experimental or innovative personnel development programs;

(2) Development or modification of instructional materials; and

(3) Dissemination of significant information derived from educational research and demonstration projects.

(e) Each annual program plan must provide that the State educational agency insures that ongoing inservice training programs are available to all personnel who are engaged in the education of handicapped children, and that these programs include:

(1) The use of incentives which insure participation by teachers (such as released time, payment for participation, options for academic credit, salary step credit, certification renewal, or updating professional skills);

(2) The involvement of local staff; and

(3) The use of innovative practices which have been found to be effective.

(f) Each annual program plan must:

(1) Describe the process used in determining the inservice training needs of personnel engaged in the education of handicapped children;

(2) Identify the areas in which training is needed (such as individualized education programs, non-discriminatory testing, least restrictive environment, procedural safeguards, and surrogate parents);

(3) Specify the groups requiring training (such as special teachers, regular teachers, administrators, psychologists, speech-language pathologists, audiologists, physical education teachers, therapeutic recreation specialists, physical therapists, occupational therapists, medical personnel, parents, volunteers, hearing officers, and surrogate parents);

(4) Describe the content and nature of training for each area under paragraph (f) (2) of this section;

(5) Describe how the training will be provided in terms of (i) geographical scope (such as Statewide, regional, or local), and (ii) staff training source (such as college and university staffs, State and local educational agency personnel, and non-agency personnel);

(6) Specify: (i) The funding sources to be used, and

(ii) The time frame for providing it; and

(7) Specify procedures for effective

evaluation of the extent to which program objectives are met.
(20 U.S.C. 1413 (a) (3).)

§ 121a.383   Personnel development plan.

Each annual program plan must: (a) Include a personnel development plan which provides a structure for personnel planning and focuses on preservice and inservice education needs;

(b) Describe the results of the needs assessment under § 121a.382 (b) (1) with respect to identifying needed areas of training, and assigning priorities to those areas; and

(c) Identify the target populations for personnel development, including general education and special education instructional and administrative personnel, support personnel, and other personnel (such as paraprofessionals, parents, surrogate parents, and volunteers).
(20 U.S.C. 1413 (a) (3).)

§ 121a.384   Dissemination.

(a) Each annual program plan must include a description of the State's procedures for acquiring, reviewing, and disseminating to general and special educational instructional and support personnel, administrators of programs for handicapped children, and other interested agencies, and organizations (including parent, handicapped, and other advocacy organizations) significant information and promising practices derived from educational research, demonstration, and other projects.

(b) Dissemination includes:

(1) Making those personnel, administrators, agencies, and organizations aware of the information and practices;

(2) Training designed to enable the establishment of innovative programs and practices targeted on identified local needs; and

(3) Use of instructional materials and other media for personnel development and instructional programming.
(20 U.S.C. 1413 (a) (3).)

§ 121a.385   Adoption of educational practices.

(a) Each annual program plan must provide for a statewide system designed to adopt, where appropriate, promising educational practices and materials proven effective through research and demonstration.

(b) Each annual program plan must provide for thorough reassessment of educational practices used in the State.

(c) Each annual program plan must provide for the identification of State, local, and regional resources (human and material) which will assist in meeting the State's personnel preparation needs.
(20 U.S.C. 1413 (a) (3).)

§ 121a.386   Evaluation.

Each annual program plan must include:

(a) Procedures for evaluating the overall effectiveness of:

(1) The comprehensive system of personnel development in meeting the needs for personnel, and

(2) The procedures for administration of the system; and

(b) A description of the monitoring activities that will be undertaken to assure the implementation of the comprehensive system of personnel development.
(20 U.S.C. 1413 (a)) (3).)

§ 121a.387   Technical assistance to local educational agencies.

Each annual program plan must include a description of technical assistance that the State educational agency gives to local educational agencies in their implementation of the State's comprehensive system of personnel development.
(20 U.S.C. 1413 (a)) (3).)

Subpart D—Private Schools

HANDICAPPED CHILDREN IN PRIVATE
SCHOOLS PLACED OR REFERRED
BY PUBLIC AGENCIES

§ 121a.400 Applicability of §§ 121a.401-121a.403.

Sections 121a.401-121a.403 apply only to handicapped children who are or have been placed in or referred to a private school or facility by a public agency as a means of providing special education and related services.
(20 U.S.C. 1413 (a) (4) (B).)

§ 121a.401 Responsibility of State educational agency.

Each State educational agency shall insure that a handicapped child who is placed in or referred to a private school or facility by a public agency:

(a) Is provided special education and related services:

(1) In conformance with an individualized education program which meets the requirements under §§ 121a.-340-121a.349 of Subpart C;

(2) At no cost to the parents; and

(3) At a school or facility which meets the standards that apply to State and local educational agencies (including the requirements in this part); and

(b) Has all of the rights of a handicapped child who is served by a public agency.
(20 U.S.C. 1413 (a) (4) (B).)

§ 121a.402 Implementation by State educational agency.

In implementing § 121a.401, the State educational agency shall:

(a) Monitor compliance through procedures such as written reports, on-site visits, and parent questionnaires;

(b) Disseminate copies of applicable standards to each private school and facility to which a public agency has referred or placed a handicapped child; and

(c) Provide an opportunity for those private schools and facilities to par-ticipate in the development and revision of State standards which apply to them.
(20 U.S.C. 1413 (a) (4) (B).)

§ 121a.403 Placement of children by parents.

(a) If a handicapped child has available a free appropriate public education and the parents choose to place the child in a private school or facility, the public agency is not required by this part to pay for the child's education at the private school or facility. However, the public agency shall make services available to the child as provided under §§ 121a.450-121a.460.

(b) Disagreements between a parent and a public agency regarding the availability of a program appropriate for the child, and the question of financial responsibility, are subject to the due process procedures under §§ 121a.500-121a.514 of Subpart E.
(20 U.S.C. 1412 (2) (B); 1415.)

HANDICAPPED CHILDREN IN PRIVATE
SCHOOLS NOT PLACED OR REFERRED
BY PUBLIC AGENCIES

§ 121a.450 Applicability of §§ 121a.451-121a.460.

As used in §§ 121a.451-121a.460, "private school handicapped children" means handicapped children enrolled in private schools or facilities other than handicapped children covered under §§ 121a.400-121a.403.
(20 U.S.C. 1413 (a) (4) (A).)

§ 121a.451 State educational agency responsibility.

The State educational agency shall insure that:

(a) To the extent consistent with their number and location in the State, provision is made for the participation of private school handicapped children in the program assisted or carried out under this part by providing them with special education and related services; and

(b) The other requirements in §§ 121a.452-121a.460 are met.
(20 U.S.C. 1413 (a) (4) (A).)

§ 121a.452 Local educational agency responsibility.

(a) Each local educational agency shall provide special education and related services designed to meet the needs of private school handicapped children residing in the jurisdiction of the agency.

(b) Each local educational agency shall provide private school handicapped children with genuine opportunities to participate in special education and related services consistent with the number of those children and their needs.
(20 U.S.C. 1413 (a) (4) (A); 1414 (a) (6).)

§ 121a.453 Determination of needs, number of children, and types of services.

The needs of private school handicapped children, the number of them who will participate under this part, and the types of special education and related services which the local educational agency will provide for them must be determined after consultation with persons knowledgeable of the needs of these children, on a basis comparable to that used in providing for the participation under this part of handicapped children enrolled in public schools.
(20 U.S.C. 1413 (a) (4) (A).)

§ 121a.454 Service arrangements.

Services to private school handicapped children may be provided through such arrangements as dual enrollment, educational radio and television, and the provision of mobile educational services and equipment.
(20 U.S.C. 1413 (a) (4) (A).)

§ 121a.455 Differences in services to private school handicapped chlidren.

A local educational agency may provide special education and related services to private school handicapped children which are different from the special education and related services it provides to public school children, if:

(a) The differences are necessary to meet the special needs of the private school handicapped children, and

(b) The special education and related services are comparable in quality, scope, and opportunity for participation to those provided to public school children with needs of equal importance.
(20 U.S.C. 1413 (a) (4) (a); *Wheeler v. Barrera,* 417 U.S. 402 (1974).)

§ 121a.456 Personnel.

(a) Public school personnel may be made available in other than public school facilities only to the extent necessary to provide services required by the handicapped children for whose needs those services were designed, and only when those services are not normally provided by the private school.

(b) Each State or local educational agency providing services to children enrolled in private schools shall maintain continuing administrative control and direction over those services.

(c) The services provided with funds under Part B of the Act for eligible handicapped children enrolled in private schools may not include:

(1) The payment of salaries of teachers or other employees of private schools except for services performed outside their regular hours of duty and under public supervision and control; or

(2) The construction of private school facilities.
(20 U.S.C. 1413 (a) (4) (A).)

§ 121a.457 Equipment.

(a) Equipment acquired with funds under Part B of the Act may be placed on private school premises for a limited period of time, but the title to and administrative control over all equipment must be retained and exercised by a public agency.

(b) In exercising administrative control, the public agency shall keep records of and account for the equipment, and shall insure that the equipment is used solely for the purposes of the program or project, and remove the equipment from the private school premises if necessary to avoid its being used for other purposes or if it is no longer needed for the purposes of the program or project.
(20 U.S.C. 1413 (a) (4) (A).)

§ 121a.458 Prohibition of segregation.

Programs or projects carried out in public facilities, and involving joint participation by eligible handicapped children enrolled in private schools and handicapped children enrolled in public schools, may not include classes that are separated on the basis of school enrollment or the religious affiliations of the children.
(20 U.S.C. 1413 (a) (4) (A).)

§ 121a.459 Funds and property not to benefit private school.

Funds provided under Part B of the Act and property derived from those funds may not inure to the benefit of any private school.
(20 U.S.C. 1413 (a) (4) (A).)

§ 121a.460 Existing level of instruction.

Provisions for serving private school handicapped children may not include the financing of the existing level of instruction in the private schools.
(20 U.S.C. 1413 (a) (4) (A).)

Subpart E—Procedural Safeguards

DUE PROCESS PROCEDURES FOR
PARENTS AND CHILDREN

§ 121a.500 Definitions of "consent," "evaluation," and "personally identifiable."

As used in this part: "Consent" means that: (a) The parent has been fully informed of all information relevant to the activity for which consent is sought, in his or her native language, or other mode of communication;

(b) The parent understands and agrees in writing to the carrying out of the activity for which his or her consent is sought, and the consent describes that activity and lists the records (if any) which will be released and to whom; and

(c) The parent understands that the granting of consent is voluntary on the part of the parent and may be revoked at any time.

"Evaluation" means procedures used in accordance with §§ 121a.530-121a.-534 to determine whether a child is handicapped and the nature and extent of the special education and related services that the child needs. The term means procedures used selectively with an individual child and does not include basic tests administered to or procedures used with all children in a school, grade, or class.

"Personally identifiable" means that information includes:

(a) The name of the child, the child's parent, or other family member;

(b) The address of the child;

(c) A personal identifier, such as the child's social security number or student number; or

(d) A list of personal characteristics or other information which would make it possible to identify the child with reasonable certainty.
(20 U.S.C. 1415, 1417 (c).)

§ 121a.501 General responsibility of public agencies.

Each State educational agency shall insure that each public agency establishes and implements procedural safeguards which meet the requirements of §§ 121a.500-121a.514.
(20 U.S.C. 1415 (a).)

§ 121a.502 Opportunity to examine records.

The parents of a handicapped child shall be afforded, in accordance with the procedures in §§ 121a.562-121a.569

an opportunity to inspect and review all education records with respect to:

(a) The identification, evaluation, and educational placement of the child, and

(b) The provision of a free appropriate public education to the child. (20 U.S.C. 1415 (b) (1) (A).)

§ 121a.503 Independent educational evaluation.

(a) *General.* (1) The parents of a handicapped child have the right under this part to obtain an independent educational evaluation of the child, subject to paragraphs (b) through (e) of this section.

(2) Each public agency shall provide to parents, on request, information about where an independent educational evaluation may be obtained.

(3) For the purposes of this part:

(i) "Independent educational evaluation" means an evaluation conducted by a qualified examiner who is not employed by the public agency responsible for the education of the child in question.

(ii) "Public expense" means that the public agency either pays for the full cost of the evaluation or insures that the evaluation is otherwise provided at no cost to the parent, consistent with § 121a.301 of Subpart C.

(b) *Parent right to evaluation at public expense.* A parent has the right to an independent educational evaluation at public expense if the parent disagrees with an evaluation obtained by the public agency. However, the public agency may initiate a hearing under § 121a.506 of this subpart to show that its evaluation is appropriate. If the final decision is that the evaluation is appropriate, the parent still has the right to an independent educational evaluation, but not at public expense.

(c) *Parent initiated evaluations.* If the parent obtains an independent educational evaluation at private expense,

the results of the evaluation:

(1) Must be considered by the public agency in any decision made with respect to the provision of a free appropriate public education to the child, and

(2) May be presented as evidence at a hearing under this subpart regarding that child.

(d) *Requests for evaluations by hearing officers.* If a hearing officer requests an independent educational evaluation as part of a hearing, the cost of the evaluation must be at public expense.

(e) *Agency criteria.* Whenever an independent evaluation is at public expense, the criteria under which the evaluation is obtained, including the location of the evaluation and the qualifications of the examiner, must be the same as the criteria which the public agency uses when it initiates an evaluation. (20 U.S.C. 1415 (b) (1) (A).)

§ 121a.504 Prior notice; parent consent.

(a) *Notice.* Written notice which meets the requirements under § 121a.-505 must be given to the parents of a handicapped child a reasonable time before the public agency:

(1) Proposes to initiate or change the identification, evaluation, or educational placement of the child or the provision of a free appropriate public education to the child, or

(2) Refuses to initiate or change the identification, evaluation, or educational placement of the child or the provision of a free appropriate public education to the child.

(b) *Consent.* (1) Parental consent must be obtained before:

(i) Conducting a preplacement evaluation; and

(ii) Initial placement of a handicapped child in a program providing special education and related services.

(2) Except for preplacement evaluation and initial placement, consent may

not be required as a condition of any benefit to the parent or child.

(c) *Procedures where parent refuses consent.* (1) Where State law requires parental consent before a handicapped child is evaluated or initially provided special education and related services, State procedures govern the public agency in overriding a parent's refusal to consent.

(2) (i) Where there is no State law requiring consent before a handicapped child is evaluated or initially provided special education and related services, the public agency may use the hearing procedures in §§ 121a.506-121a.508 to determine if the child may be evaluated or initially provided special education and related services without parental consent.

(ii) If the hearing officer upholds the agency, the agency may evaluate or initially provide special education and related services to the child without the parent's consent, subject to the parent's rights under §§ 121a.510-121a.513.

(20 U.S.C. 1415 (b) (1) (C), (D).)

Comment. 1. Any changes in a child's special education program, after the initial placement, are not subject to the prior notice requirement in paragraph (a) and the individualized education program requirements in Subpart C.

2. Paragraph (c) means that where State law requires parental consent before evaluation or before special education and related services are initially provided, and the parent refuses (or otherwise withholds) consent, State procedures, such as obtaining a court order authorizing the public agency to conduct the evaluation or provide the education and related services, must be followed.

If, however, there is no legal requirement for consent outside of these regulations, the public agency may use the due process procedures under this subpart to obtain a decision to allow the evaluation or services without parental consent. The agency must notify the

parent of its actions, and the parent has appeal rights as well as rights at the hearing itself.

§ 121a.505 **Content of notice.**

(a) The notice under § 121a.504 must include:

(1) A full explanation of all of the procedural safeguards available to the parents under Subpart E;

(2) A description of the action proposed or refused by the agency, an explanation of why the agency proposes or refuses to take the action, and a description of any options the agency considered and the reasons why those options were rejected;

(3) A description of each evaluation procedure, test, record, or report the agency uses as a basis for the proposal or refusal; and

(4) A description of any other factors which are relevant to the agency's proposal or refusal.

(b) The notice must be:

(1) Written in language understandable to the general public, and

(2) Provided in the native language of the parent or other mode of communication used by the parent, unless it is clearly not feasible to do so.

(c) If the native language or other mode of communication of the parent is not a written language, the State or local educational agency shall take steps to insure:

(1) That the notice is translated orally or by other means to the parent in his or her native language or other mode of communication;

(2) That the parent understands the content of the notice, and

(3) That there is written evidence that the requirements in paragraph (c) (1) and (2) of this section have been met.

(20 U.S.C. 1415 (b) (1) (D).)

§ 121a.506 **Impartial due process hearing.**

(a) A parent or a public educational

agency may initiate a hearing on any of the matters described in § 121a.504 (a) (1) and (2).

(b) The hearing must be conducted by the State educational agency or the public agency directly responsible for the education of the child, as determined under State statute, State regulation, or a written policy of the State educational agency.

(c) The public agency shall inform the parent of any free or low-cost legal and other relevant services available in the area if:

(1) The parent requests the information; or

(2) The parent or the agency initiates a hearing under this section. (20 U.S.C. 1416 (b) (2).)

Comment: Many States have pointed to the success of using mediation as an intervening step prior to conducting a formal due process hearing. Although the process of mediation is not required by the statute or these regulations, an agency may wish to suggest mediation in disputes concerning the identification, evaluation, and educational placement of handicapped children, and the provision of a free appropriate public education to those children. Mediations have been conducted by members of State educational agencies or local educational agency personnel who were not previously involved in the particular case. In many cases, mediation leads to resolution of differences between parents and agencies without the development of an adversarial relationship and with minimal emotional stress. However, mediation may not be used to deny or delay a parent's rights under this subpart.

§ 121a.507   Impartial hearing officer.

(a) A hearing may not be conducted:

(1) By a person who is an employee of a public agency which is involved in the education or care of the child, or

(2) By any person having a personal or professional interest which would conflict with his or her objectivity in the hearing.

(b) A person who otherwise qualifies to conduct a hearing under paragraph (a) of this section is not an employee of the agency solely because he or she is paid by the agency to serve as a hearing officer.

(c) Each public agency shall keep a list of the persons who serve as hearing officers. The list must include a statement of the qualifications of each of those persons. (20 U.S.C. 1414 (b) (2).)

§ 121a.508   Hearing rights.

(a) Any party to a hearing has the right to:

(1) Be accompanied and advised by counsel and by individuals with special knowledge or training with respect to the problems of handicapped children;

(2) Present evidence and confront, cross-examine, and compel the attendance of witnesses;

(3) Prohibit the introduction of any evidence at the hearing that has not been disclosed to that party at least five days before the hearing;

(4) Obtain a written or electronic verbatim record of the hearing;

(5) Obtain written findings of fact and decisions. (The public agency shall transmit those findings and decisions, after deleting any personally identifiable information, to the State advisory panel established under Subpart F.)

(b) Parents involved in hearings must be given the right to:

(1) Have the child who is the subject of the hearing present; and

(2) Open the hearing to the public. (20 U.S.C. 1415 (d).)

§ 121a.509   Hearing decision; appeal.

A decision made in a hearing conducted under this subpart is final, unless a party to the hearing appeals the

decision under § 121a.510 or § 121a.511.
(20 U.S.C. 1415 (c).)

§ 121a.510 Administrative appeal; impartial review.

(a) If the hearing is conducted by a public agency other than the State educational agency, any party aggrieved by the findings and decision in the hearing may appeal to the State educational agency.

(b) If there is an appeal, the State educational agency shall conduct an impartial review of the hearing. The official conducting the review shall:

(1) Examine the entire hearing record;

(2) Insure that the procedures at the hearing were consistent with the requirements of due process;

(3) Seek additional evidence if necessary. If a hearing is held to receive additional evidence, the rights in § 121a.508 apply;

(4) Afford the parties an opportunity for oral or written argument, or both, at the discretion of the reviewing official;

(5) Make an independent decision on completion of the review; and

(6) Give a copy of written findings and the decision to the parties.

(c) The decision made by the reviewing official is final, unless a party brings a civil action under § 121a.512. (20 U.S.C. 1415 (c), (d); H. Rep. No. 94-664, at p. 49 (1975).)

Comment. 1. The State educational agency may conduct its review either directly or through another State agency acting on its behalf. However, the State educational agency remains responsible for the final decision on review.

2. All parties have the right to continue to be represented by counsel at the State administrative review level, whether or not the reviewing official determines that a further hearing is necessary. If the reviewing official decides to hold a hearing to receive additional evidence, the other rights in section 121a.508, relating to hearings, also apply.

§ 121a.511 Civil action.

Any party aggrieved by the findings and decision made in a hearing who does not have the right to appeal under § 121a.510 of this subpart, and any party aggrieved by the decision of a reviewing officer under § 121a.510 has the right to bring a civil action under section 615 (a) (2) of the Act.
(20 U.S.C. 1415.)

§ 121a.512 Timelines and convenience of hearings and reviews.

(a) The public agency shall insure that not later than 45 days after the receipt of a request for a hearing:

(1) A final decision is reached in the hearing; and

(2) A copy of the decision is mailed to each of the parties.

(b) The State educational agency shall insure that not later than 30 days after the receipt of a request for a review:

(1) A final decision is reached in the review; and

(2) A copy of the decision is mailed to each of the parties.

(c) A hearing or reviewing officer may grant specific extensions of time beyond the periods set out in paragraphs (a) and (b) of this section at the request of either party.

(d) Each hearing and each review involving oral arguments must be conducted at a time and place which is reasonably convenient to the parents and child involved.
(20 U.S.C. 1415.)

§ 121a.513 Child's status during proceedings.

(a) During the pendency of any administrative or judicial proceeding regarding a complaint, unless the public agency and the parents of the child agree otherwise, the child involved in the complaint must remain in his or her present educational placement.

(b) If the complaint involves an application for initial admission to public school, the child, with the consent of the parents, must be placed in the public school program until the completion of all the proceedings. (20 U.S.C. 1415 (e) (3).)

Comment. Section 121a.513 does not permit a child's placement to be changed during a complaint proceeding, unless the parents and agency agree otherwise. While the placement may not be changed, this does not preclude the agency from using its normal procedures for dealing with children who are endangering themselves or others.

§ 121a.514 Surrogate parents.

(a) *General.* Each public agency shall insure that the rights of a child are protected when:

(1) No parent (as defined in § 121a.-10) can be identified;

(2) The public agency, after reasonable efforts, cannot discover the whereabouts of a parent; or

(3) The child is a ward of the State under the laws of that State.

(b) *Duty of public agency.* The duty of a public agency under paragraph (a) of this section includes the assignment of an individual to act as a surrogate for the parents. This must include a method (1) for determining whether a child needs a surrogate parent, and (2) for assigning a surrogate parent to the child.

(c) *Criteria for selection of surrogates.* (1) The public agency may select a surrogate parent in any way permitted under State law.

(2) Public agencies shall insure that a person selected as a surrogate:

(i) Has no interest that conflicts with the interests of the child he or she represents; and

(ii) Has knowledge and skills, that insure adequate representation of the child.

(d) *Non-employee requirement; compensation.* (1) A person assigned as a surrogate may not be an employee of a public agency which is involved in the education or care of the child.

(2) A person who otherwise qualifies to be a surrogate parent under paragraph (c) and (d) (1) of this section, is not an employee of the agency solely because he or she is paid by the agency to serve as a surrogate parent.

(e) *Responsibilities.* The surrogate parent may represent the child in all matters relating to:

(1) The identification, evaluation, and educational placement of the child, and

(2) The provision of a free appropriate public education to the child. (20 U.S.C. 1415 (b) (1) (B).)

PROTECTION IN EVALUATION PROCEDURES

§ 121a.530 General.

(a) Each State educational agency shall insure that each public agency establishes and implements procedures which meet the requirements of §§ 121a.530-121a.534.

(b) Testing and evaluation materials and procedures used for the purposes of evaluation and placement of handicapped children must be selected and administered so as not to be racially or culturally discriminatory. (20 U.S.C. 1412 (5) (C).)

§ 121a.531 Preplacement evaluation.

Before any action is taken with respect to the initial placement of a handicapped child in a special education program, a full and individual evaluation of the child's educational needs must be conducted in accordance with the requirements of § 121a.532. (20 U.S.C. 1412 (5) (C).)

§ 121a.532 Evaluation procedures.

State and local educational agencies shall insure, at a minimum, that:

(a) Tests and other evaluation materials:

(1) Are provided and administered in the child's native language or other mode of communication, unless it is clearly not feasible to do so;

(2) Have been validated for the specific purpose for which they are used; and

(3) Are administered by trained personnel in conformance with the instructions provided by their producer;

(b) Tests and other evaluation materials include those tailored to assess specific areas of educational need and not merely those which are designed to provide a single general intelligence quotient;

(c) Tests are selected and administered so as best to ensure that when a test is administered to a child with impaired sensory, manual, or speaking skills, the test results accurately reflect the child's aptitude or achievement level or whatever other factors the test purports to measure, rather than reflecting the child's impaired sensory, manual, or speaking skills (except where those skills are the factors which the test purports to measure);

(d) No single procedure is used as the sole criterion for determining an appropriate educational program for a child; and

(e) The evaluation is made by a multidisciplinary team or group of persons, including at least one teacher or other specialist with knowledge in the area of suspected disability.

(f) The child is assessed in all areas related to the suspected disability, including, where appropriate, health, vision, hearing, social and emotional status, general intelligence, academic performance, communicative status, and motor abilities.

(20 U.S.C. 1412 (5) (C).)

Comment. Children who have a speech impairment as their primary handicap may not need a complete battery of assessments (e.g., psychological, physical, or adaptive behavior). However, a qualified speech-language pathologist would (1) evaluate each speech impaired child using procedures that are appropriate for the diagnosis and appraisal of speech and language disorders, and (2) where necessary, make referrals for additional assessments needed to make an appropriate placement decision.

§ 121a.533   Placement procedures.

(a) In interpreting evaluation data and in making placement decisions, each public agency shall:

(1) Draw upon information from a variety of sources, including aptitude and achievement tests, teacher recommendations, physical condition, social or cultural background, and adaptive behavior;

(2) Insure that information obtained from all of these sources is documented and carefully considered;

(3) Insure that the placement decision is made by a group of persons, including persons knowledgeable about the child, the meaning of the evaluation data, and the placement options; and

(4) Insure that the placement decision is made in conformity with the least restrictive environment rules in

§§ 121a.550-121a.554.

(b) If a determination is made that a child is handicapped and needs special education and related services, an individualized education program must be developed for the child in accordance with §§ 121a.340-121a.349 of Subpart C.

(20 U.S.C. 1412 (5) (C); 1414 (a) (5).)

Comment. Paragraph (a) (1) includes a list of examples of sources that may be used by a public agency in making placement decisions. The agency would not have to use all the sources in every instance. The point of the requirement is to insure that more than one source is used in interpreting evaluation data and in making placement decisions. For example, while all of the named sources would have to be used for a child whose suspected disability is mental retardation, they would not be necessary for certain other handicapped children, such as a child who has a severe articulation disorder as his primary handicap. For such a child, the speech-language pathologist, in complying with the multisource requirement, might use (1) a standardized test of articulation, and (2) observation of the child's articulation behavior in conversational speech.

§ 121a.534   Reevaluation.

Each State and local educational agency shall insure:

(a) That each handicapped child's individualized education program is reviewed in accordance with §§ 121a.-340-121a.349 of Subpart C, and

(b) That an evaluation of the child, based on procedures which meet the requirements under § 121a.532, is conducted every three years or more frequently if conditions warrant or if the child's parent or teacher requests an evaluation.

(20 U.S.C. 1412 (5) (c).)

LEAST RESTRICTIVE ENVIRONMENT

§ 121a.550   General.

(a) Each State educational agency shall insure that each public agency establishes and implements procedures which meet the requirements of §§ 121a.550-121a.556.

(b) Each public agency shall insure;

(1) That to the maximum extent appropriate, handicapped children, including children in public or private institutions or other care facilities, are educated with children who are not handicapped, and

(2) That special classes, separate schooling or other removal of handicapped children from the regular educational environment occurs only when the nature or severity of the handicap

is such that education in regular classes with the use of supplementary aids and services cannot be achieved satisfactorily.

(20 U.S.C. 1412 (5) (B); 1414 (a) (1) (C) (iv).)

§ 121a.551   Continuum of alternative placements.

(a) Each public agency shall insure that a continuum of alternative placements is available to meet the needs of handicapped children for special education and related services.

(b) The continuum required under paragraph (a) of this section must:

(1) Include the alternative placements listed in the definition of special education under § 121a.13 of Subpart A (instruction in regular classes, special classes, special schools, home instruction, and instruction in hospitals and institutions), and

(2) Make provision for supplementary services (such as resource room or itinerant instruction) to be provided in conjunction with regular class placement.

(20 U.S.C. 1412 (5) (B).)

§ 121a.552   Placements.

Each public agency shall insure that:

(a) Each handicapped child's educational placement:

(1) Is determined at least annually,

(2) Is based on his or her individualized education program, and

(3) Is as close as possible to the child's home;

(b) The various alternative placements included under § 121a.551 are available to the extent necessary to implement the individualized education program for each handicapped child;

(c) Unless a handicapped child's individualized education program requires some other arrangement, the child is educated in the school which he or she would attend if not handicapped; and

(d) In selecting the least restrictive

environment, consideration is given to any potential harmful effect on the child or on the quality of services which he or she needs.
(20 U.S.C. 1412 (5) (B).)

Comment. Section 121a.552 includes some of the main factors which must be considered in determining the extent to which a handicapped child can be educated with children who are not handicapped. The overriding rule in this is that placement decisions must be made on an individual basis. The section also requires each agency to have various alternative placements available in order to insure that each handicapped child receives an education which is appropriate to his or her individual needs.

The analysis of the regulations for Section 504 of the Rehabilitation Act of 1973 (45 CFR Part 84—Appendix, Paragraph 24) includes several points regarding educational placements of handicapped children which are pertinent to this section:

1. With respect to determining proper placements, the analysis states: " * * * it should be stressed that, where a handicapped child is so disruptive in a regular classroom that the education of other students is significantly impaired, the needs of the handicapped child cannot be met in that environment. Therefore regular placement would not be appropriate to his or her needs * * *."

2. With respect to placing a handicapped child in an alternate setting, the analysis states that among the factors to be considered in placing a child is the need to place the child as close to home as possible. Recipients are required to take this factor into account in making placement decisions. The parent's right to challenge the placement of their child extends not only to placement in special classes or separate schools, but also to placement in a distant school, particularly in a residential program. An equally appropriate education program may exist

closer to home; and this issue may be raised by the parent under the due process provisions of this subpart.

§ 121a.553 Nonacademic settings.

In providing or arranging for the provision of nonacademic and extracurricular services and activities, including meals, recess periods, and the services and activities set forth in § 121a.306 of Subpart C, each public agency shall insure that each handicapped child participates with nonhandicapped children in those services and activities to the maximum extent appropriate to the needs of that child.
(20 U.S.C. 1412 (5) (B).)

Comment. Section 121a.553 is taken from a new requirement in the final regulations for Section 504 of the Rehabilitation Act of 1973. With respect to this requirement, the analysis of the Section 504 Regulations includes the following statement: "[A new paragraph] specifies that handicapped children must also be provided nonacademic services in as integrated a setting as possible. This requirement is especially important for children whose educational needs necessitate their being solely with other handicapped children during most of each day. To the maximum extent appropriate, children in residential settings are also to be provided opportunities for participation with other children." (45 CFR Part 84—Appendix, Paragraph 24.)

§ 121a.554 Children in public or private institutions.

Each State educational agency shall make arrangements with public and private institutions (such as a memorandum of agreement or special implementation procedures) as may be necessary to insure that § 121a.550 is effectively implemented.
(20 U.S.C. 1412 (5) (B).)

Comment. Under section 612 (5) (B) of the statute, the requirement to educate handicapped children with nonhandicapped children also applies to children in public and private institutions or other care facilities. Each State educational agency must insure that each applicable agency and institution in the State implements this requirement. Regardless of other reasons for institutional placement, no child in an institution who is capable of education in a regular public school setting may be denied access to an education in that setting.

§ 121a.555 Technical assistance and training activities.

Each State educational agency shall carry out activities to insure that teachers and administrators in all public agencies:

(a) Are fully informed about their responsibilities for implementing § 121a.550, and

(b) Are provided with technical assistance and training necessary to assist them in this effort.

(20 U.S.C. 1412 (5) (B).)

§ 121a.556 Monitoring activities

(a) The State educational agency shall carry out activities to insure that § 121a.550 is implemented by each public agency.

(b) If there is evidence that a public agency makes placements that are inconsistent with § 121a.550 of this subpart, the State educational agency:

(1) Shall review the public agency's justification for its actions, and

(2) Shall assist in planning and implementing any necessary corrective action.

(20 U.S.C. 1412 (5) (B).)

CONFIDENTIALITY OF INFORMATION

§ 121a.560 Definitions.

As used in this subpart:

"Destruction" means physical destruction or removal of personal identifiers from information so that the information is no longer personally identifiable.

"Education records" means the type of records covered under the definition of "education records" in Part 99 of this title (the regulations implementing the Family Educational Rights and Privacy Act of 1974).

"Participating agency" means any agency or institution which collects, maintains, or uses personally identifiable information, or from which information is obtained, under this part. (20 U.S.C. 1412 (2) (D); 1417 (c).)

§ 121a.561 Notice to parents.

(a) The State educational agency shall give notice which is adequate to fully inform parents about the requirements under § 121a.128 of Subpart B, including:

(1) A description of the extent to which the notice is given in the native languages of the various population groups in the State;

(2) A description of the children on whom personally identifiable information is maintained, the types of information sought, the methods the State intends to use in gathering the information (including the sources from whom information is gathered), and the uses to be made of the information;

(3) A summary of the policies and procedures which participating agencies must follow regarding storage, disclosure to third parties, retention, and destruction of personally identifiable information; and

(4) A description of all of the rights of parents and children regarding this information, including the rights under section 438 of the General Education Provisions Act and Part 99 of this title (the Family Educational Rights and Privacy Act of 1974, and implementing regulations).

(b) Before any major identification, location, or evaluation activity, the notice must be published or announced in newspapers or other media, or both, with circulation adequate to notify parents throughout the State of the activity.

(20 U.S.C. 1412 (2) (D); 1417 (c).)

§ 121a.562 Access rights.

(a) Each participating agency shall permit parents to inspect and review any education records relating to their children which are collected, maintained, or used by the agency under this part. The agency shall comply with a request without unnecessary delay and before any meeting regarding an individualized education program or hearing relating to the identification, evaluation, or placement of the child, and in no case more than 45 days after the request has been made.

(b) The right to inspect and review education records under this section includes:

(1) The right to a response from the participating agency to reasonable requests for explanations and interpretations of the records;

(2) The right to request that the agency provide copies of the records containing the information if failure to provide those copies would effectively prevent the parent from exercising the right to inspect and review the records; and

(3) The right to have a representative of the parent inspect and review the records.

(c) An agency may presume that the parent has authority to inspect and review records relating to his or her child unless the agency has been advised that the parent does not have the authority under applicable State law governing such matters as guardianship, separation, and divorce.
(20 U.S.C. 1412 (2) (D); 1417 (c).)

§ 121a.563 Record of access.

Each participating agency shall keep a record of parties obtaining access to education records collected, maintained, or used under this part (except access by parents and authorized employees of the participating agency), including the name of the party, the date access was given, and the purpose for which the party is authorized to use the records.
(20 U.S.C. 1412 (2) (D); 1417 (c).)

§ 121a.564 Records on more than one child.

If any education record includes information on more than one child, the parents of those children shall have the right to inspect and review only the information relating to their child or to be informed of that specific information.
(20 U.S.C. 1412 (2) (D); 1417 (c).)

§ 121a.565 List of types and locations of information.

Each participating agency shall provide parents on request a list of the types and locations of education records collected, maintained, or used by the agency.
(20 U.S.C. 1412 (2) (D); 1417 (c).)

§ 121a.566 Fees.

(a) A participating education agency may charge a fee for copies of records which are made for parents under this part if the fee does not effectively prevent the parents from exercising their right to inspect and review those records.

(b) A participating agency may not charge a fee to search for or to retrieve information under this part.
(20 U.S.C. 1412 (2) (D); 1417 (c).)

§ 121a.567 Amendment of records at parent's request.

(a) A parent who believes that information in education records collected, maintained, or used under this part is inaccurate or misleading or violates the privacy or other rights of the child, may request the participating agency which maintains the information to amend the information.

(b) The agency shall decide whether to amend the information in accordance with the request within a reasonable period of time of receipt of the request.

(c) If the agency decides to refuse

to amend the information in accordance with the request it shall inform the parent of the refusal, and advise the parent of the right to a hearing under § 121a.568.

(20 U.S.C. 1412 (2) (D); 1417 (c).)

§ 121a.568   Opportunity for a hearing.

The agency shall, on request, provide an opportunity for a hearing to challenge information in education records to insure that it is not inaccurate, misleading, or otherwise in violation of the privacy or other rights of the child.

(20 U.S.C. 1412 (2) (D); 1417 (c).)

§ 121a.569   Result of hearing.

(a) If, as a result of the hearing, the agency decides that the information is inaccurate, misleading or otherwise in violation of the privacy or other rights of the child, it shall amend the information accordingly and so inform the parent in writing.

(b) If, as a result of the hearing, the agency decides that the information is not inaccurate, misleading, or otherwise in violation of the privacy or other rights of the child, it shall inform the parent of the right to place in the records it maintains on the child a statement commenting on the information or setting forth any reasons for disagreeing with the decision of the agency.

(c) Any explanation placed in the records of the child under this section must:

(1) Be maintained by the agency as part of the records of the child as long as the record or contested portion is maintained by the agency; and

(2) If the records of the child or the contested portion is disclosed by the agency to any party, the explanation must also be disclosed to the party.

(20 U.S.C. 1412 (2) (D); 1417 (c).)

§ 121a.570   Hearing procedures.

A hearing held under § 121a.568 of this subpart must be conducted according to the procedures under § 99.22 of this title.

(20 U.S.C. 1412 (2) (D); 1417 (c).)

§ 121a.571   Consent.

(a) Parental consent must be obtained before personally identifiable information is:

(1) Disclosed to anyone other than officials of participating agencies collecting or using the information under this part, subject to paragraph (b) of this section; or

(2) Used for any purpose other than meeting a requirement under this part.

(b) An educational agency or institution subject to Part 99 of this title may not release information from education records to participating agencies without parental consent unless authorized to do so under Part 99 of this title.

(c) The State educational agency shall include policies and procedures in its annual program plan which are used in the event that a parent refuses to provide consent under this section.

(20 U.S.C. 1412 (2) (D); 1417 (c).)

§ 121a.572   Safeguards.

(a) Each participating agency shall protect the confidentiality of personally identifiable information at collection, storage, disclosure, and destruction stages.

(b) One official at each participating agency shall assume responsibility for insuring the confidentiality of any personally identifiable information.

(c) All persons collecting or using personally identifiable information must receive training or instruction regarding the State's policies and procedures under § 121a.129 of Subpart B and Part 99 of this title.

(d) Each participating agency shall maintain, for public inspection, a current listing of the names and positions of those employees within the agency who may have access to personally identifiable information.

(20 U.S.C. 1412 (2) (D); 1417 (c).)

§ 121a.573 Destruction of information.

(a) The public agency shall inform parents when personally identifiable information collected, maintained, or used under this part is no longer needed to provide educational services to the child.

(b) The information must be destroyed at the request of the parents. However, a permanent record of a student's name, address, and phone number, his or her grades, attendance record, classes attended, grade level completed, and year completed may be maintained without time limitation. (20 U.S.C. 1412 (2) (D); 1417 (c).)

Comment. Under section 121a.573, the personally identifiable information on a handicapped child may be retained permanently unless the parents request that it be destroyed. Destruction of records is the best protection against improper and unauthorized disclosure. However, the records may be needed for other purposes. In informing parents about their rights under this section, the agency should remind them that the records may be needed by the child or the parents for social security benefits or other purposes. If the parents request that the information be destroyed, the agency may retain the information in paragraph (b).

§ 121a.574 Children's rights.

The State educational agency shall include policies and procedures in its annual program plan regarding the extent to which children are afforded rights of privacy similar to those afforded to parents, taking into consideration the age of the child and type or severity of disability. (20 U.S.C. 1412 (2) (D); 1417 (c).)

Comment. Note that under the regulations for the Family Educational Rights and Privacy Act (45 CFR 99.4 (a)), the rights of parents regarding education records are transferred to the student at age 18.

§ 121a.575 Enforcement.

The State educational agency shall describe in its annual program plan the policies and procedures, including sanctions, which the State uses to insure that its policies and procedures are followed and that the requirements of the Act and the regulations in this part are met. (20 U.S.C. 1412 (2) (D); 1417 (c).)

§ 121a.576 Office of Education.

If the Office of Education or its authorized representatives collect any personally identifiable information regarding handicapped children which is not subject to 5 U.S.C. 552a (The Privacy Act of 1974), the Commissioner shall apply the requirements of 5 U.S.C. section 552a (b) (1)-(2), (4)-(11); (c); (d); (e) (1), (2), (3) (A), (B), and (D), (5)-(10); (h); (m); and (n), and the regulations implementing those provisions in Part 5b of this title. (20 U.S.C. 1412 (2) (D); 1417 (c).)

OFFICE OF EDUCATION PROCEDURES

§ 121a.580 Opportunity for a hearing.

The Commissioner gives a State educational agency reasonable notice and an opportunity for a hearing before taking any of the following actions:

(a) Disapproval of a State's annual program plan under § 121a.113 of Subpart B.

(b) Withholding payments from a State under § 121a.590 or under section 434 (c) of the General Education Provisions Act .

(c) Waiving the requirement under § 121a.589 of this subpart regarding supplementing and supplanting with funds provided under Part B of the Act. (20 U.S.C. 1232c (c); 1413 (a) (9) (B); 1413 (c); 1416.)

§ 121a.581 Hearing panel.

The Commissioner appoints a Hearing Panel consisting of not less than three persons to conduct any hearing under § 121a.530 of this subpart. (20 U.S.C. 1232c (c); 1413 (a) (9) (B); 1413 (c); 1416.)

§ 121a.582 Hearing procedures.

(a) (1) If the Hearing Panel determines that oral testimony would not materially assist the resolution of disputed facts, the Panel shall give each party an opportunity for presenting the case:

(i) In whole or in part in writing, or

(ii) In an informal conference before the Hearing Panel.

(2) The Hearing Panel shall give each party:

(i) Notice of the issues to be considered (if this notice has not already been given); and

(ii) An opportunity to be represented by counsel.

(b) If the Hearing Panel determines that oral testimony would materially assist the resolution of disputed facts, the Panel shall give each party, in addition to the requirements under paragraph (a) (2) of this section:

(1) An opportunity to obtain a record of the proceedings;

(2) An opportunity to present witnesses on the party's behalf; and

(3) An opportunity to cross-examine witnesses either orally or with written questions. (20 U.S.C. 1232c (c); 1413 (a) (9) (B); 1413 (c); 1416.)

§ 121a.583 Initial decision; final decision.

(a) The Hearing Panel shall prepare an initial written decision which includes findings of fact and the conclusions based on those facts.

(b) The Hearing Panel shall mail a copy of the initial decision to each party (or to the party's counsel) and to the Commissioner, with a notice that each party has an opportunity to submit written comments regarding the decision to the Commissioner within a specified reasonable time.

(c) The initial decision of the Hearing Panel is the final decision of the Commissioner unless, within 25 days after the end of the time for receipt of written comments, the Commissioner informs the Panel in writing that the decision is being reviewed.

(d) Review by the Commissioner is based on the decision, the written record, if any, of the Hearing Panel's proceedings, and written comments or oral arguments by the parties.

(e) No decision under this section becomes final until it is served on the State educational agency or its attorney. (20 U.S.C. 1232c (c); 1413 (a) (9) (b); 1413 (c); 1416.)

§ 121a.589 Waiver of requirement regarding supplementing and supplanting with Part B funds.

(a) Under sections 613 (a) (9) (B) and 614 (a) (2) (B) (ii) of the Act, State and local Educational agencies must insure that Federal funds provided under Part B of the Act are used to supplement the level of State and local funds expended for the education of handicapped children, and in no case to supplant those State and local funds. Beginning with funds appropriated for fiscal year 1979 and for each following fiscal year, the nonsupplanting requirement only applies to funds allocated to local educational agencies. (See § 121a.372.)

(b) If the State provides clear and convincing evidence that all handicapped children have available to them a free appropriate public education, the Commissioner may waive in part the requirement under section 613 (a) (9) (B) and 614 (a) (2) (B) (ii) of the Act if the Commissioner concurs with the evidence provided by the State.

c) If a State wishes to request a waiver, it must inform the Commissioner in writing. The Commissioner then provides the State with a finance and membership report form which provides the basis for the request.

(d) In its request for a waiver, the State shall include the results of a special study made by the State to obtain evidence of the availability of a free appropriate public education to all handicapped children. The special study must include statements by a representative sample of organizations which deal with handicapped children, and parents and teachers of handicapped children, relating to the following areas:

(1) The adequacy and comprehensiveness of the State's system for locating, identifying, and evaluating handicapped children, and

(2) The cost to parents, if any, for education for children enrolled in public and private day schools, and in public and private residential schools and institutions, and

(3) The adequacy of the State's due process procedures.

(e) In its request for a waiver, the State shall include finance data relating to the availability of a free appropriate public education for all handicapped children, including:

(1) The total current expenditures for regular education programs and special education programs by function and by source of funds (State, local, and Federal) for the previous school year, and

(2) The full-time equivalent membership of students enrolled in regular programs and in special programs in the previous school year.

(f) The Commissioner considers the information which the State provides under paragraph (d) and (e) of this section, along with any additional information he may request, or obtain through on-site reviews of the State's education programs and records, to determine if all children have available to them a free appropriate public education, and if so, the extent of the waiver.

(g) The State may request a hearing under §§ 121a.580-121a.583 with re-gard to any final action by the Commissioner under this section.

(20 U.S.C. 1411 (c) (3); 1413 (a) (9) (B).)

§ 121a.590 Withholding payments.

(a) The Commissioner may make the following findings only after reasonable notice and an opportunity for a hearing under §§ 121a.580-121a.583 to the State educational agency involved (and to any local educational agency affected by any failure described in paragraph (a) (2) of this section):

(1) That there has been a failure to comply substantially with the provisions of section 612 and 613 of the Act, or

(2) That in the administration of the annual program plan there is a failure to comply with any provision of this part or with any requirement in the application of a local educational agency approved by the State educational agency under the annual program plan.

(b) After making either of the findings in paragraph (a) of this section, the Commissioner:

(1) Shall, after notifying the State educational agency, withhold any further payments to the State under this part, and

(2) May, after notifying the State educational agency, withhold further payments to the State under the Federal programs referred to in § 121a.139 of Subpart B which are within his jurisdiction, to the extent that funds under those programs are available for the provision of assistance for the education of handicapped children.

(c) If the Commissioner withholds payments under paragraph (b) of this section he may determine:

(1) That withholding is limited to programs or projects under the annual program plan, or portions of it, affected by the failure, or

(2) That the State educational agency must not make further payments under Part B of the Act to

specified local educational agencies affected by the failure.
(20 U.S.C. 1416 (a).)

§ 121a.591 Reinstating payments.

Until the Commissioner is satisfied that there is no longer any failure to comply with the provisions of this part, as specified in § 121a.590 (a):

(a) No further payments shall be made to the State under this part or under the Federal programs specified in section 613 (a) (2) of the Act which are within his jurisdiction to the extent that funds under those programs are available for the provision of assistance for the education of handicapped children, or

(b) Payments by the State educational agency under this part shall be limited to local educational agencies whose actions did not cause or were not involved in the failure.
(20 U.S.C. 1416 (a).)

§ 121a.592 Public notice by State and Commission's final action on annual program plan.

Any State educational agency and local educational agency which receives a notice under § 121a.590 (a) shall by means of a public notice, take any necessary measures to inform the public within the agency's jurisdiction of the pendency of the action.
(20 U.S.C. 1416 (a).)

§ 121a.593 Judicial review of local educational agencies.

If any State is dissatisfied with the Commissioner's final action with respect to its annual program plan submitted under Subpart B, the State may under section 616 (b) of the Act, within sixty days after notice of the action, file a petition for review of that action with the United States Court of Appeals for the circuit in which the State is located.
(20 U.S.C. 1416 (b).)

Subpart F—State Administration

STATE EDUCATIONAL AGENCY
RESPONSIBILITIES: GENERAL

§ 121a.600 Responsibility for all educational programs.

(a) The State educational agency is responsible for insuring;

(1) That the requirements of this part are carried out; and

(2) That each educational program for handicapped children administered within the State, including each program administered by any other public agency:

(i) Is under the general supervision of the persons responsible for educational programs for handicapped children in the State educational agency, and

(ii) Meets education standards of the State educational agency (including the requirements of this part).

(b) The State must comply with paragraph (a) of this section through State statute, State regulation, signed agreement between respective agency officials, or other documents.
(20 U.S.C. 1412 (6).)

Comment. The requirement in § 121a.600 (a) is taken essentially verbatim from section 612 (6) of the statute and reflects the desire of the Congress for a central point of responsibility and accountability in the education of handicapped children within each State. With respect to State educational agency responsibility, the Senate Report on P.L. 94-142 includes the following statements:

This provision is included specifically to assure a single line of responsibility with regard to the education of handicapped children, and to assure that in the implementation of all provisions of this Act and in carrying out the right to education for handicapped children, the State educational agency shall be the responsible agency * * *.

Without this requirement, there is an abdication of responsibility for the education of handicapped children. Presently, in many States, responsibility is divided, depending upon the age of the handicapped child, sources of funding, and type of services delivered. While the Committee understands that different agencies may, in fact, deliver services, the responsibility must remain in a central agency overseeing the education of handicapped children, so that failure to deliver services or the violation of the rights of handicapped children is squarely the responsibility of one agency. (Senate Report No. 94-168, p. 24 (1975))

In meeting the requirements of this section, there are a number of acceptable options which may be adopted, including the following:

(1) Written agreements are developed between respective State agencies concerning State educational agency standards and monitoring. These agreements are binding on the local or regional counterparts of each State agency.

(2) The Governor's Office issues an administrative directive establishing the State educational agency responsibility.

(3) State law, regulation, or policy designates the State educational agency as responsible for establishing standards for all educational programs for the handicapped, and includes responsibility for monitoring.

(4) State law mandates that the State educational agency is responsible for all educational programs.

§ 121a.601 **Monitoring and evaluation activities.**

Each State educational agency shall:

(a) Undertake monitoring and evaluation activities to insure compliance of all public agencies within the State with the requirements of Subparts C, D, and E.

(b) Develop procedures (including specific timelines) for monitoring and evaluating public agencies involved in that education of handicapped children.

These procedures must include:

(1) Collection of data and reports;
(2) Conduct of on-site visits;
(3) Audit of Federal fund utilization; and
(4) Comparison of a sampling of individualized education programs with the programs actually provided.
(20 U.S.C. 1412 (6); 1413 (a) (11).)

Comment: In carrying out the requirements of paragraph (b) of this section, State educational agencies could include additional procedures, such as involving parents or representatives of parent organizations in on-site visits and other monitoring activities.

§ 121a.602 **Adoption of complaint procedures.**

(a) Each State educational agency shall adopt effective procedures for reviewing, investigating, and acting on any allegations of substance, which may be made by public agencies, or private individuals, or organizations, of actions taken by any public agency that are contrary to the requirements of this part.

(b) In carrying out the requirements in paragraph (a) of this section, the State educational agency shall:

(1) Designate specific individuals within the agency who are responsible for implementing the requirements;
(2) Provide for negotiations, technical assistance activities, and other remedial action to achieve compliance; and
(3) Provide for the use of sanctions, including the withholding of Part B funds in accordance with § 121a.194. (20 U.S.C. 1412 (6).)

USE OF FUNDS

§ 121a.620 **Federal funds for State administration.**

A State may use five per cent of the total State allotment in any fiscal year under Part B of the Act, or $200,000, whichever is greater, for administrative costs related to carrying out sections

612 and 613 of the Act. However, this amount cannot be greater than the amount which the State may use under § 121a.704 or § 121a.705, as the case may be.
(20 U.S.C. 1411 (b), (c).)

§ 121a.621   Allowable costs.

(a) The State educational agency may use funds under § 121a.620 of this Subpart for:

(1) Administration of the annual program plan and for planning at the State level, including planning, or assisting in the planning, of programs or projects for the education of handicapped children;

(2) Approval, supervision, monitoring, and evaluation of the effectiveness of local programs and projects for the education of handicapped children;

(3) Technical assistance to local educational agencies with respect to the requirements of this part;

(4) Leadership services for the program supervision and management of special education activities for handicapped children; and

(5) Other State leadership activities and consultative services.

(b) The State educational agency shall use the remainder of its funds under § 121a.620 in accordance with § 121a.370 of Subpart C.
(20 U.S.C. 1411 (b), (c).)

STATE ADVISORY PANEL

§ 121a.650   Establishment.

(a) Each State shall establish, in accordance with the provisions of this subpart, a State advisory panel on the education of handicapped children.

(b) The advisory panel must be appointed by the Governor or any other official authorized under State law to make those appointments.

(c) If a State has an existing advisory panel that can perform the functions in § 121a.652, the State may modify the existing panel so that it fulfills all of the requirements of this subpart, instead of establishing a new advisory panel.
(20 U.S.C. 1413 (a) (12).)

§ 121a.651   Membership.

(a) The membership of the State advisory panel must be composed of persons involved in or concerned with the education of handicapped children. The membership must include at least one person representative of each of the following groups:

(1) Handicapped individuals.

(2) Teachers of handicapped children.

(3) Parents of handicapped children.

(4) State and local educational officials.

(5) Special education program administrators.

(b) The State may expand the advisory panel to include additional persons in the groups listed in paragraph (a) of this section and representatives of other groups not listed.
(20 U.S.C. 1413 (a) (12).)

Comment. The membership of the State advisory panel, as listed in paragraphs (a) (1)-(5), is required in section 613 (a) (12) of the Act. As indicated in paragraph (b), the composition of the panel and the number of members may be expanded at the discretion of the State. In adding to the membership, consideration could be given to having:

(1) An appropriate balance between professional groups and consumers (i.e., parents, advocates, and handicapped individuals);

(2) Broad representation within the consumer-advocate groups, to insure that the interests and points of view of various parents, advocates and handicapped individuals are appropriately represented;

(3) Broad representation within professional groups (e.g., (a) regular education personnel, (b) special educators, including teachers, teacher trainers, and administrators, who can properly rep-

resent various dimensions in the education of handicapped children, and (c) appropriate related services personnel); and

(4) Representatives from other State advisory panels (such as vocational education).

If a State elects to maintain a small advisory panel (e.g., 10-15 members), the panel itself could take steps to insure that it (1) consults with and receives inputs from various consumer and special interest professional groups, and (2) establishes committees for particular short-term purposes composed of representatives from those input groups.

§ 121a.652 Advisory panel functions.

The State advisory panel shall:

(a) Advise the State educational agency of unmet needs within the State in the education of handicapped children;

(b) Comment publicly on the State annual program plan and rules or regulations proposed for issuance by the State regarding the education of handicapped children and the procedures for distribution of funds under this part; and

(c) Assist the State in developing and reporting such information and evaluations as may assist the Commissioner in the performance of his responsibilities under section 618.

(20 U.S.C. 1413 (a) (12).)

§ 121a.653 Advisory panel procedures.

(a) The advisory panel shall meet as often as necessary to conduct its business.

(b) By July 1 of each year, the advisory panel shall submit an annual report of panel activities and suggestions to the State educational agency. This report must be made available to the public in a manner consistent with other public reporting requirements under this part.

(c) Official minutes must be kept on all panel meetings and shall be made available to the public on request.

(d) All advisory panel meetings and agenda items must be publicly announced prior to the meeting, and meetings must be open to the public.

(e) Interpreters and other necessary services must be provided at panel meetings for panel members or participants. The State may pay for these services from funds under § 121a.620.

(f) The advisory panel shall serve without compensation but the State must reimburse the panel for reasonable and necessary expenses for attending meetings and performing duties. The State may use funds under § 121a.620 for this purpose.

(20 U.S.C. 1413 (a) (12).)

Subpart G—Allocation of Funds; Reports

ALLOCATIONS

§ 121a.700 Special definition of the term State.

For the purposes of § 121a.701, § 121a.702, and §§ 121a.704-121a.708, the term "State" does not include Guam, American Samoa, the Virgin Islands, and the Trust Territory of the Pacific Islands.

(20 U.S.C. 1411 (a) (2).)

§ 121a.701 State entitlement; formula.

(a) The maximum amount of the grant to which a State is entitled under section 611 of the Act in any fiscal year is equal to the number of handicapped children aged three through 21 in the State who are receiving special education and related services, multiplied by the applicable percentage, under paragraph (b) of this section, of the average per pupil expenditure in public elementary and secondary schools in the United States.

(b) For the purposes of the formula in paragraph (a) of this section, the applicable percentage of the average per pupil expenditure in public elementary and secondary schools in the United States for each fiscal year is:

(1) 1978—5 percent,
(2) 1979—10 percent,
(3) 1980—20 percent,
(4) 1981—30 percent, and
(5) 1982, and for each fiscal year after 1982, 40 percent.
(20 U.S.C. 1411 (a) (1).)

(c) For the purposes of this section, the average per pupil expenditure in public elementary and secondary schools in the United States, means the aggregate expenditures during the second fiscal year preceding the fiscal year for which the computation is made (or if satisfactory data for that year are not available at the time of computation, then during the most recent preceding fiscal year for which satisfactory data are available) of all local educational agencies in the United States (which, for the purpose of this section, means the fifty States and the District of Columbia), plus any direct expenditures by the State for operation of those agencies (without regard to the source of funds from which either of those expenditures are made), divided by the aggregate number of children in average daily attendance to whom those agencies provided free public education during that preceding year.
(20 U.S.C. 1411 (a) (4).)

§ 121a.702 Limitations and exclusions.

(a) In determining the amount of a grant under § 121a.701 of this subpart, the Commissioner may not count:

(1) Handicapped children in a State to the extent that the number of those children is greater than 12 percent of the number of all children aged five through 17 in the State;

(2) Children with specific learning disabilities to the extent that the number of those children is greater than two percent of the number of all children aged five through 17 in the State; and

(3) Handicapped children who are counted under section 121 of the Elementary and Secondary Education Act of 1965.

(b) For the purposes of paragraph (a) of this section, the number of children aged five through 17 in any State shall be determined by the Commissioner on the basis of the most recent satisfactory data available to him.
(20 U.S.C. 1411 (a) (5).)

§ 121a.703 Ratable reductions.

(a) *General.* If the sums appropriated for any fiscal year for making payments to States under section 611 of the Act are not sufficient to pay in full the total amounts to which all States are entitled to receive for that fiscal year, the maximum amount which all States are entitled to receive for that fiscal year shall be ratably reduced. In case additional funds become available for making payments for any fiscal year during which the preceding sentence is applicable, those reduced amounts shall be increased on the same basis they were reduced.
(20 U.S.C. 1411 (g) (1).)

(b) *Reporting dates for local educational agencies and reallocations.*

(1) In any fiscal year in which the State entitlements have been ratably reduced, and in which additional funds have not been made available to pay in full the total of the amounts under paragraph (a) of this section, the State educational agency shall fix dates before which each local educational agency shall report to the State the amount of funds available to it under this part which it estimates it will expend.

(2) The amounts available under paragraph (a) (1) of this section, or any amount which would be available to any other local educational agency if it were to submit an application meeting the requirements of this part, which the State educational agency determines will not be used for the period of its availability, shall be available for allocation to those local educational agencies, in the manner provided

in § 121a.707, which the State educational agency determines will need and be able to use additional funds to carry out approved programs.
(20 U.S.C. 1411 (g) (2).)

§ 121a.704 Hold harmless provision.

No State shall receive less than the amount it received under Part B of the Act for fiscal year 1977.
(20 U.S.C. 1411 (a) (1).)

§ 121a.705 Within-State distribution: fiscal year 1978.

Of the funds received under § 121a.701 of this subpart by any State for fiscal year 1978:

(a) 50 percent may be used by the State in accordance with the provisions of § 121a.620 of Subpart F and § 121a.370 of Subpart C, and

(b) 50 percent shall be distributed to local educational agencies in the State in accordance with § 121a.707.
(20 U.S.C. 1411 (b) (1).)

§ 121a.706 Within-State distribution: fiscal year 1979 and after.

Of the funds received under § 121a.701 by any State for fiscal year 1979, and for each fiscal year after fiscal year 1979:

(a) 25 percent may be used by the State in accordance with § 121a.620 of Subpart F and § 121a.370 of Subpart C, and

(b) 75 percent shall be distributed to the local educational agencies in the State in accordance with § 121a.707.
(20 U.S.C. 1411 (c) (1).)

§ 121a.707 Local educational agency entitlements; formula.

From the total amount of funds available to all local educational agencies, each local educational agency is entitled to an amount which bears the same ratio to the total amount as the number of handicapped children aged three through 21 in that agency who are receiving special education and related services bears to the aggregate number of handicapped children aged three through 21 receiving special education and related services in all local educational agencies which apply to the State educational agency for funds under Part B of the Act.
(20 U.S.C. 1411 (d).)

§ 121a.708 Reallocation of local educational agency funds.

If a State educational agency determines that a local educational agency is adequately providing a free appropriate public education to all handicapped children residing in the area served by the local agency with State and local funds otherwise available to the local agency, the State educational agency may reallocate funds (or portions of those funds which are not required to provide special education and related services) made available to the local agency under § 121a.707, to other local educational agencies within the State which are not adequately providing special education and related services to all handicapped children residing in the areas served by the other local educational agencies.
(20 U.S.C. 1414 (e).)

§ 121a.709 Payments to Secretary of Interior.

(a) The Commissioner is authorized to make payments to the Secretary of the Interior according to the need for that assistance for the education of handicapped children on reservations serviced by elementary and secondary schools operated for Indian children by the Department of the Interior.

(b) The amount of those payments for any fiscal year shall not exceed one percent of the aggregate amounts available to all States for that fiscal year under Part B of the Act.
(20 U.S.C. 1411 (f) (1).)

§ 121a.710 Entitlements to jurisdictions.

(a) The Jurisdictions to which this section applies are Guam, American

Samoa, the Virgin Islands, and the Trust Territory of the Pacific Islands.

(b) Each jurisdiction under paragraph (a) of this section is entitled to a grant for the purposes set forth in section 601 (c) of the Act. The amount to which those jurisdictions are so entitled for any fiscal year shall not exceed an amount equal to 1 percent of the aggregate of the amounts available to all States under this part for that fiscal year. Funds appropriated for those jurisdictions shall be allocated proportionately among them on the basis of the number of children aged three through twenty-one in each jurisdiction. However, no jurisdiction shall receive less than $150,000, and other allocations shall be ratably reduced if necessary to insure that each jurisdiction receives at least that amount.

(c) The amount expended for administration by each jurisdiction under this section shall not exceed 5 percent of the amount allotted to the jurisdiction for any fiscal year, or $35,000, whichever is greater.

(20 U.S.C. 1411 (e).)

REPORTS

§ 121a.750 Annual report of children served—report requirement.

(a) The State educational agency shall report to the Commissioner no later than April 1 of each year the number of handicapped children aged three through 21 residing in the State who are receiving special education and related services.

(b) The State educational agency shall submit the report on forms provided by the Commissioner.

(20 U.S.C. 1411 (a) (3).)

Comment. It is very important to understand that this report and the requirements that relate to it are solely for allocation purposes. The population of children the State may count for allocation purposes may differ from the population of children to whom the State must make available a free appro-

priate public education. For example, while section 611 (a) (5) of the Act limits the number of children who may be counted for allocation purposes to 12 percent of the general school population aged five through seventeen, a State might find that 14 percent (or some other percentage) of its children are handicapped. In that case, the State must make free appropriate public education available to all of those handicapped children.

§ 121a.751 Annual report of children served—information required in the report.

(a) In its report, the State educational agency shall include a table which shows:

(1) The number of handicapped children receiving special education and related services on October 1 and on February 1 of that school year, and the average of the numbers for those two dates;

(2) The number of those handicapped children within each disability category, as defined in the definition of "handicapped children" in § 121a.5 of Subpart A; and

(3) The number of those handicapped children within each of the following age groups:

(i) Three through five;
(ii) Six through seventeen; and
(iii) Eighteen through twenty-one.

(b) A child must be counted as being in the age group corresponding to his or her age on the date of the count: October 1 or February 1, as the case may be.

(c) The State educational agency may not report a child under more than one disability category.

(d) If a handicapped child has more than one disability, the State educational agency shall report that child in accordance with the following procedure:

(1) A child who is both deaf and blind must be reported as "deaf-blind."

(2) A child who has more than one disability (other than a deaf-blind child) must be reported as "multi-handicapped."
(20 U.S.C. 1411 (a) (3); 1411 (a) (5) (A) (ii); 1418 (b).)

§ 121a.752 Annual report of children served—certification.

The State educational agency shall include in its report a certification signed by an authorized official of the agency that the information provided is an accurate and unduplicated count of handicapped children receiving special education and related services on the dates in question.
(20 U.S.C. 1411 (a) (3); 1417 (b).)

§ 121a.753 Annual report of children served—criteria for counting children.

(a) The State educational agency may include handicapped children in its report who are enrolled in a school or program which is operated or supported by a public agency, and which either:

(1) Provides them with both special education and related services; or

(2) Provides them only with special education if they do not need related services to assist them in benefitting from that special education.

(b) The State educational agency may not include handicapped children in its report who:

(1) Are not enrolled in a school or program operated or supported by a public agency;

(2) Are not provided special education that meets State standards;

(3) Are not provided with a related service that they need to assist them in benefitting from special education;

(4) Are counted by a State agency under section 121 of the Elementary and Secondary Education Act of 1965, as amended; or

(5) Are receiving special education funded solely by the Federal Govern-

ment. However, the State may count children covered under § 121a.186 (b) of Subpart B.
(20 U.S.C. 1411 (a) (3); 1417 (b).)

Comment. 1. Under paragraph (a), the State may count handicapped children in a Head Start or other preschool program operated or supported by a public agency if those children are provided special education that meets State standards.

2. "Special education," by statutory definition, must be at no cost to parents. As of September 1, 1978, under the free appropriate public education requirement, both special education and related services must be at no cost to parents.

There may be some situations, however, where a child receives special education from a public source at no cost, but whose parents pay for the basic or regular education. This child may be counted. The Office of Education expects that there would only be limited situations where special education would be clearly separate from regular education — generally, where speech therapy is the only special education required by the child. For example, the child might be in a regular program in a parochial or other private school but receiving speech therapy in a program funded by the local educational agency. Allowing these children to be counted will provide incentives (in addition to complying with the legal requirement in section 613 (a) (4) (A) of the Act regarding private schools) to public agencies to provide services to children in private schools, since funds are generated in part on the basis of the number of children provided special education and related services. Agencies should understand, however, that where a handicapped child is placed in or referred to a public or private school for educational purposes, special education includes the entire educational program provided to the child. In that case, parents may not be charged for any part of the child's education.

A State may not count Indian children on or near reservations and children on military facilities if it provides them no special education. If a State or local educational agency is responsible for serving these children, and does provide them special education and related services, they may be counted.

§ 121a.754   Annual report of children served—other responsibilities of the State educational agency.

In addition to meeting the other requirements in this subpart, the State educational agency shall:

(a) Establish procedures to be used by local educational agencies and other educational institutions in counting the number of handicapped children receiving special education and related services;

(b) Set dates by which those agencies and institutions must report to the State educational agency to insure that the State complies with § 121a.750 (a);

(c) Obtain certification from each agency and institution that an unduplicated and accurate count has been made;

(d) Aggregate the data from the count obtained from each agency and institution, and prepare the reports required under this subpart; and

(e) Insure that documentation is maintained which enables the State and the Commissioner to audit the accuracy of the count.

(20 U.S.C. 1411 (a) (3); 1417 (b).)

Comment. States should note that the data required in the annual report of children served are not to be transmitted to the Commissioner in personally identifiable form. States are encouraged to collected these data in non-personally identifiable form.

APPENDIX A—ANALYSIS OF FINAL REGULATION (45 CFR PART 121a) UNDER PART B OF THE EDUCATION OF THE HANDICAPPED ACT

These regulations set forth requirements to be followed by States and localities if they are to receive funds under Part B of the Education of the Handicapped Act. The regulations cover matters such as the identification, location, and evaluation of handicapped children; the provision of free appropriate public education; the establishment of a full educational opportunity goal; the count of handicapped children for allocation purposes; priorities in the use of Part B funds; the proper use of Part B funds; the development of an individualized education program; the creation of a comprehensive personnel development system; procedural safeguards (e.g. right to notice and conduct of hearings); methods to guarantee public participation; and details about State annual program plans and local educational agency applications.

RELATIONSHIP BETWEEN REGULATIONS UNDER PART B AND REGULATIONS UNDER SECTION 504

The regulations under section 504 of the Rehabilitation Act of 1973 (45 CFR Part 84; published at 42 FR 22675; May 4, 1977) deal with non-discrimination on the basis of handicap and basically require that recipients of Federal funds provide equal opportunities to handicapped persons (for example, that they meet the needs of handicapped persons to the same extent that the needs of nonhandicapped persons are met). Subpart D of the section 504 regulations ("Preschool, Elementary, and Secondary Education") contains requirements very similar to those in Part B of the Education of the Handicapped Act.

Basically, both require that handicapped persons be provided a free appropriate public education; that handicapped students be educated with non-handicapped students to the extent appropriate; that educational agencies identify and locate all unserved handicapped children; that evaluation procedures be adopted to insure appropriate classification and educational services; and that procedural safeguards be established.

In several respects, however, the section 504 regulations are broader in coverage than Part B. For example, the definition of "handicapped person" and "qualified handicapped person" under section 504 covers a broader population than the definition of "handicapped children" under Part B. Under the Part B definition, a handicapped child is a child who has one of the impairments listed in the Act, who because of that impairment requires special education and related services. Under section 504, a handicapped person is a person who has a physical or mental impairment that substantially limits one or more major life activities, has a record of that type of impairment, or is regarded as having that impairment (§ 84.3 (j)).

The regulations for section 504 also deal with a number of subjects not covered by the Part B regulations (for example, barrier-free facilities and program accessibility; employment; postsecondary education and health, welfare and social services). On the other side, Part B contains a substantial number of administrative requirements not included under section 504 (for example, annual program plans and local applications) and requires more detailed procedures and policies in many instances (such as due process procedures).

In several instances, the section 504 regulations specifically reference where a requirement may be met by complying with a requirement under Part B. For example, § 84.33 (b) (2), dealing with appropriate education, cites im-

plementation of an individualized education program as one means of meeting the requirement. Section 84.33 (d) has a September 1, 1978 outside date for providing an appropriate education to qualified handicapped persons (conforming to the timelines in Part B). Section 84.35 (d) indicates that a re-evaluation procedure consistent with the Part B requirements is one means of meeting the reevaluation requirements under section 504. Section 84.36, dealing with due process requirements, indicates that compliance with the procedural safeguards in Part B is one means of meeting those requirements.

It should be noted that the term "free appropriate public education" (FAPE) has different meanings under Part B and section 504. For example, under Part B, "FAPE" is a statutory term which requires special education and related services to be provided in accordance with an individualized education program. However, under section 504, each recipient must provide an education which includes "the provision of regular or special education and related aids and services that (i) are designed to meet individual educational needs of handicapped persons as adequately as the needs of nonhandicapped persons are met * * *"

There is also a major difference between Part B and the section 504 regulations concerning the matter of exclusion of handicapped children from school. As of the effective date of the section 504 regulations (June 3, 1977), exclusion of handicapped children from school constitutes a violation of those requirements. However, under Part B, States are not required to serve all handicapped children aged 3-18 until September 1, 1978. As stated in Appendix A of the section 504 regulations:

The EHA requires a free appropriate education to be provided to handicapped children "no later than September 1, 1978," but section 504 contains no authority for delaying enforcement. To resolve this problem, a new paragraph (d) has been added to § 84.33. Section 84.33 (d) requires recipients to achieve full compliance with the free appropriate public education requirements of § 84.33 as expeditiously as possible, but in no event later than September 1, 1978. The provision also makes clear that, as of the effective date of this regulation, no recipient may exclude a qualified handicapped child from its educational program. This provision against exclusion is consistent with the order of providing services set forth in section 612 (3) of the EHA, which places the highest priority on providing services to handicapped children who are not receiving an education.

PART 121a—ASSISTANCE TO STATES FOR EDUCATION OF HANDICAPPED CHILDREN

SUBPART A—GENERAL

Subpart A sets forth the purposes and applicability of these regulations and includes definitions of statutory terms (e.g. free appropriate public education, special education, and related services) and other definitions related to those terms.

The following comments were received regarding Subpart A.

APPLICABILITY OF REGULATIONS TO STATE, LOCAL AND PRIVATE AGENCIES (§ 1218.2)

Comment: A commenter felt that the statement regarding the applicability of the regulations was not clear, and should be revised to indicate that the requirements apply to any public agency serving handicapped children, even if the agency does not receive Part B funds.

Response: A definition of "public agency" has been added to the regulations. The definition includes all political subdivisions in the State that are responsible for educating handicapped children. Throughout the regu-

lation, the term "public agency" has been used to make it clear where the requirements do not apply only to State and local educational agencies. In addition, an explanatory comment was added after section 121a.2 to make it clear that the requirements under Part B are binding on each public agency in the State that has direct or delegated authority for the education of handicapped children, regardless of whether that agency receives Part B funds.

DEFINITIONS (§§ 121a.4-121a.15)

Comment: Hundreds of comments were received regarding definitions in the proposed rules. Commenters requested that new definitions be added, or sought changes in existing definitions, especially definitions of various disability categories and the various types of related services. In many instances, revisions were sought to conform to the most recent definitions adopted or used by professional associations.

Response: Definitions of terms used in the regulations are taken from various statutes, Congressional reports, or materials provided by professional associations and other groups. Where appropriate, the Office of Education has attempted to incorporate changes recommended by commenters, and has made other changes to clarify the definitions. In addition, the following new terms were added:

Definitions of "deaf-blind" and "multi-handicapped" were added because these are recognized categories of handicapped children in most States.

A definition of "qualified" was added in order to be able to use a consistent term in referring to the qualifications of the various personnel.

The definition of "handicapped children" has been modified only by making certain clarifying changes. Although some commenters requested additional changes in the definitions of the various disability categories, it is felt that the definitions in this regulation must closely conform to current usage in the States and professions.

The related services definition was expanded to include "school health services." In addition, changes were made in the definitions of the individual terms included under "related services" (e.g., psychological services and recreation) to conform to recommendations of professional associations.

SUBPART B—STATE ANNUAL PROGRAM
PLANS AND LOCAL APPLICATIONS

Subpart B includes the requirements relating to State annual program plans, local educational agency applications, participation by the Bureau of Indian Affairs, and public participation.

Two new sections (sections 121a.150 and 121a.239) have been added to require assurances from the State educational agencies and local educational agencies that the program under Part B will be operated in compliance with the section 504 regulations, including the requirements under section 606 of the Education of the Handicapped Act regarding employment of qualified handicapped individuals in programs assisted under the Act. (The Office for Civil Rights has been delegated authority for enforcing section 606.)

A substantial number of commenters were concerned with the following major issues in this subpart: (1) the amount of data required of State and local educational agencies; (2) the excess costs, nonsupplanting and comparability requirements; and (3) the public participation requirements. In addition, as with other subparts, many commenters objected to statutory requirements and sought interpretations of the statute and regulations.

ANNUAL PROGRAM PLANS
CONDITION OF ASSISTANCE (§ 121a.110)

Section 434 (b) of the General Education Provisions Act (GEPA), as amended by Pub. L. 93-380, requires each State to submit (1) a general application containing five assurances, and (2) an annual program plan for each Office of Education program under which funds are provided to local educational agencies through, or under the supervision of, the State educational agency. Under Section 434 (b), and the implementing regulations (45 CFR 100b, Subpart B), the general application and an annual program plan take the place of a State plan for Part B (45 CFR 100b.19).

The five assurances required under section 434 (b) of the GEPA cover proper administration, fiscal control and accounting, reports, supplanting, and submission of the annual program plan. Where Part B contains plan requirements covering the same subject matters, submission of those plan requirements is satisfied by the State's submission of the general application. They do not have to be submitted as part of the annual plan. The Part B plan provisions which do not have to be submitted in the annual program plan are referenced in 45 CFR § 100b.17 (c) (2) (iv). Note that a substantive section on the nonsupplanting requirement for local educational agencies is set out in § 121a.230.

Under 45 CFR 100b.18 (c), material may be incorporated by reference in an annual program plan if the material is in a document previously approved by the Commissioner and on file in the Office of Education. This should save paperwork, particularly in the years after the first annual program plan (for school year 1977-1978) is submitted under these regulations.

The provisions to be included in the annual program plan for Part B are set forth in §§ 121a.120-121a.151 of these regulations (which include the conditions of eligibility and the State plan requirements under sections 612 and 613 of the Act and section 434 (b) (1) (B) (ii) of the GEPA (which requires each annual program plan to "set forth a statement describing the purposes for which Federal funds will be expended during the fiscal year for which the annual program plan is submitted"). APPROVAL; DISAPPROVAL (§ 121a.113)

The following is clarification about the submission of draft annual program plans for review by the Office of Education and how this would affect the issuance of grant award documents:

A State educational agency may elect to send a copy of its proposed annual program plan to the Commissioner for technical assistance purposes at the same time that the plan is being made available for public comment. However, funds cannot be obligated by a State before the date on which its official adopted plan is received in substantially approvable form by the Federal Government. (See 45 CFR 100b.35.)

EXAMPLE: A State educational agency's proposed plan for a particular school year is received by the Bureau of Education for the Handicapped on June 1. Its official plan is received on August 1. When BEH approves the plan (e.g. September 1), the State educational agency will receive a grant award document which will show August 1, as the earliest date of obligation under that plan.

EFFECTIVE PERIOD OF ANNUAL PROGRAM PLAN
(§ 121a.114)

The Office of Education is proposing to use the period July 1-June 30 for State annual program plans in those programs where appropriations become available for obligation by the Federal Government each July 1 (the so-called "advance funded" programs). The purpose of this is to meet the statutory requirement for an annual program plan covering a 12-month period and at the same time to conform as closely as possible to the regular school year. However, even if the proposed procedure is adopted, the obligational period of State and local agencies for

funds from any fiscal year would not be changed. If a State submits its annual program plan and receives its grant on the earliest possible date (July 1), the funds are available for obligation at the State and local level for 27 months, subject to submission or extension of the annual program plan for the following year. (This period includes the 12-month carryover provision under the Tydings Amendment. See 45 CFR 100b.55 (Obligation by recipients).) For example, if a State received its grant for fiscal year 1978 on July 1, 1977, the funds would be available for obligation at the State and local level from July 1, 1977 through September 30, 1979. The rules which govern when an annual program plan becomes effective, and State and local authority to obligate the Federal funds are located in 45 CFR Part 100b, Subpart B.

PUBLIC PARTICIPATION (§ 121a.120)

Comment: Commenters wanted this section to be expanded to require the States to describe in detail a number of additional specific steps to be taken in complying with the public participation requirements of the Act. For example, they wanted States to develop a roster of interested persons to whom plans and other documents would routinely be sent. The commenters felt that these steps would be necessary to insure full public participation.

Response: Requirements have been added (in §§ 121a.280 et seq.) to spell out in more detail the State's duties regarding public participation in development of the annual program plan (for example, indicating in the notice of public hearings of the plan the timetable for developing the final plan and submittting it to the Commissioner). A requirement has also been added to specify that the plan must be available for comment at least 30 days following the date notice is given.

Another revised section indicates that

the public participation requirements for local educational agencies are to be comparable to those required of the State, except that public hearings are not required (§ 121a.234).

FULL EDUCATIONAL OPPORTUNITY
GOAL REQUIREMENTS
(§§ 121a.124-121a.126)

Comment: Commenters disagreed about the amount of data which should be required under this (and other) sections. Some commenters sought to have the regulations require a substantial amount of additional data (about the population of handicapped children and their placements) on the grounds that it is needed for effective monitoring. Others sought to have the amount of data to be reported substantially reduced as unnecessary and fulfilling no useful purpose.

Response: The final regulations eliminate the data requirements in proposed section 121a.24 (a) for school year 1977-1978. Since the funds for FY 1978 became available for obligation by the Federal government on July 1, 1977, the States began submitting annual program plans for school year 1977-1978 before these regulations were published. Therefore, it would be inappropriate to impose a retroactive data requirement. No substantive change has been made in the data requirement for school years 1978-1979 and thereafter. The Office of Education believes that the remaining amount of data sought is necessary and adequate to provide information on what and how children are being served. Additional information may be sought on a case by case basis from each State where necessary to monitor compliance with Part B. In addition, requirements have been added to Subpart F to increase each State's monitoring and enforcement obligations.

Comment: Commenters requested that the data requirements regarding

personnel needed to meet the full educational opportunity goal include various other professional groups, such as physical therapists, or use terms currently accepted by the professions, such as "therapeutic recreation specialists" rather than "recreation therapists."

Response: These changes have been made to cover the various personnel who provide special education or related services and to use terms currently recognized by the appropriate professional associations.

LOCAL EDUCATIONAL AGENCY
APPLICATIONS

PARENT INVOLVEMENT (§ 121a.226)

Comment: Commenters wanted the regulations to require the establishment of a parent advisory committee in each school district.

Response: No change has been made. Extensive public and parental participation is already required under sections 121a.226 and 121a.234.

EXCESS COST REQUIREMENTS
(§§ 121a.182-121a.186)

Comment: A substantial number of commenters requested clarification and explanation of the excess cost requirement.

Response: The section on excess costs has been broken out into five sections for easier reading. Section 121a.184 specifies that a local educational agency must spend a certain minimum amount for the education of handicapped children before Part B funds may be used. A detailed example of determining the minimum amount follows revised section 121a.184.

NONSUPPLANTING AND COMPARABLE
SERVICES (§§ 121a.230-121a.231)

Comment: A substantial number of commenters requested clarification of these requirements. Some commenters proposed detailed procedures and urged that the regulations require the reporting of a substantial amount of data to monitor compliance with these requirements. Some commenters felt the comparability requirement should be met by comparing expenses for regular and special education.

Response: These sections have been substantially revised to attempt to explain these requirements. Detailed procedures and reporting requirements are not adopted at this time because local educational agencies are otherwise required to maintain auditable records to document their compliance with these and other requirements.

Regarding nonsupplanting, the regulation provides that the requirement applies to total aggregate funds and particular costs. A local educational agency meets the requirement if (1) the total amount or average per capita amount of State and local school funds budgeted by the local educational agency for expenditures in the current fiscal year for the education of handicapped children is at least equal to the total amount or average per capita amount of State and local school funds actually expended for their education in the most recent preceding fiscal year for which information is available. Allowances may be made for decreases in enrollment of handicapped children and unusually large amounts of funds expended for long-term purposes (construction); and (2) Part B funds are not used to displace State or local funds for any particular cost.

The statutory requirement for comparability is implemented by prohibiting a local educational agency from using funds under Part B to provide services to handicapped children, unless the agency uses State and local funds to provide services to those children which, taken as a whole, are at least comparable to services provided to other handicapped children in that local educational agency. This should insure that handicapped children who receive services with Part B funds are treated equally with handicapped children who do not receive services with Part B funds. It would be too difficult to make an objective comparison between special and regular education. The concern of the commenters who asked for this comparison should be met by the excess cost requirement, which provides that a local educational agency must spend a minimum amount, on the average, for each of its handicapped children.

Comment: Commenters requested that the regulations make it clear that the local applications must meet the requirements imposed on the State in Subpart B.

Response: A section has been added to make it clear that each local application must include additional procedures and other information which the State educational agency may require in order to meet the State annual program plan requirements in Subpart B. The requirement for local educational agencies to be consistent with the annual program plan is set forth in section 121a.236.

APPLICATION FROM SECRETARY OF INTERIOR (§§ 121a.260-121a.261)

These sections have been rewritten to clarify that the annual application by the Secretary of the Interior for schools operated for Indian children must meet the applicable requirements of section 614 (a), include other material as agreed to by the Commissioner and the Secretary of the Interior, and meet monitoring and public participation requirements.

PUBLIC PARTICIPATION

See the comments on Section 121a.-120.

SUBPART C—SERVICES

Subpart C contains regulations governing the major service components required under Part B of the Act. These include free appropriate public education, the full educational opportunity goal, priorities in the use of Part B funds, individualized education programs, direct services by the State educational agency, and the State comprehensive system of personnel development.

FREE APPROPRIATE PUBLIC EDUCATION

FREE APPROPRIATE PUBLIC EDUCATION REQUIREMENTS (§§ 121a.300-121a.303)

Comment: Commenters disagreed with the interpretation of "State law or practice" in the proposed regulations. Some commenters felt the exception to the requirement to make free appropriate public education (FAPE) available to children in the age ranges three through five and 18 through 21 applies only if State law (or a court order) specifically prohibits services, or only if the State's practice is to provide services to less than a majority of the State's handicapped children. Others felt the requirement does not apply to the lower and upper age ranges unless the State is in fact serving all nonhandicapped children in those age ranges.

Response: The requirement has been redrafted to clarify the use of the exception and to insure at a minimum that handicapped children in any of these age ranges are served to the extent nonhandicapped children are served (to be consistent with nondiscrimination requirements under section 504).

Section 121a.300 ("Timelines for free appropriate public education") breaks "practice" down by individual public agency, disability category, and age group. This revision is designed to maximize the number of handicapped children aged 3-5 and 18-21 who receive services. It should reduce the reluctance of agencies wishing to serve children in those age groups, because services to a few handicapped children will not require services to all handicapped children in all of the disabilities.

Section 121a.300 also includes an amendment designed to insure that each time a public agency elects to serve a handicapped child, the child receives the full range of rights and services, whether or not FAPE is mandated for that age range.

FREE APPROPRIATE PUBLIC EDUCATION METHODS AND PAYMENTS (§ 121a.301-121a.303)

Comment: Commenters disagreed on which agencies or parties should bear the costs of educating a handicapped child, especially room and board costs. Commenters sought clarification of when the costs must be borne by the State or local educational agency.

Response: The proposed regulation on methods and costs for FAPE (proposed § 121a.201) has been redrafted and expanded as follows:

(1) A new paragraph has been added to section 121a.301; which states: "Nothing in this part relieves an insurer or similar third party from an otherwise valid obligation to provide or to pay for services provided to a handicapped child."

(2) Section 121a.302 states that if placement in a public or private residential program is necessary to provide FAPE to a handicapped child, the program (including non-medical care and room and board) must be at no cost to the child's parents.

Both of these changes have been made to conform to the regulations implementing section 504.

Other Changes: A new section 121a-303 has been added regarding the proper functioning of hearing aids. This section is based on a special study conducted by the Office of Education ("The Condition of Hearing Aids as Worn by Children in Public Schools," GPO publication date Summer, 1977).

FULL EDUCATIONAL OPPORTUNITY GOAL (§§ 121a.304-121a.306)

The statutory terms "free appropriate public education" and "full educational opportunity goal" are distinguished in this regulation as follows:

"Free appropriate public education" (FAPE) must (1) be made available to all handicapped children within the mandated time lines and age ranges set forth in the Act, and (2) include special education and related services which are provided in accordance with an individualized education program.

"Full educational opportunity goal" is broader in scope than "FAPE." It is an all-encompassing term, which (1) covers all handicapped children aged birth through twenty-one, (2) includes a basic planning dimension (including making projections of the estimated numbers of handicapped children), (3) permits each agency to establish its own timetable for meeting the goal, and (4) calls for the provision of additional facilities, personnel, and services to further enrich a handicapped child's educational opportunity beyond that mandated under the "FAPE" requirement. The term "goal" means an end to be sought. However, while an agency may never achieve its goal in the absolute sense, it must be committed to implementing this provision, and must be in compliance with the policies and procedures in the Annual Program Plan under this provision. Further, the agency is not relieved from its obligations under the "FAPE" requirement.

The proposed rule on full educational opportunity goal has been revised as follows: Proposed paragraph (a) (Program options) is now § 121a.305 and proposed paragraph (b) (Non-academic services) is now § 121a306. A new § 121a.304 has been added which (1) requires each State educational agency to insure that each public agency establishes and implements a goal of providing full educational opportunity to all handicapped children, and (2) authorizes State and local educational agencies to use Part B funds to provide the facilities, personnel and services necessary to meet the goal.

A comment has been added following section 121a.304 which points to Congressional interest in having artistic and cultural activities included in programs supported under this part, subject to the priorities.

Comment: Many commenters asked that additional areas be added to the program options requirement (e.g., leisure education, cultural and performing arts, and occupational education). Other commenters requested that the term "consumer and homemaking education" be substituted for "home economics" in order to be consistent with the vocational education amendments of 1976 (Pub. L. 94-482).

Response: No substantive change was made in this requirement. The program options included are examples and the list is not exhaustive. Under the regulation implementing section 504, any program provided to nonhandicapped students must also be made available to handicapped pupils. The language conforming to the vocational education amendments was added.

Comment: Commenters requested that under the requirement on non-academic services the term "cocurricular" be substituted for "extra curricular" and that intramural, extramural, and interscholastic athletics be included in order to insure consistent use of terminology as it applies nationally. Another commenter suggested that specific language be included regarding participation of visually handicapped persons.

Response: The suggested terms were not adopted. This section conforms to the language in the final regulations under section 504. Also, the suggested language on visually handicapped was not included. This requirement applies to all handicapped individuals, including those with visual handicaps.

PHYSICAL EDUCATION (§ 121a.307)

Comment: Some commenters felt that the section on physical education

(PE) needed to be clarified, particularly the conditions under which a handicapped child would not be required to participate in the regular PE program; (e.g., the child (a) is enrolled fulltime in a separate facility, (b) needs specially designed PE, or (c) the parents and agency agree that the child should not participate). The main concern dealt with the parent-agency agreement, because it appeared to provide a loophole in which a child would not be required to participate in any PE activity.

Response: The statement on parent-agency agreement was deleted. With this change, a handicapped child attending a regular school would participate in the regular PE program, unless the child needs specially designed PE as prescribed in his or her individualized education program (IEP). Parent-agency agreement is inherent in the development of a child's IEP. The decision as to whether the child should be in the regular PE program or receive specially designed PE is made in the IEP meeting in which the parent and agency personnel are represented.

It should be noted that every handicapped child would participate in some type of PE activity. Specially designed PE could involve arrangements for a child to participate in some individual sport or physical activity (e.g., weight lifting, bowling, or an exercise or motor activity program).

Other changes: Proposed section 121a.204 (Incidental use of property) has been deleted.

PRIORITIES IN THE USE OF PART B FUNDS

As part of the provision on free appropriate public education, the law requires each State and local educational agency to establish priorities, first with respect to handicapped children not receiving an education (defined as "first priority children" in the regulations) and second with respect to handicapped children, within each disability, with the most severe handicaps who are receiving an inadequate education (defined as "second priority children"). The law further requires that, except for State administration funds, each State and local educational agency must use its full entitlement under part B "in accordance with the priorities." The regulations which implement these priority requirements are included in section 121a.320-121a.324.

PRIORITIES (§ 121a.321)

Comment: Many commenters were concerned that first priority expenditures cannot be used for inservice training for personnel who can serve those students, and stated that such inservice training activities may be an essential component toward achieving the first priority.

Response: The proposed rules have been redrafted and expanded in order to address the above concerns. A new section was added to make it clear that an agency may use Part B funds for inservice training concurrently with placing a first priority child in school (in an interim program, if a component of the child's program is missing). However, the provision of inservice training may not be used as a pre-condition for service to the child.

The intent of Congress with respect to the education of first priority children is both long-standing (dating back to Pub. L. 93-380) and very clear, as reflected in the following statements:

(1) The Congress has a responsibility "* * * to see that all persons are assured equal opportunity. For handicapped children, this means, at the very least, that they must be educated * * * These funds must be focused in such a way that we are assured that handicapped children are provided their right to education." (Congressional Record—Senate, June 18, 1975, p. S10969)

(2) "First priority for spending under

the legislation is to provide services for handicapped children who are not now being served. The flexible approach in the Conference Report with respect to the current fiscal year, fiscal year 1977 and fiscal year 1978 will allow for concentrations of moneys so that this priority can be met." (Congressional Record — House of Representatives, November 18, 1975, p. H12348)

(3) "There are millions of children with handicapping conditions who are receiving no services at all. And since we must have a place to start, it is appropriate that we give priority to those who are receiving no services at all first, and then try to reach those with the most severe handicaps who have traditionally received only minimal attention second." (Congressional Record—Senate, June 18, 1975, p. S10961)

Comment: Several commenters requested clarification regarding whether the requirements on the use of funds for priorities apply within or among local educational agencies (e.g., if an agency is serving all of its first priority children, could a State give that agency's entitlement to another agency which is not serving all of its first priority children?).

Response: No change has been made. The statute does not permit the State to take away a local educational agency's Part B funds solely because the local educational agency is serving all of its first priority children. For the limited circumstances where a local educational agency's funds may be reallocated, see section 121a.708.

Other changes: A new paragraph (c) has been added to section 121a.321, which provides that Part B funds cannot be used for preservice training. This addition was made to implement Congressional intent expressed in Senate Report No. 94-168, p. 34 (1975), in which it was stated that funds for preservice training are available under the training program under Part D of the

Act, and that Part B funds should not be used for this purpose.

INDIVIDUALIZED EDUCATION PROGRAM

The requirements on individualized education programs (IEPs) in Subpart C have been reorganized and redrafted substantially, based largely on comments received. (These sections have been renumbered, starting with section 121a.340.) A summary of these changes is included below:

(1) A definition of IEP has been added which states that the term "IEP" means a written statement on a handicapped child that is developed and implemented in accordance with sections 121a.341-121a.349 of Subpart C.

(2) The proposed section entitled, "Scope" has been deleted and the substance combined with the section on "State educational agency responsibility."

(3) The proposed section on "Local educational agency responsibility" has been replaced by two new sections ("When IEPs must be in effect" and "Meetings").

(4) The section on "Participants in meetings" has been redrafted to adopt essentially verbatim the language in the Act and to add a new paragraph on participation of evaluation personnel.

(5) The proposed section on "Parent participation" has been amended to include specific provisions regarding notifying parents about the IEP meetings.

(6) The substance under the proposed section on "Content of IEP" has been replaced with the statutory language.

(7) The proposed section on "Private school placements" has been reorganized into two sections to conform to the two groups of private school handicapped children in Subpart D, and has been expanded to spell out in more detail the responsibilities of State and local educational agencies in administering this provision.

(8) A new section was added, entitled, "IEP—accountability."

TIMING OF IEP MEETINGS
(§§121a.342-121a.343)

Comment: Many commenters felt that the final rules should provide more flexibility to agencies in terms of when IEP meetings are conducted.

Response: The following changes were made in the proposed rules in an attempt to clarify this provision. First, the regulations now specify the dates on which IEP's must be in effect (October 1, 1977, and the beginning of each school year thereafter). Second, except for new handicapped children (those initially evaluated after October 1, 1977), the timing of meetings to develop, review and revise IEPs is left to the discretion of each agency. (For a new handicapped child, a meeting must be held within thirty days of a determination that he or she needs special education.) The regulations are flexible on the schedule to be followed by public agencies in meeting the above dates.

PARTICIPANTS IN IEP MEETINGS
(§ 121a.344)

Comment: A number of commenters recommended that personnel from specific disciplines be participants at IEP meetings (e.g., physicians, health care personnel, psychologists, and representatives from other agencies, such as Head Start). Some commenters felt that the meetings should include all direct service personnel who work with a handicapped child. Other commenters suggested cutting back on the number of people who participate.

Response: The final regulations only require the participants listed in the statute, except in the case of a child who has been evaluated for the first time. (NOTE: Participation of evaluation personnel in IEP meetings is covered under the next comment-response sequence.)

Generally, having a large group of people at an IEP meeting may be unproductive and very costly, and could essentially defeat the purpose of insuring active, open parent involvement.

While it is necessary to insure that all direct services personnel who work with a handicapped child are informed about and involved in implementing the child's IEP, this does not mean that they should attend the IEP meetings. The mechanism for insuring the involvement of all IEP implementers is left to the discretion of each agency (e.g., the child's teacher, or principal, or supervisor could have that responsibility). However, this is a basic administrative procedure which can be handled outside of the context of the IEP meeting.

The statute does not require all IEP implementers to be involved in the meetings. In fact, the definition of IEP in section 602 (19) of the Act includes only four people (e.g., a special education provider or supervisor, the teacher, the parent, and the child, where appropriate). Moreover, it was the intent of Congress that IEP meetings generally be small. This position is reflected in the following statement by Senator Randolph in the June 18, 1975 Congressional Record:

In answer to my colleague, it was the intent, and I believe, I can speak for the subcommittee and the committee in this matter, that these meetings * * * be small meetings; that is, confined to those persons who have, naturally an intense interest in a particular child, i.e., the parent or parents, and in some cases the guardian of the child. Certainly the teacher involved or even more than one teacher would be included. In addition, there should be a representative of the local educational agency who is qualified to provide, or supervise the provision of, specially designed instruction to meet the unique needs of handicapped children.

These are the persons that we

thought might well be included. That is why we have called them "individualized planning conferences." We believe that they are worthwhile, and we discussed this very much as we drafted the legislation.

While very large IEP meetings might generally be inappropriate, there may be specific instances where additional participants are essential. In order to enable other persons to be included, the Office of Education retained a provision from the proposed rules which authorized the attendance of "other participants, at the discretion of the agency or parents."

Comment: Some commenters recommended that members of the evaluation team participate in IEP meetings.

Response: A new paragraph has been added which states, in effect, that an evaluation person must participate in any IEP meetings conducted for handicapped children who have been evaluated for the first time (i.e., the preplacement evaluation required under section 121a.531 of Subpart E). Since the meeting is intended to develop an education program for the child, it is essential that someone at the meeting be familiar with the child's evaluation.

Comment: Several commenters recommended that the representative of the agency be qualified in the disability area in which the IEP is written.

Response: A comment has been added following section 121a.344 which suggests (but does not require) that either the teacher or the agency representative should be qualified in the area of suspected disability. At the time of the meeting, the public agency may not yet have hired a person qualified to provide special education with respect to that suspected disability.

PARENT PARTICIPATION (§ 121a.345)

Comment: Some commenters stated that documenting efforts to involve parents would be difficult and time consuming. One commenter felt it was important to retain the general state-ment requiring agencies to involve parents, but recommended that the details in the parent participation section be deleted from the final regulation. Another commenter recommended that the section be dropped because it is not required in the law and is "* * * utterly paternalistic. If a local education agency is foolish enough to keep inadequate records on transactions with parents, it alone stands in jeopardy; there is no damage to parents or to handicapped children."

Response: The comments have not been adopted. The Office of Education believes that it is important to retain this section in the final regulations, for the following reasons:

First, the section provides rules that allow agencies to proceed in conducting IEP meetings in cases where parents cannot or will not attend. Without this authorization, the IEP process might come to a halt in some cases, since the law states that an IEP must be developed at a meeting with the parents.

Second, the section is designed to protect agencies by setting the conditions under which they can proceed.

Third, the section is designed to protect the rights of the parents. The Congress intended that IEP meetings be utilized as an extension of the procedural protections guaranteed under Pub. L. 93-380. However, if the regulations provided an authorization for agencies to proceed without the parents, there is a potential problem that the authorization (without documentation) might be inappropriately applied in individual cases, which could result in parents' rights not being protected.

Comment: A few commenters suggested using surrogate parents if a child's parents could not attend an IEP meeting. One commenter recommended adding a provision to enable the parents to designate a person to represent them at a meeting.

Response: The Office of Education

elected not to write regulations on either of these suggestions.

First, a surrogate parent is appointed only in accordance with the procedural safeguards in Subpart E. The provision was not meant to apply in situations when parents are unwilling to participate, or when an agency makes unsuccessful efforts to communicate with a known parent. A surrogate parent is appointed only when the parents are unknown, unavailable or the child is a ward of the state. However, a surrogate parent appointed under appropriate circumstances would attend the IEP meetings and represent the child in all matters relating to the provision of a free appropriate public education to the child.

Second, with respect to parent designated representatives, the Office of Education does not feel that any change in the regulation is warranted. Parents unable to attend an IEP meeting, who are interested enough in their child's education to seek a third party representative, would have direct input in developing the child's IEP through individual or conference telephone calls or other methods authorized under paragraph (c) of section 121a.345.

Other changes. A new paragraph (f) has been added to require that parents be given a copy of the IEP on request. This should help to insure that the parents are fully informed of the program for their child, and will assist them in participating in future meetings on the IEP.

CONTENT OF IEP (§ 121a.346)

Comment: Hundreds of commenters responded to this section. Some commenters requested that additional services or other items be added. Other commenters recommended that the section be sharply cut back, because they felt that this went unnecessarily beyond the items listed in the statute. Many of the commenters wanted the specific service areas they represent added to the list of services to be provided in the IEP. Others felt that this went unnecessarily beyond the items listed in the statute.

Response: The Office of Education has elected to amend this section by adopting substantially verbatim the language from section 602 (19) of the statute. The regulation retains one clarification from the proposed rules, that the individualized education program must include related services to be provided to the child, as well as special education and the extent to which the child can participate in regular education programs. However, given the controversy over this section and whether it is appropriate to add items not specifically covered in the statute, the Office of Education has decided that some experience operating under the statute would be useful before considering whether further regulations on this point would be appropriate.

IEP—ACCOUNTABILITY (§ 121a.349)

Comment: In the preamble to the proposed rules, a statement was made that the IEP is not a legally binding document. Many commenters recommended that this statement should be included in the body of the final regulations. Other commenters felt that the statement needed to be clarified.

Response: The Office of Education has added a new section, which states, in effect, that each public agency must provide special education and related services in accordance with a handicapped child's IEP. However, Part B does not require that the agency, the teacher, or other persons be held accountable if the child does not achieve the growth projected in the written statement.

COLLECTIVE BARGAINING

Comment: Numerous commenters recommended that the regulations deal with the fact that the required participation of teachers (and other agency staff) in the meetings to develop IEP's would require modification of collective bargaining agreements. Some commenters urged that the regulations require additional compensation for teachers to participate in these meetings, prescribe or limit any after-school-hours participation, and specify arrangements for relieving teachers from classroom duties for the meetings.

Response: No change has been made in the regulation. The requirement for teacher participation in developing IEPs is statutory. The Commissioner understands that collective bargaining agreements and individual annual contracts for teachers vary greatly among local educational agencies and may or may not deal with additional duties and compensation for after-hour activities. In some instances, especially in urbanized and highly unionized areas, collective bargaining agreements may have to be renegotiated to cover employee participation in IEPs. However, this is an area which is solely within the authority of the public agency and its employees (and their union representative, if any). It would be inappropriate and beyond the scope of the Commissioner's authority to prescribe how this requirement must be met. Where collective bargaining agreements must be modified, the public agency must negotiate the appropriate modifications to comply with the statute. The public agency is also responsible for insuring that the IEP meetings are conducted at a time reasonably convenient to parents. (In some cases this may be during school hours; in others, after hours.) The agency also must make its own arrangements for covering classrooms when teachers are absent.

DIRECT SERVICES BY THE STATE EDUCATIONAL AGENCY

The direct services provision of this subpart includes sections on (1) use of local educational agency (LEA) funds, (2) nature and location of services, (3) use of the State's (SEA's) entitlement, and (4) a State matching requirement.

The section on the use of LEA allocations (renumbered section 121a.360) has been redrafted to combine the proposed paragraphs (a) and (b) into a single paragraph. This paragraph sets out the conditions under which an SEA may use an LEA's entitlement.

A new paragraph (b) has been added to section 121a.360, which states that in meeting the requirements of this section, the SEA may provide special education and related services directly, by contract, or through other arrangements.

A new paragraph (c) has been added, which repeats the statutory provision that the excess cost requirement does not apply to State educational agencies.

Section 121a.360 (Nature and location of services) has been amended to correct an error made in the proposed rule. The proposed regulation stated that the least restrictive environment (LRE) provisions do not apply when the SEA provides direct services. The amended rule now states that the manner in which the education and services are provided must be consistent with the requirements of this part (including the LRE provisions).

The regulation on "State matching" was not substantially changed. However, a comment was added after this section to make it clear that the requirement would be satisfied if the State can document that the amount of State funds expended on each major program area (e.g., the comprehensive system of personnel development) is at least equal to the expenditure of Federal funds in that program area.

Comment: In the preamble to the proposed rules under the direct services provision, a point was made that an LEA would not be in compliance with the section 504 regulations if that agency did not make available a free appropriate public education (FAPE) to all of its handicapped children. A commenter, in responding to this statement, pointed out that the term FAPE has different meanings under section 504 and Pub. L. 94-142; and, therefore, an LEA would not have to meet the requirements of Pub. L. 94-142 in order to be in compliance with section 504.

Response. Under Part B, "FAPE" is a statutory term which requires services to be provided in accordance with an IEP. However, under the section 504 regulations, each recipient must provide an education which includes services that are "designed to meet individual educational needs of handicapped persons as adequately as the needs of nonhandicapped persons are met * * *" Those regulations state that implementation of an IEP, in accordance with Part B, is one means of meeting the "FAPE" requirement. (NOTE.—A more detailed description of the relationship between section 504 and Pub. L. 94-142 is included in this appendix.)

Other changes: A new section 121a.-372 has been added to implement section 611 (c) (3) of the Act. This section provides that the nonsupplanting requirement does not apply to the State's expenditure of its allocation beginning with funds appropriated for Fiscal Year 1979 and for each following fiscal year.

COMPREHENSIVE SYSTEM OF PERSONNEL DEVELOPMENT
GENERAL

The proposed rules in this section created some controversy over the amount of detail contained in the regulations. Comments ranged from requests for more specificity to suggestions that everything be deleted except the statutory language.

The statute is very clear in requiring that a "comprehensive system of personnel development" be implemented in each State. Since this is a broad requirement, challenging each State to reach out to the expansive community of agencies involved in preparing personnel to educate the handicapped, many of which are private and not under the control of the State, it was felt that a regulation was needed that would provide sufficient information for the State and involved agencies to understand their responsibilities in achieving compliance.

SCOPE OF SYSTEM (§ 121a.380)

Comment: A commenter suggested that inservice education be available to all special, regular, and related service personnel.

Response: Paragraph (a) of section 121a.380 was changed to read "the inservice training of general and special educational instructional, related services, and support personnel."

Comment: A commenter suggested that all personnel preparation services be conducted in accredited institutions granting advanced degrees and that "no less than ten percent of the money under this Act be contracted to institutions of higher education." Another commenter recommended the earmarking of a percentage of funds for staff and program development.

Response: No change has been made in the regulations. The Office of Education believes that each State must have maximum latitude in decisions regarding the types of facilities and personnel that are used to implement the comprehensive system of personnel development.

With respect to targeting funds for training, the Office of Education feels that such a step would be inappropriate at this time.

Part B is a unique Federal statute in that it imposes requirements on States which must be implemented, regardless of the amount of Federal funds available. Given the scope and magnitude of the law, the Office of Education believes that each State should have maximum latitude in terms of how its Part B funds are used to implement the various statutory provisions, subject, of course, to the priority requirements in Subpart C.

DEFINITION OF "APPROPRIATELY AND ADEQUATELY PREPARED AND TRAINED" (PROPOSED § 121a.261)

A number of comments were received on the definition of "appropriately and adequately prepared and trained" which was in § 121a.261 of the proposed rules. The definition has been deleted in the final regulations. Instead, the term "qualified" is used, as defined in § 121a.12.

Comment: A commenter suggested that nationwide certification requirements be mandated to allow for the mobility of personnel.

Response: No change has been made. The intent of the Act is to insure that all personnel necessary to carry out the purposes of the Act are qualified. The Act does not authorize the establishment of national certification standards.

Comment: A commenter suggested that early childhood be required as an area for certification.

Response: No change has been made. These personnel must be included under the State's comprehensive personnel development system.

Comment: Several commenters expressed the belief that certification should not be required for all personnel directly serving the handicapped, or that such a requirement would result in great expense for the State. Still others felt that competency based systems should be used as opposed to the requirement for certification, registration, or licensing.

Response: The statutory language "appropriately and adequately prepared and trained" has been interpreted, by use of the term "qualified," to mean certification, registration, or licensing.

These are commonly accepted procedures for determining if personnel are "appropriately and adequately prepared and trained."

PARTICIPATION OF OTHER AGENCIES AND INSTITUTIONS (§ 121a.381)

The comments on the level and intensity of the "participation" required in this section ranged from the belief expressed that special meetings on components of the state plan are not required in the Act, therefore the "participation" envisioned in section 121a.381 should be eliminated, to the suggested requirement that organizations not only have an opportunity to participate, but that they "must participate." The comprehensive system of personnel development is such a specialized aspect of the Act, necessarily involving agencies not under the jurisdiction of the State that "participation" is fully warranted, though not mandated in the statute. Thus, the regulations set a requirement for the State to insure that those agencies with an interest in the preparation of personnel for the education of the handicapped have an opportunity to participate fully in the development, review, and updating of the system. This is a reasonable requirement, especially considering the critical effect the system will have on those agencies preparing the personnel. Rather than a burden on the State, the "participation" should provide the direct opportunity for the State to encourage the development of quality personnel preparation programs, a factor essential to the provision of a "free appropriate public education."

Comment: Several commenters suggested that "representatives from each group be included in the planning" as well as parents. One commenter suggested that disability categories and groups be listed in the proposed rule.

Response: The regulation has been altered to include representatives of handicapped and parent organizations.

This wording should be sufficient to involve all relevant groups.

Comment: A commenter suggested the addition of a subsection (3) to section 121a381 (b) that would require the annual program plan to include a description of agency responsibilities with respect to research and evaluation of exemplary programs that could be implemented in local educational settings.

Response: Sections 121a.385 and 121a.386 have been modified to classify agency responsibilities.

INSERVICE TRAINING (§ 121a.382)

Comment: There were a number of contrasting points of view and suggestions on this section ranging from requests to mandate greater detail in the proposed rules, to the suggestion that the section be deleted altogether. Those proposing greater detail suggested that specific knowledge and areas of learning be emphasized and that teachers be trained "by having them work one-to-one with specialists" and that "inservice training be mandated at the local level, a county being the largest unit possible, to prevent the State from using the money for ineffectual regional workshops." Also, there were suggestions that where academic credit is to be made available that this be done only in institutions of higher education with State approved programs.

On the other extreme there were suggestions that this section "exceeds statutory requirements" and "federal rules should not say how a task is accomplished" and "(state) provides adequate training and inservice and does not need more obstacles and regulations."

Response: The statute clearly requires inservice education as a central part of the comprehensive system of personnel development and it is appropriate for the rules to detail the nature and extent of the inservice education that is required. This has been accomplished through the outlining of procedures which define inservice education, its parameters, and relationship to required needs assessments. However, the rules do not define the specific nature of the training to be accomplished. Thus, the rules have been designed to outline the foundation for an adequate program of inservice education, without stifling the creativity of State and local personnel in their efforts to plan and implement such a system.

Comment: A commenter suggested that the statement "in cooperation with institutions of higher education" be inserted in section 121a.383 (b) (1).

Response: No change has been made. However, involvement of institutions of higher education is required under § 121a.381 (a).

Comment: A number of commenters suggested the addition of specific disciplines and professionals to this section, constituting an itemized list of personnel to be trained or involved in the review of training needs.

Response: No change has been made. The State's plan must include all personnel who need training.

Comment: Several commenters suggested wording changes designed to clarify the text of the proposed rule on inservice training.

Response: Changes were made where necessary to bring the regulation into conformity with current usage.

Comment: There were a number of suggestions concerning the financial arrangements for conducting inservice training. Some commenters advocated the funding of parent groups to conduct inservice training. Others suggested financial support for trainees involved in their programs. One commenter urged that the rule allow for contracting with other than non-profit organizations. One suggested contracts with institutions of higher education to carry out personnel development programs. Another suggested incentives for teacher participation, including released time and college credit. One suggested that inservice be provided during contract time, not involving extra hours.

Response: No substantive changes have been made. All of the suggestions in the above comments are authorized under these regulations.

PERSONNEL DEVELOPMENT PLAN
(§ 121a.383)

Comment: Several commenters asked for special attention to physical education and service delivery models which take into account problems of rural families.

Response: No change has been made. Specialized needs in physical education and the unique aspects of providing services in rural settings should be addressed as appropriate in the needs assessment and plan.

Comment: One commenter objected to including preservice training under this section.

Response: No change has been made. The term "inservice" education is used in the Act. However, since the Act clearly requires that a "comprehensive system of personnel development" be developed, such a system must include the consideration of preservice training.

NOTE.—The data required in sections 121a.124 and 121a.126 of Subpart B on the numbers of handicapped children and the kind and number of personnel needed will serve as the uniform data base within the State for the personnel development system under § 121a.383 of this subpart. The data may also be used by institutions of higher education and other nonprofit educational training agencies in submitting personnel preparation applications under Part D of the Act. Section 121f.9 of the regulations under Part D (45 CFR 121f.9) provides as follows:

§ 121f.9   *State personnel needs.*

Each application shall include (a) a statement by the State educational agency of personnel needs for educa-

tion of the handicapped and a statement by the applicant of how the proposed program relates to those stated needs, and (b) a description of the ways in which the recipient's program goals and objectives relate to the purposes of Part D of the Act.
(20 U.S.C. 1431, 1432, 1434)

DISSEMINATION (121a.384)

Comment: One commenter suggested that "teachers organizations" be specified as recipients of information.

Responses: No change has been made. Teacher organizations are included under the phrase "other interested agencies and organizations."

SUBPART D—PRIVATE SCHOOLS

The proposed rules created a certain amount of confusion among commenters in distinguishing between handicapped children placed in or referred to private schools by the State or by local educational agencies and handicapped children whose parents choose to educate them in private schools. The major difference between these two groups of children is in who bears the cost of the private school.

A free appropriate public education must be made available to each handicapped child by the public agencies of the State. Subject to the requirements on least restrictive environment, this could include placement in or referral to a private school or facility. Such a placement or referral must be at no cost to the parent.

On the other hand, even if a free appropriate public education is available, the parent may choose not to accept it. The parent may choose to send the child to a private school rather than take advantage of the free public education. If this happens the Act does not require the State or local educational agency to bear the cost of the private school. For children placed in private schools by their parents, the

State and its local educational agencies have a different duty. They must design their program so that handicapped children in those private schools can participate in special education and related services offered by the local educational agencies if the parents of those children so desire.

The regulations have been reorganized to make these distinctions clearer. The first set of sections (121a-400-121a.403) now cover children placed in or referred to private schools or facilities by a public agency in order to provide them with special education or related services. (These sections replace sections 121a.320-121a.323 of the proposed rules.)

Since the "State" includes all of its political subdivisions, the term "public agency" is used, as elsewhere in the regulations, to mean all of the political subdivisions of the State which are responsible for providing special education or related services to handicapped children.

The second set of sections (121a.-450-121a.460) apply to handicapped children enrolled in private schools or facilities but who are not placed or referred there by a public agency to receive special education or related services. (These sections replace sections 121a.300-121a.306 of the proposed rules.)

The following comments were made regarding proposed Subpart D. Comments which asked for changes not authorized under the statute are not summarized. (Commenters who are concerned about the cost of room and board as a "related service" are referred to section 121a.302 and the discussion of that section in this preamble.) The comments are arranged in order of the final rules.

RESPONSIBILITY OF STATE EDUCATIONAL AGENCY (§ 121a.401)

Comment: A commenter asked that paragraph (a)(3) be deleted, which

required that the special education given to a handicapped child placed by a public agency must meet the education standards of the State educational agency (SEA). The commenter stated that otherwise there would be conflicts between the SEA's standards and those of other agencies, in the day care area, for example.

Response. Paragraph (a)(3) cannot be deleted, since it is derived from a statutory requirement. However, it has been revised by using the language of the statute. This will broaden the types of standards that the SEA may apply, and therefore avoid conflict with other mandatory standards. Of course, those standards cannot override the provisions in Part B of the Act.

Comment: A commenter asked that provision be made for interstate referrals to private schools and communication among States regarding those referrals.

Response: No change has been made in the regulation. Referrals between States are to be handled under existing procedures. Unless a problem develops in this area that seriously interferes with the rights of handicapped children or their parents under Part B, the Office of Education is reluctant to regulate the mechanisms by which the States arrange to provide services.

IMPLEMENTATION BY SEA (§ 121a.402)

Comment: A commenter suggested that the State educational agency insure the monitoring of private schools, dissemination of standards to them, and involving them in developing State standards, rather than the State educational agency doing it directly.

Response: No change has been made. The statute places direct responsibility on the State educational agency to administer and monitor the requirements under Part B. While the State educational agency in many areas need only insure that the Part B requirements are met, monitoring must be done by the agency itself. Dissemination of standards could be done in a variety of ways. Involvement in development of State standards would have to be done directly by the State educational agency if it is the agency that develops those standards.

PLACEMENT OF CHILDREN BY PARENTS
(§ 121a.403)

Comment: Commenters were concerned with the effect of this section on the rights of handicapped children in private schools and felt that the section was worded in a manner that would limit those rights.

Response: The section has been revised to make it clear that a free appropriate public education (FAPE) must be made available to each handicapped child. This would include the development of an individualized education program and placement in the least restrictive environment. Free appropriate public education must be made available at no cost to the parents. If the parents felt that services were not adequate, they may have a due process hearing to show that more or better services must be provided to give their child FAPE. However, if the parents choose not to educate their child in the public school system, they are not required to do so. In that case, the relevant public agency has the remaining duty of offering special education and related services under sections 121a.450-121a.460, but does not have the duty of insuring that the private school meets the requirements of Part B (unless other handicapped children have been placed in or referred to that private school by the agency), or of paying for the cost of the private school. Language has been added to clarify the public agency's duties under sections 121a.450-121a.460.

Other changes: Proposed section 121a.323 (Placements in another State) has been deleted. It would have required private schools to meet the standards of both the sending and receiving States. This would have been an unreasonable burden on the receiving State to enforce.

HANDICAPPED CHILDREN IN PRIVATE SCHOOLS NOT PLACED OR REFERRED BY PUBLIC AGENCIES
(§§ 121a.450-121a.460)

Comments: A number of commenters felt that clarification was needed in these sections. There was also some concern expressed regarding the State's legal authority to provide services to children enrolled in private schools.

Response: The regulations have been amended to conform more closely to those under Title I of the Elementary and Secondary Education Act of 1965 (education of educationally deprived children) (45 CFR, Section 116a.23). As under Title I, a balance is drawn between the statutory requirement to provide services, and the constitutional necessity of avoiding excessive entanglements between public agencies and church-related institutions. It is also important for the Office of Education to have a uniform policy regarding services to private school children under all Federal education programs it administers. The amendments to the proposed rules should serve all of these purposes.

SUBPART E—PROCEDURAL SAFEGUARDS

This subpart implements the procedural safeguards set forth in the Act, including due process procedures for parents and children, protection in evaluation procedures, least restrictive environment, confidentiality of information, and procedures of the Office of Education.

A substantial number of detailed comments were received on these sections. Many concerned the statute rather than the regulations or did not state what changes in the regulations were desired. Others requested revisions which did not appear to involve substantive changes. Some comments sought substantially more detailed specification of due process rights while others indicated that the statute itself was so detailed in the due process area that the regulations should not go beyond the statute.

As stated earlier in this preamble, the Office of Education's position, while incorporating a number of the suggestions in the final regulations, is still to adopt minimum regulations in this area at this time, review experience under the regulations, and then made a determination as to whether more detailed regulations are required.

DUE PROCESS PROCEDURES FOR PARENTS AND CHILDREN
DEFINITIONS (§ 121a.500)

Comment: Commenters recommended that the phrase "unless it is clearly not feasible to do so" be deleted from the definition of consent and that consent may be revoked and may not be made a precondition to the child's right to participate in basic educational programs. The effect of deleting the phrase would be to require that a consent is not valid unless the parent is informed in every case of the information relevant to the consent.

Response: The phrase has been deleted. The deletion of the phrase will help to assure an informed consent in every case, regardless of the parent's language or other mode of communication. A phrase has been added to make it clear that parents have the right to revoke consent. A separate section 121a.504 states that consent may not improperly be made a precondition of services. While public agencies must obtain consent for preplacement evaluations or for initial placement, a public agency may not coerce parents to consent by withholding or threatening to withhold other regular education services or extracurricular activities unless the parent consents.

Comment: Several commenters requested changes in the definition of

"evaluation" to indicate that an evaluation must be conducted by qualified personnel, that the findings must be reduced to writing, and that it must take into account the child's assets as well as deficits.

Response: No change has been made. The suggestion regarding qualified personnel is covered under section 121a.532. The Office of Education expects that evaluations will be in writing and that a child's assets will be considered. If a problem develops in this area, the Office of Education will reconsider the necessity for further regulations.

GENERAL RESPONSIBILITY OF PUBLIC AGENCIES (§ 121a.501)

Comment: Commenters suggested that parents have the right to complain and that agencies should be required to respond to them outside of the context of a hearing.

Response: No change has been made in the regulation. However, agencies should certainly seek to respond to complaints by informal discussions and negotiations. A comment section has been added which notes that mediation may be useful in some instances. In any case, negotiations may not delay a hearing if a parent has requested it.

INDEPENDENT EDUCATIONAL EVALUATION (§ 121a.503)

Comment: Commenters disagreed as to whether the parent's right to an independent evaluation should be broadened or narrowed.

Response: The section has been rewritten to require public agencies to provide parents information, upon request, of where an independent educational evaluation may be obtained. Also, "public expense" has been defined. However, the interpretation in the proposed regulations is retained. The evaluation must be at public expense if the parent disagrees with the evaluation by the public agency, unless the public agency initiates a hearing to show that its evaluation is appropriate. If upheld, the expense of the independent evaluation does not have to be borne by the agency. The independent evaluation must be considered in any hearing.

There are several competing interests which the regulation seeks to balance. The statutory right of the parent to an independent educational evaluation must be preserved. On the other hand, the public agencies should not be asked to bear the cost of unreasonably expensive independent evaluations. Also, for the independent evaluation to be useful, it must meet the same criteria as evaluations conducted by public agencies under this part.

PRIOR NOTICE; PARENT CONSENT AND CONTENT OF NOTICE (§§ 121a.504-121a.505)

Comment: Commenters sought further specificity as to the detail of information provided to parents in the notice. Other commenters felt that the requirements were too demanding. Some commenters asked that consent be required for preplacement evaluation and prior notice for reevaluation; and that consent be extended to include permission for placement. Other commenters sought to delete the consent requirement on the grounds that educational judgments should be final.

Response: The basic notice requirements in sections 121a.504 and 121a.-505 were not changed. However, the following changes were made in the consent requirements:

(1) Consent was expanded to include permission for initial placement of a handicapped child in a special education program. Many commenters had requested this addition; and the Office of Education agrees that this requirement is as essential as consent for preplacement evaluation.

(2) The proposed consent rule was changed from consent for all evaluations to consent for the initial or preplacement evaluation. This change is essentially consistent with the section 504 final regulations (45 CFR Part 84, § 84.35 (a)). The Office of Education agrees with commenters that there is no need to require consent for reevaluation. If a handicapped child is initially placed in accordance with section 121a.504, and if his or her individualized education program is annually reviewed in accordance with section 121a.343 of Subpart C, a requirement is not necessary. However, prior notice would have to be provided.

Comment: Commenters were especially concerned that clarification be added regarding procedures for overriding parents' refusal to consent.

Response: A subsection has been added to set out procedures for dealing with parental refusal to consent (see section 121a.504 (c) and the comment following that section).

The procedures are designed not to interfere with existing State laws which may require consent. Where State law does not require consent, the parent is afforded a due process hearing under this Part. These rules should provide protection to the parent, the child, and the public agency.

IMPARTIAL DUE PROCESS HEARING (§ 121a.506)

Comment: A commenter asked that the regulations specify that the public agency must pay for the hearing.

Response: The change requested by the commenter has not been made. Since the statute requires that the public agency must afford parents an opportunity for a hearing, the agency must bear the cost of the hearing, except for paying for parents' representatives and witnesses. However, section 121a.506 has been amended to require agencies to provide parents with information about free or low-cost legal and other relevant services that are available.

IMPARTIAL HEARING OFFICER
(§ 121a.507)

Comment: Commenters sought to have three-person panels, including parents, serve as the hearing officials. Some sought to allow and others sought not to allow school board officials from serving as hearing officials. Commenters also asked that lists of hearing officers be required, including their qualifications.

Response: A requirement has been added that each public agency keep a list of persons who serve as hearing officers and a statement of their qualifications. This should help to ensure that the requirement for impartiality is met. No other substantive change has been made. A three-person panel could be used under the existing rules, as long as the conditions of impartiality are met. However, a parent of the child in question and school board officials are disqualified under section 121a.508.

HEARING RIGHTS (§ 121a.508)

Comment: Commenters disagreed as to whether hearing rights set forth in the proposed rules should be expanded or restricted. Among the additional rights sought were the right to compel the attendance of witnesses, prohibit the introduction of evidence not disclosed prior to the hearing, allow the child to be present and the hearing to be open to the public at the parents' discretion, and to specify whether the record of the hearing must be free or at reasonable cost.

Response: The section has been revised to add rights for any party to prohibit the introduction of evidence not previously disclosed to the other party and for the child to be present and the hearing to be open to the public. The purpose of hearings under this part is to ensure that handicapped children are provided free appropriate public education. Opening up the hearing and the evidence that may be presented should serve to insure that the result of a hearing will be in the best interests of the child. No provision has been added relating to cost. However, it is expected that a copy of any decision would be provided to the parent at no cost.

HEARING DECISION; APPEAL
(§ 121a.509)

Comment: A commenter sought to add a requirement that specifies that the hearing officer has the power to order any educational program for the child and that his or her power not be limited to accepting or rejecting the program by the public agency or parent.

Response: No change is necessary. The hearing officer has the function to decide what placement is appropriate, if that is the subject of the hearing.

ADMINISTRATIVE APPEAL; IMPARTIAL REVIEW (§ 121a.510)

Comment: Commenters disagreed on whether to reduce or expand the requirements in this section. Some commenters wanted short, specific timelines set out for various actions and specification of the rights that apply at the review level.

Response: The section has been revised to specify other duties and powers of the reviewing official, in addition to those already set out. For example, the official may seek additional evidence if necessary, including holding a new hearing and affording the parties an opportunity for written as well as oral argument (at the reviewing official's discretion). The reviewing official must give a copy of the written findings and decision to the parties. These duties and powers are regarded as necessary to insure that a full review will be conducted and that all parties will be informed of the result of the review. Revisions to timelines for any hearing or review are set out in section 121a.512.

CIVIL ACTION (§ 121a.511)

Comment: Commenters wanted the regulations revised to allow for direct appeal to the courts without first using administrative hearing and review procedures if those procedures would be futile, the timelines or adequacy of the administrative proceedings are being challenged, or a class action is involved. Commenters cited language in the Congressional Record in support of this interpretation (121 Cong. Rec. S20433 daily ed., November 19, 1975).

Response: No change has been made. The legislative history cited is nongermane as it was made in reference to the Senate Bill (S. 6) which did not contain the final statutory provision on civil actions. The provision on civil action was added as a Conference substitute. The issue of exhaustion of remedies will be up to the courts to resolve.

TIMELINES AND CONVENIENCE OF HEARINGS AND REVIEWS (§ 121a.512)

Comment: Commenters wanted clarification of the 45-day time limit for commencing and completing a hearing and review set out in the proposed regulations. They disagreed on whether the time should be shortened or lengthened.

Response: The section has been revised to set a 45 day time limit for a hearing and a 30 day limit for a State level review. In both instances, a decision must be reached and mailed to each of the parties within the time limits set. A hearing or reviewing officer may grant specific extensions, at his or her discretion, at the request of either party. The Office of Education believes reasonable outside time limits must be set to insure resolution of any dispute quickly so that the child's special education may proceed. Discretion for specific extensions is consistent with normal judicial and administrative practice.

CHILD'S STATUS DURING PROCEEDINGS (§ 121a.513)

Comment: Commenters suggested a provision be added to allow change of placement for health or safety reasons. One commenter requested that the regulations indicate that suspension not be considered a change in placement. Another commenter wanted more specificity to make it clear that where an initial placement is involved, the child be placed in the regular education program or, if the parents agree, in an interim special placement.

Response: A comment has been added to make it clear that this section would not preclude a public agency from using its regular procedures for dealing with emergencies.

SURROGATE PARENTS (§ 121a.514)

Comment: Commenters requested that the regulations clarify when surrogates may be appointed. One reason given was to insure that agencies do not attempt to appoint surrogates when parents are uncooperative or nonresponsive.

Response: The section has been revised to make it clear that the requirements for appointing surrogates apply only when no parent can be identified, the agency after reasonable efforts cannot discover the whereabouts of a parent, or the child is a ward of the State. Agencies are not allowed to appoint surrogates when parents are uncooperative or nonresponsive.

Comment: Commenters requested that the regulations further specify procedures to be used for the appointment of surrogates, including administrative proceedings with notice to interested parties and the right of interested parties to seek a review of the decision.

Response: No change has been made. State procedures for the appointment of surrogates will be followed. Disagreements about the choice of surrogates may be the subject of a due process hearing under section 121a.506.

Comment: A number of commenters suggested that the regulations provide more detail about the qualifications of the surrogates (for example, requiring training and a commitment to becoming acquainted with the child).

Response: No change has been made. The Office of Education believes these concerns are covered by section 121a.-514 (c) (2) which requires that the surrogate have knowledge and skills that insure adequate representation of the child.

Comment: A number of commenters were concerned about the legal liability of surrogates. Some commenters wanted the regulations to protect surrogates from any legal liability.

Response: No change has been made. The legal liability of surrogates will be determined under State law relating to such matters as breach of fiduciary duty, negligence, and conflict of interest. The Federal government has no authority to limit legal liability.

Comment: A number of commenters sought clarification regarding which agency employees could serve as surrogates. For example, one commenter wanted the regulations to indicate whether the head of a State institution could serve as the surrogate.

Response: The regulation has been reworded to make it clear that no employee of any agency involved in the education or care of the child may serve as the surrogate parent.

PROTECTION IN EVALUATION PROCEDURES

Section 612 (5) (C) of the Act requires States to establish nondiscriminatory testing procedures for use in the evaluation and placement of handicapped children. The requirements for public agencies to follow in carrying out this provision are set forth in sections 121a.530-121a.534 of Subpart E. (These section numbers have been changed to correspond with other number changes in Subpart E.)

The evaluation procedures in the proposed rules have been changed to conform to the corresponding requirements in the final regulations for section 504 of the Rehabilitation Act of 1973 (45 CFR Part 84, § 84.35) and in response to other comments received. (Many of the comments dealing with the language and substance of the proposed evaluation procedures are covered by the above conforming changes.) A summary of the changes in these procedures is included below:

(1) Proposed section 121a.431 ("Evaluation; change in placement") has been replaced with new section 121a.531 ("Preplacement evaluation"). This corresponds to section 84.35 (a) of Part 84.

(2) Proposed section 121a.432 ("Evaluation procedures") has been divided into two sections (section 121a.-532 "Evaluation procedures" and section 121a.533, "Placement procedures"). The new section on evaluation procedures (a) incorporates essentially verbatim the language of section 84.35 (b) of part 84, (b) adds two additional requirements from section 612 (5) (C) of the Act which are not in Part 84 (e.g., the provision on native language, and the requirement that "No single procedure is used as the sole criterion for determining an appropriate educational program for a child"), and (c) requires that the evaluation be made by a "multidisciplinary team * * * including at least one teacher or other specialist with knowledge in the area of identified disability * * *"

(3) The new section on placement procedures incorporates essentially verbatim the language in section 84.35 (c) of Part 84. In addition, the section ties the development of an individualized education program to the placement procedures.

The following additional comments were made regarding evaluation procedures:

Comment: Several commenters felt that the regulations should require State and local educational agencies to develop procedures for the conduct of evaluations. This would make it possible to determine the adequacy of the evaluations and to insure uniformity in basic procedures.

Response: A paragraph was added to section 121a.530 (General) which requires the State educational agency to insure that each public agency establishes and implements evaluation—placement procedures.

Comment: Several commenters felt that timelines should be set for implementing the evaluation process (e.g., for initial referral to evaluation and placement).

Response: No change has been made. The Office of Education has elected to impose very few absolute timelines in the regulations for this part, because of the potential administrative and legal problems they can cause. Imposing timelines can actually delay the provision of a service (for example, if the time periods are regarded as both minimum and maximum times for implementing a procedure).

A child should be evaluated as soon as possible following referral. Any undue delay in providing the evaluation would raise the question of the State and local educational agencies' compliance with sections 121a.128 and 121a.220 (identification and evaluation of all handicapped children).

Comment: Some commenters requested clarification regarding whether a reevaluation is needed, as required by proposed section 121a.431 (a) (2), if the parents and agency agree that the child should be transferred from a special education program to a full time regular class placement.

Response: This specific section has been deleted in the final regulations. However, any changes in a child's placement (including a transfer to a regular class) would not be made until after a meeting is held to review the child's individualized education program in accordance with the requirements under sections 121a.340-121a.-

349 of Subpart C. If the parents and agency agree that the child no longer needs special education, a reevaluation would not be necessary. Section 121a.531 requires an evaluation before initial placement only. Reevaluations are covered under section 121a.534.

LEAST RESTRICTIVE ENVIRONMENT

Section 612 (5) (B) of the Act requires States to establish policies and procedures to insure that "to the maximum extent appropriate, handicapped children * * * are educated with nonhandicapped children * * *." The regulations for implementing this provision are set out in sections 121a.550-121a.556 of Subpart E.

A new paragraph was added to section 121a.550 which requires the State to insure that all public agencies establish and implement procedures in accordance with the requirements of this subpart. In addition, a new section, entitled "Nonacademic settings" was added. This section is taken from a new requirement in the section 504 regulations (45 CFR Part 84, § 84.34).

GENERAL (§ 121a.550)

Comment: A number of commenters requested that provisions be made for special support in the regular classroom in order to accommodate handicapped children (e.g., including reducing the pupil-teacher ratio and assigning aides to the room).

Response: No change was made, since the statute already authorizes the use of supplementary aids and services as a means of enabling a handicapped child to be educated with nonhandicapped children.

CONTINUUM OF ALTERNATIVE PLACEMENTS (§ 121a.551)

Comment: Many commenters responded to this requirement. Some felt that terms other than "continuum" should be used (e.g., "range of programs" and "variety of services"). A large number of commenters felt that "continuum" carried negative connotations (e.g., statements were made that the concept undermines the ideals of Pub. L. 94-142, that it implies best-to-worst, etc.). Other commenters felt that it discriminated against residential or private schools, and suggested that efforts be made to counteract this bias.

Response: No change has been made in this section. The term "continuum," as with "least restrictive environment" (LRE), is commonly used by agencies, advocates, and parents. However, there is nothing to prohibit an agency from using terms such as those included above in administering these provisions.

As with "LRE," the term that is used is not as important as the basic provision and how that provision is implemented. The purpose of a continuum is to be able to accommodate to differences between handicapped children in terms of the degree of special assistance they need to receive a free appropriate public education. This matter was dealt with directly in the June 26, 1975 Report of the House of Representatives on HR 7217 (H. Rept. No. 94-332, p. 9):

The Committee understands the importance of providing educational services to each handicapped child according to his or her individual needs. These needs may entail instruction to be given in varying environments, i.e., hospital, home, school or institution. The Committee urges that where possible and where most beneficial to the child, special educational services be provided in a classroom situation. An optimal situation, of course, would be one in which the child is placed in a regular classroom. The Committee recognizes that this is not always the most beneficial place of instruction. No child should be denied an educational opportunity; therefore, H.R. 7217 expands special educational services to be pro-

vided in hospitals, in the home, and in institutions.

When it is clear that, because of the nature or severity of a child's handicap, the child must be educated in a setting other than the regular class, it is appropriate to implement such a placement. However, the LRE provision is also designed as a rights provision to protect against indiscriminate placement of a child in a separate facility solely because the child is handicapped and not because special education is needed in that type of setting.

Even wtih respect to severely handicapped children, it may be possible to meet the "regular education setting" goal by having a separate class or separate wing in a regular school building.

PLACEMENTS (§ 121a.552)

Comment: Many commenters were concerned that there may be an overzealous implementation of the LRE provision without regard to the needs of individual handicapped or nonhandicapped children.

Response: No substantive change has been made in this section, because the Office of Education feels that the section includes necessary safeguards to insure protection against the above concerns. With respect to those concerns, the overriding rule is that each child's placement must be determined annually and be based on his or her individualized education program.

With respect to concerns about the harmful effect of placing handicapped children in regular classes, the analysis of the section 504 regulations indicates: "* * * it should be stressed that, where a handicapped child is so disruptive in a regular classroom that the education of other students is significantly impaired, the needs of the handicapped child cannot be met in that environment. Therefore regular placement would not be appropriate to his or her needs * * *" (45 CFR Part 84—Appendix, paragraph 24)

Comment: A commenter requested that a new provision be added which requires State and local educational agencies to utilize community-based early childhood development programs for 3-5 year old handicapped children. The main intent of the new provision is "aimed solely at assuring maximum appropriate mainstreaming."

Response: No change was made in the section. The existing provisions are considered to be adequate to cover the intent of this request.

CONFIDENTIALITY OF INFORMATION NOTICE TO PARENTS (§ 121a.561)

Comment: Commenters asked that the detailed content of the notice requirements be deleted as excessive.

Response: No change has been made. The Office of Education believes the provisions require that States provide necessary information to inform parents about the type of information collected about handicapped children to meet the requirements of this part.

ACCESS RIGHTS (§ 121a.562)

Comment: Commenters requested that this section be expanded to require that access to records be given in no case less than five days prior to meetings to develop individualized education programs or any hearing and to permit authorized representatives of the parent to inspect the record. A commenter felt the 45-day outside time limitation could be misinterpreted to mean an agency need not comply at all after 45 days from the date of the request.

Response: Language has been added to make it clear that an agency must comply with a request for access before any meeting regarding an individualized education program. This will help insure that interested parents are able to familiarize themselves with their child's records prior to any meeting

and be able to participate more knowledgeably. The prohibition against unnecessary delay places an obligation on the agency to make the records available in a timely manner so that the Office of Education does not believe it is necessary to specify a specific time limitation. Section 121a.562 has been amended to give parents the right to have an authorized representative inspect their child's education records.

The 45-day time limitation is not subject to the misinterpretation the commenter fears. This language is from the Family Educational Rights and Privacy Act, section 438 of the General Education Provisions Act (specifically section 432 (a) (1) (A)), to which these regulations are tied (by statute).

FEES (§ 121a.566)

Comment: A commenter felt the first copy of a record should be given free upon request from the parents.

Response: No change has been made. The prohibition against charging a fee if it would effectively prevent the parents from inspecting and reviewing the record is based on a requirement in the Family Educational Rights and Privacy Act, to which these regulations are limited by statute (section 612 (2) (C)). Agencies may of course adopt policies of making copies available free of charge and are encouraged to do so.

HEARING PROCEDURES (§ 121a.570)

Comment: A commenter requested clarification of who conducts a hearing.

Response: The section states that the procedures under § 99.22 (the hearing procedures in the regulations for the Family Educational Rights and Privacy Act) be used. Section 99.22 (b) states the hearing may be conducted by any party, including an official of the educational agency or institution, who does not have a direct interest in the outcome of the hearing.

CONSENT (§ 121a.571)

Comment: Commenters requested that "advanced students," "persons acting as practicum advisors," and researchers be given access to records without consent.

Response: No change has been made. The Family Educational Rights and Privacy Act specifically lists parties and conditions where records may be released without parental consent.

SAFEGUARDS (§ 121a.572)

Comment: A commenter requested a list of positions rather than a list of names of employees who may have access to personally identifiable information.

Response: The requirement has been modified to require a list of names and positions to more fully inform parents and the public of the categories of individuals given access to data as well as the specific individuals who may have access.

DESTRUCTION OF INFORMATION (§ 121a.573)

Comment: A number of commenters were concerned about the destruction requirements. The principle concern was that detailed records might be needed by the handicapped individuals to show proof of need for further services from other agencies. One recommendation was that the parent and child be notified of the existence of the records at the time of graduation and informed that they would be destroyed only upon request of the parent or child. Another commenter suggested that records be maintained, but that parents be given the option to have them destroyed.

Response: The requirement has been revised to permit the parents to request that the information be destroyed and to require the public agency to inform the parents of the destruction option and their right to have the records destroyed upon request. The notice would normally be given at the time a child graduates or otherwise leaves the agency. The purpose of the destruction option is to insure that nonessential records about a child's behavior, performance, and abilities, which may possibly by stigmatizing and are highly personal, are not kept after they are no longer needed for educational purposes. Destruction of these records is the best protection against improper or unauthorized disclosures. However, the handicapped child or his or her parents may need certain records for other purposes (such as proof of eligibility for benefits).

Comment: Commenters asked that notice be given to a child who has reached the age of majority.

Response: No change has been made. Section 121a.574 requires the State educational agency to have policies and procedures regarding children's privacy rights. Where education records are maintained by an agency covered under the Family Educational Rights and Privacy Act, these rights must include transfer of the rights of parents to the child when he or she reaches 18 or the post-secondary education level.

Other Changes: The regulations have been revised to make it clear that the records covered under this Act are the same as the type of records covered under the Family Educational Rights and Privacy Act. Consistency in coverage is necessary to avoid undue administrative burdens on public agencies covered by both laws.

OFFICE OF EDUCATION PROCEDURES

General: The requirements in these sections largely repeated the statute. Perhaps for this reason, few comments were received on the Office of Education procedures.

WAIVER OF REQUIREMENT REGARDING SUPPLEMENTING AND SUPPLANTING WITH PART B FUNDS
(§ 121a.589)

Comment: A commenter requested that the special study to determine if a waiver of the requirement should be granted include a review of whether grievance procedures are operational. Other commenters disagreed on the need for this study.

Response: A requirement has been added to have the study cover the adequacy of the State's due process procedures, as this is an important part of insuring that grievances are heard and to determine if parents and other parties are satisfied with the adequacy of the State's programs for handicapped children.

WITHHOLDING PAYMENTS (§ 121a.590)

Comment: Commenters asked for definitions of "substantial compliance" and "failure to comply." Commenters also urged that the Office of Education, the Office for Civil Rights, and Departmental audit officials apply the same criteria.

Response: No change has been made. The Office of Education believes these terms will have to be defined on a case-by-case basis.

The Office of Education and the Office for Civil Rights will coordinate and cooperate in enforcing requirements under this Part and Part 84 (the regulations for section 504 of the Rehabilitation Act of 1973) where identical requirements are involved. The Office of Education will make every effort to insure that auditing officials understand and apply any criteria used by program officials.

SUBPART F—STATE ADMINISTRATION

This subpart has been expanded with requirements set out under the major headings: State Educational Agency Responsibilities, Use of Funds, and State Advisory Panel.

STATE EDUCATIONAL AGENCY RESPONSIBILITIES

Provisions on State educational agency responsibilities have been redrafted (and relocated from proposed section 121a.34) in response to comments, to better summarize general administrative and supervisory responsibilities in section 612 (6) and other sections of the Act. A section on complaint procedures, which was included in previous regulations for Part B (prior section 121a.14) and inadvertently not included in the proposed regulations has been added.

Comment: Commenters requested addition of a new section on State educational agencies' responsibilities for monitoring, evaluation, and enforcement activities to insure compliance throughout the State with the requirements of this part. The commenters made specific suggestions for implementing such a section, including collection of data, conduct of on-site visits, audit of fund utilization, comparison of written individualized education programs with programs actually provided, meetings with parents and parent groups, public hearings, development of detailed criteria for evaluating program quality and effectiveness, and detailed procedures for enforcing requirements against noncomplying agencies.

Response: A new section has been added to require each State educational agency to develop procedures and specific timelines for monitoring and evaluating public agencies involved in the education of handicapped children. These are minimal requirements. Adoption of the other suggestions made by the commenters is encouraged but not required.

ALLOWABLE COSTS (§ 121a.621)

Comment: A number of commenters requested that the limitation on State administrative funds be raised and that provisions be added to allow local educational agencies to use funds for administrative costs.

Response: No change has been made on the State limit as it is a statutory limitation.

Comment: Commenters requested that the regulations require each State educational agency to use its funds for specific purposes. One recommendation was that ten percent of the administrative funds be used to train persons in local communities to assist and represent parents and to prepare and disseminate to parents information about their rights under these regulations. Another was that they be used to disseminate instructional material.

Response: No change has been made. The Office of Education does not believe it is appropriate to dictate to States how to use their limited administrative funds.

STATE ADVISORY PANEL ESTABLISHMENT (§ 121a.650)

Comment: One commenter recommended that local panels be required.

Response: No change has been made. The statute only requires a State advisory panel. A State may, of course, decide to establish local panels.

MEMBERSHIP (§ 121a.651)

Comment: A substantial number of commenters requested additions to the list of representatives to be included on the panel, including professional groups, legal advocacy groups, and employees of State and local agencies. Some commenters recommended that handicapped individuals or their parents make up specific percentages of the panel.

Response: A provision has been added to make it clear that a State may expand the advisory panel to include additional persons in the groups listed (which are statutory) and representatives of other groups. The Office of Education does not believe it is appropriate to prescribe specific percentages, as the States should have some discretion to determine the proper mix of representatives. A comment has been added to indicate factors a State may consider in determining balanced membership of the panel.

ADVISORY FUNCTIONS AND ADVISORY PANEL PROCEDURES (§§121a.652-121a.653)

Comment: Commenters recommended that the regulations indicate that the panel must comment publicly on the State annual program plan as well as on any rules and regulations regarding education of handicapped children, review annual evaluations, and act as ombudspersons to hear complaints.

Response: A change has been made to require the panel to comment on the annual program plan. The annual program plan is an extremely important document and this addition makes it clear that the advisory panel must be involved in reviewing it. The other recommendations are legitimate activities but not ones the Federal government believes should be required by these regulations at this time.

Comment: Commenters requested that the regulations provide that panel members be reimbused for reasonable and necessary expenses for attending meetings and performing duties.

Response: This change has been made. It is reasonable to require reimbursement for expenses so that persons will be able to participate without financial sacrifice.

SUBPART G—ALLOCATIONS OF FUNDS; REPORTS

ALLOCATIONS

This major section of Subpart G is entirely statutory; therefore, there are no comments of substance on which to respond.

REPORTS—ANNUAL REPORT OF CHILDREN
SERVED (§§ 121a.750-121a.754)

The following comments were received regarding the annual report by the States of the number of children receiving special education and related services. This report is the basis for each State's allocation of funds under Part B, and serves as a mechanism for the Commissioner to meet some of his reporting requirements to Congress under section 618 of the Act. Some commenters recommended changes that would require amendment of the Act. These have not been summarized except where further explanation seemed to be useful.

AMOUNT OF INFORMATION REQUIRED IN THE REPORT

Comment: Commenters varied in their views on what information should be included in the report. It was suggested that additional information be collected for compliance purposes. Objections were made to the requirement for reporting information by disability category, and for reporting the 0-2 year old population. On the other hand, some commenters recommended that additional categories be added to the report, particularly for deaf-blind children and for multihandicapped children.

Response: Two categories of handicapped children have been added to the report—one for multihandicapped children and one for deaf-blind children. These terms are defined in section 121a.5 of Subpart A. No other changes have been made on the amount of information to be reported.

The additional categories should help to insure that no handicapped child is counted more than once, since the States will not have to decide in which of two or more disability categories to count, a multihandicapped child. The changes conform to existing reporting requirements used by the States.

The annual report of children served is not a compliance document. It is only used to determine each State's allocation and to assist the Commissioner in meeting his reporting requirements to the Congress under section 618. Under section 611 of the Act, allocations are based on the number of handicapped children in each State receiving special education and related services. Compliance with requirements such as "least restrictive environment" will be achieved through other mechanisms, including the State's annual program plan, the local educational agency's application, and monitoring by the State educational agency and the Office of Education.

As explained in the preamble to the proposed rules published in the FEDERAL REGISTER on September 8, 1976, the report requirements are the minimum needed by the Commissioner to carry out the Act. (See 41 FR 37814.) While the Commissioner is concerned about the possible harmful effects of "labeling" children, the Act requires that the Commissioner report a substantial amount of information, to Congress by disability category. For this reason, and for the other reasons stated in the September 8, 1976, FEDERAL REGISTER, there appears to be no workable alternative to retaining the categories in the States' annual reports. The various disability categories, as well as the requirements to use them in the Commissioner's reports to the Congress, are statutory.

WHO MAY BE COUNTED

Comment: Commenters disagreed as to whether handicapped children should be counted if their special education is paid for solely from private sources or solely from Federal funds (such as children living on military bases). Some thought that only publicly-funded special education should qualify, while others argued that since all children have a right to a free appropriate public education the source of funding (other than the parent) should not matter.

Response: Section 121a.753 has been amended to provide that handicapped children (including such children in Head Start or other preschool programs) may be counted only if they (1) are enrolled in a school or program which is operated or supported by a public agency, and (2) receive special education that meets State standards.

A State may not count a child whose special education is paid for solely by the Federal government, unless the child is in one of the age groups 3-5 or 18-21, and there are no local or State funds available for nonhandicapped children in that age group.

Children funded solely by the Federal government would include Indian children whose special education is paid for solely by the Federal government, as well as children on military bases whose education is paid for solely with Federal funds. This rule is consistent with the requirement that a free appropriate public education (FAPE) be made available by the State to each handicapped child. Parents are not required to take advantage of FAPE. If they choose to educate their child outside of the public school system, even though FAPE is available, the State has discharged its responsibility. However, by the same token, the child should not be counted by the State for its allocation if the child is not being provided special education at public expense. The same reasoning applies to Indian children and other children who receive their special education from the Federal government. The rule should serve as an encouragement to States to provide services to all handicapped children, however, since any child provided special education from State or local funds may be counted.

Comment: Two other provisions in the regulations were objected to by commenters. The first of these provided that handicapped children "enrolled" in schools to receive special education could be counted as receiving special education. These commenters felt that enrollment did not guarantee actual receipt of services. The second provision stated, in essence, that a child who receives special education may be counted, but not a child who receives only "related services." This was viewed as an overly restrictive reading of the Act.

Response: No change has been made in the regulations. While no system is perfect, enrollment is a legitimate way of determining the number of handicapped children receiving special education on October 1 and on February 1, the two dates on which the Act requires the count of children served. It would not be practical to make an actual head count of children in classrooms and other facilities where services are provided.

With respect to children who only receive "related services," this is governed by statutory language. "Related services" are only those "required to assist a handicapped child to benefit from special education." (Section 602 (17) of the Act.) If a child does not need special education, there can be no "related services," as that term is defined in the Act. However, section 121a.14 permits a State to define certain services as "special education," if those services are "specially designed instruction to meet the unique needs of a handicapped child." (This is taken from the definition of "special education" in section 602 (16) of the Act.)

REALLOCATION OF LOCAL EDUCATIONAL AGENCY FUNDS (§ 121a.708)

Comment: Commenters requested criteria be added for when funds may be reallocated.

Response: No criteria have been added as determinations will be made on a case-by-case basis.

Identification, location, evaluation — § 121a.128 (b) (5).
Individualized education programs — § 121a.130 (b) (2).
Least restrictive environment—§ 121a.556.
Private school children — § 121a.402 (a).
State educational agency responsibility —§ 121a.601.

NONDISCRIMINATION

Annual program requirement—§ 121a.150.
Evaluation materials and procedures—§ 121a.530.
Local application requirement—§ 121a.239.
Nonacademic services—§ 121a.306.
Private school children—§ 121a.458.
Program options—§ 121a.305.
Testing materials and procedures — § 121a.530.

NOTICE

Confidentiality of information — §§ 121a.561, 121a.573.
Individualized education program meeting—§ 121a.345.
Initiation or change of identification, evaluation, placement, or free appropriate public education—§§ 121a.504-121a.505.
Notice of opportunity for a hearing—See: Hearings.
Notice of procedural safeguards — § 121a.505.
Public notice of withholding payments —§ 121a. 592.

PERSONNEL DEVELOPMENT

Annual program plan requirement—§ 121a.139.
Comprehensive system of personnel development—§§ 121a.380-121a.387.
Included in State support services—§ 121a.370.
Least restrictive environment—§ 121a.555.
Local application requirement—§ 121a.224.

Personnel needs—§§ 121a.126; 121a.228.
Preservice training—§ 121a.321.
Trained personnel for evaluation materials—§ 121a.532.
Training regarding confidentiality of information—§ 121a.572.
Use of Part B funds for training—§§ 121a.321, 121a.322.

PHYSICAL EDUCATION

Included in special education—§ 121a.14.
Required—§ 121a.307.

PLACEMENTS

See: Evaluation.
Least Restrictive Environment.
Private schools.

PRIORITIES

See: Evaluation.
Identification, Location, Evaluation.
Annual program plan requirement—§ 121a.127.
Definitions:
First priority children—§ 121a.320 (a).
Second priority children — § 121a.320 (b).
General requirements — §§ 121a.320-121a.324.
Local application requirement—§ 121a.225.
State direct and support services — § 121a.370.

PRIVATE SCHOOL CHILDREN

Annual program plan requirement—§ 121a.140.
Confidentiality of information—§ 121a.560.
Cost of residential placement—§ 121a.302.
Handicapped children placed or referred by public agencies—§§ 121a.400-121a.403.
Handicapped children not placed or referred by public agencies—§§ 121a.450-121a.460.

Free appropriate public education—§§ 121a.122; 121a.300.

Full educational opportunity goal—§§ 121a.125; 121a.222.

Hearing decisions—§§ 121a.512; 121a.583.

Individualized education programs—§§ 121a.342; 121a.343.

Public participation in the annual program plan—§ 121a.280-121a.284.

Reevaluation—§ 121a.534.

Report of children served—§ 121a.750-121a.754.

State monitoring of public agencies—§ 121a.601.

State review of hearing decision — § 121a.512.

TRAINING

See: Personnel Development.

USE OF PART B FUNDS

Allocation formulas:
Consolidated applications—§§ 121a.190-121a.191.
Entitlements—§§ 121a.700-121a.710.

Annual program plan requirements—§§ 121a.148; 121a.149.

Department of the Interior (Indian children)—§ 121a.262.

Excess costs—§§ 121a.182-121a.186.

Local application requirement—§ 121a.238.

State and local educational agencies:
Free appropriate public education—§§ 121a.301-121a.302.
Full educational opportunity goal—§ 121a.304 (b).
Priorities—§§ 121a.320-121a.324.
Private school children—§§ 121a.450-121a.460.

State educational agencies:
Allowable costs—§ 121a.621.
Federal funds for State administration—§ 121a.620.
Matching—§ 121a.371.
State advisory panel—§ 121a.652.
Use of local allocation for direct services—§§ 121a.360-121a.361.
Use of State educational agency

allocation for direct and support services—§ 121a.370.

Supplanting—§§ 121a.230; 121a.372; 121a.589.

Training—See: Personnel Development.

5. A new Part 121m is added to read as follows:

PART 121m—INCENTIVE GRANTS

Sec.
121m.1 Scope; purpose.
121m.2 General provisions regulations.
121m.3 Eligibility.
121m.4 Application.
121m.5 Application contents.
121m.6 Participation by children not counted under Part B of the Act.
121m.8 Excess costs.
121m.9 Administration.
121m.10 Annual evaluation report.

AUTHORITY: Sec. 619 of Pub. L. 91-230, as amended, 89 Stat. 793 (20 U.S.C. 1419), unless otherwise noted.

§ 121m.1 Scope; purpose.

(a) This part applies to assistance under section 619 of the Act.

(b) The Commissioner awards a grant to each State which provides special education and related services to handicapped children ages three, four, or five.

(c) The State shall use funds provided under this part to give special education and related services to handicapped children in the age groups named in paragraph (b) of this section.

(d) The terms "special education" and "related services" have the meanings defined in § 121a.12 and § 121a.13 of this chapter.
(20 U.S.C. 1419 (c).)

§ 121m.2 General provisions regulations.

Assistance under this part is subject to the requirements in Parts 100, 100b, 100c, and 121 of this chapter (including definitions and fiscal, administrative, property management, and other matters).

(20 U.S.C. 1419).

§ 121m.3   Eligibility.

A State is eligible to receive a grant if:

(a) The Commissioner has approved its annual program plan under Part 121a of this chapter; and

(b) The State provides special education and related services to any handicapped children aged three, four, or five.

(20 U.S.C. 1419 (a).)

§ 121m.4   Application.

To receive funds under this part, a State must submit an application to the Commissioner through its State educational agency.

(20 U.S.C. 1419 (b).)

§ 121m.5   Application contents.

An application must include the following material:

(a) A description of the State's goals and objectives for meeting the educational needs of handicapped children ages three through five. These goals and objectives must be consistent with the State's full educational opportunity goal under § 121a.123 of this chapter.

(b) A description of the objectives to be supported by the grant in sufficient detail to determine what will be achieved with the grant.

(c) A description of the activities to be supported by the grant. The activities must be related to the objectives under paragraph (b) of this section and must be described in sufficient detail to determine how the grant will be used.

(d) A description of the impact the proposed activities will have on handicapped children ages three through five. This description must include evidence that the proposed activities are of sufficient size, scope, and quality to warrant the amount of the expenditure. The application must indicate the number of children to be served and the number of handicapped children who will be benefitted indirectly. If children are to be benefitted indirectly, there must be a rationale that demonstrates the benefit.

(e) The number of local educational agencies or intermediate educational units, and the number and names of other agencies which will provide contractual services under the grant, the activities they will carry out, and the reasons for selecting these agencies.

(f) The dollar amounts that will be spent for each major activity described.

(g) A description of the procedures the State will use to evaluate the extent to which the activities met the objectives described under paragraph (b) of this section.

(20 U.S.C. 1419 (b).)

§ 121m.6   Amount of grant.

(a) The amount of a grant is $300 multiplied by the average number of children ages three through five counted during the current school year under §§ 121a.750-121a.754 of this chapter.

(b) If appropriated funds are less than enough to pay in full the grants under this part, the amount of each grant is ratably reduced.

(20 U.S.C. 1419 (a), (d).)

§ 121m.7   Allowable expenditures.

(a) The State educational agency may use funds under this part to give special education and related services to handicapped children ages three through five who are not counted under §§ 121a.750-121a.754 of this chapter if the State educational agency insures that those children have all of the rights afforded under part 121a of this chapter.

(b) The State educational agency may use up to five percent of its grant for the costs of administering the funds provided under this part.

(20 U.S.C. 1419 (c).)

Comment. In carrying out the provisions of this part some activities are considered particularly appropriate for the use of these funds: (1) Providing parents with child development information; (2) assisting parents in the understanding of the special needs of their handicapped child; (3) providing parent counseling and parent training, where appropriate, to enable parents to work more effectively with their children; (4) providing essential diagnosis and assessment; (5) providing transportation essential to the delivery of services; (6) providing speech therapy, occupational therapy, or physical therapy.

§ 121m.8   Excess costs.

(a) If local or State funds are available to pay for the education of non-handicapped children of the same age as the handicapped children served with funds under this part, funds equal to that amount must also be made available for these handicapped children.

(b) If no local or State funds are available for nonhandicapped children of the same age, funds under this part may be used to pay for all of the costs directly attributable to the education of the handicapped children.

(20 U.S.C. 1419 (c).)

§ 121m.9   Administration.

(a) The State educational agency shall administer the funds provided under this part.

(b) The State educational agency may use the funds itself, or may contract with local educational agencies, intermediate educational units, or other agencies.

(20 U.S.C. 1419 (a).)

§ 121m.10   Annual evaluation report.

(a) Within 90 days after the end of the grant period, the State educational agency shall submit a report to the Commissioner on the activities carried out under this part during that period.

(b) The report must contain:

(1) The results of the evaluation under § 121m.5 (g), and

(2) In brief narrative form, the impact that these funds have had on the State's educational services to handicapped children ages three, four, and five.

(20 U.S.C. 1419 (c).)

[FR Doc. 77-24033 Filed 8-22-77; 8:45 am]

BIBLIOGRAPHY AND ORGANIZATIONS

BIBLIOGRAPHY

A Continuing Summary of Pending & Completed Litigation Regarding the Education of Handicapped Children. Abeson, A., & Bolick, N., Eds., Council for Exceptional Children, 1974.

A Directory of Organizations of the Handicapped in the United States. Massachusetts Council of Organizations of the Handicapped, 41 Woodglen Rd., Hyde Park, MA 02136.
A geographically arranged listing of self-help organizations of the physically and mentally handicapped throughout the country.

A Guide to Sources of Educational Information. Woodbury, M., Information Resources Press, 2100 M. Street, N.W., Washington, D.C. 20037, 1976.

A Primer on Due Process. Abeson, Bolic, & Haas. Council for Exceptional Children, 1920 Association Drive, Reston, VA, 1975.

A State Director Looks at the Education of Pupils with Exceptional Needs in 1985. Melcher, John. *Journal of Educational Finance,* Vol. I, No. 3, Winter, 1976.

A Summary of Selected Legislation Relating to the Handicapped 1975-76. U.S. Department of Health, Education, & Welfare, Washington, D.C. 20201: U.S. Govt. Print. Office (May, 1977).

Advocacy Manual for Parents of Handicapped Children. U.S. Government Printing Office, Supt. of Documents, Washington, D.C. 20000, 1976.

American Annals of the Deaf. Directory issue (April or May of each year, $5.00). Conference of Executives of American School for the Deaf, 5034 Wisconsin Avenue, N.W., Washington, D.C. 20016.
Lists speech and learning facilities serving the deaf, including public day schools and classes, denominational and private schools in the U.S., schools and classes.

Ballentine's Law Dictionary. Ballentine, James A. Third edition. Lawyers Cooperative Publishing Co., San Francisco, CA, 1969.
Definitions for the layman and nonspecialist.

Barriers and Bridges. California Advisory Council on Vocational Education, 708 Tenth Street, Sacramento, CA 95184.

Black's Law Dictionary, Black, Henry Campbell, Revised fourth edition. West Publishing Co., 1968.
A scholarly treatment of legal terms. Also contains the "Code of Professional Responsibility."

Child Abuse Intervention & Treatment, Ebeling, N. & Hill, D., Eds., Publishing Sciences Group, Inc., 1976.

Children, Parents and School Records, Rioux, J. & S. Sandow, National Committee for Citizens in Education, Wilde Lake Village Green, Columbia, MD 21044 (1974).

Children's Rights and the Mental Health Professions, Koocher, Gerald P., Ed., Wiley-Interscience, 1976.

Consent Handbook, American Association on Mental Deficiency, 5101 Wisconsin Avenue, N.W., Washington, D.C., 20016.

Consumer Protection in a Nutshell, Epstein, David G., West Co., St. Paul, MN., 1976.

Correctional Treatment in Community Settings, A Report of Current Research, National Institute of Mental Health, Crime & Delinquency Issues, 1974.

Directory for Exceptional Children, Porter Sargent, Publisher, 11 Beacon St., Boston, MA 02108. 7th Edition, 1972.
Concise descriptions of more than 3600 schools, homes, hospitals, treatment and training centers and psychiatric and guidance clinics includes information on: services offered, admission policies, cost and specialized instruction and care for the retarded, maladjusted or physically handicapped. Classifies facilities by special needs they serve.

Directory of Educational Facilities for the Learning Disabled. Association for Children with Learning Disabilities, 5th edition, Academic Therapy Publications, 1539 Fourth St., San Rafael, CA 94901 (1973).

Directory of Facilities for the Learning Disabled and Handicapped, Ellingson, Careth and Cass, James. Harper and Row Publishers, 10 E. 53rd St., NY, NY, 10022.
This directory includes analytical descriptions of diagnostic facilities, as well as descriptions of remedial, therapeutic and developmental programs.

Directory of Federal Programs for the Handicapped. Council for Exceptional Children, 1920 Association Drive, Reston, VA.

Directory of Residential Facilities for the Mentally Retarded. American Association on Mental Deficiency, 5201 Connecticut Avenue, N.W., Washington, D.C. 20015.
A national directory of public and private facilities (schools, hospitals, homes) in the U.S. and Canada. Also includes a list of state authorities for licensing private residential facilities and an index of administrative offices of residential facilities.

Directory of Organizations Interested in the Handicapped. People to People Program, Suite 610, La Salle Bldg., Connecticut Ave. & L. St., Washington, D.C. 20036 (1974).
Contains descriptions of the organization and programs of more than

sixty governmental and private agencies, as well as information on the utilization of volunteer workers and international programs.

Due Process and the Exceptional Child: A Guide for Parents. The Education Law Center, Inc., 1976.

Educating Children with Learning Disabilities: Selected Readings. Frierson, Edward, & Bache, Walter B., Eds., New York. Appleton-Century Crofts, 1967.

Education & Training of the Mentally Retarded. Council for Exceptional Children, 1920 Association Drive, Reston, VA 22091.

Encyclopedia of Associations, Fisk, Margaret, Ed., Vol. 1, National Organizations of the U.S., Detroit, MI, Gale Research Co., 1977.

Ethical & Legal Issues in the Practice of School Psychology. Temple University, Philadelphia, PA, 1975.

ERIC Clearinghouse on Early Childhood Education, 805 W. Pennsylvania Avenue, University of Illinois, Urbana, Illinois 61801.

ERIC Clearinghouse on Handicapped & Gifted, CEC Information Center, 1920 Association Drive, Reston, VA 22091.

ERIC Processing & Reference Facility, 4833 Rugby Avenue, Suite 303, Bethesda, MD 20014.

Exceptional Child. Council for Exceptional Children, 1920 Association Drive, Reston, VA 22091.

Films and Filmstrips on Legal and Law Related Subjects, American Bar Association, Division of Communications, ABA Press, Chicago, Illinois, 1974.

Financing Educational Services for the Handicapped, Bernstein, Hartman, Kirst, Marshall, Council for Exceptional Children, 1976.

Freedom of Information Clearinghouse, P.O. Box 19367, Washington, D.C. 20036.

Handbook on the Legal Rights of Handicapped People. U.S. Government Printing Office, Supt. of Documents, Washington, D.C. 20402, 1976. Handicapped citizens have fundamental rights guaranteed them by law This book outlines these rights as they exist in the District of Columbia, Maryland, and Virginia, in such areas as employment, hospitalization and medical care, education, and transportation.

Hearing Officers Handbook, Division of Special Education, Pennsylvania Department of Education, 1976.

Insanity Inside Out, Donaldson, K., Crown Publishers, Inc., 1976.

Insight: The Council for Exceptional Children Government Report. Ballard, Joseph, Ed., The Council for Exceptional Children, Reston, VA, January, 1976.

Instructional Materials for the Handicapped: Birth Through Early Childhood. Thorum, A.R. Olumpus Publishing Co., Salt Lake City, Utah, 1976.

Integrated Education. Healey, William C., *The Volta Review,* Washington, D.C., Alexander Graham Bell Association for the Deaf, Inc., May, 1976.
Key Federal Regulations Affecting the Handicapped, 1975-1976. U.S. Department of Health, Education and Welfare, Washington, D.C. 20201, U.S. Govt. Print. Office (Sept. 1977).
Law and the Handicapped, Science & Children, March 1976.
Law and the Mental Health Professions: Friction at the Interface. Barton, Walter E. and Sanborn, Charlotte, Editors. International Universities Press, 1977.
Law and the School Psychologist: Challenge & Opportunity, Cardon, Bartell & Peter Kuriloff, Human Sciences Press, New York, 1975.
Law and the Sovereigns of Childhood, Coons, John E., *Phi Delta Kappan,* Vol. 58, No. 1, Sept. 1976.
Law Books in Print, Jacobstein, J. Myron and Meira G. Pimsleur. Three Volumes, Glanville Publishers, 1971.
   Listings by author/title, subject and publishers of books covering legal topics.
Law Books Published, Glanville Publishers, 1970. Cumulative supplements to *Law Books in Print.*
Law, Language and Communication, Probert, Walter, & Thomas, Charles. Thomas Publishing Co, Springfield, Illinois, 1972.
Legal Challenges to Behavior Modification, Martin, R., Research Press, 2612 N. Mattis, Champaign, Illinois 61820.
Legal Change for the Handicapped Through Litigation. Council for Exceptional Children, 1920 Association Drive, Reston VA 22091.
Legal Research in a Nutshell. Cohen Morris L., West Publishing Co., 1971.
   A short concise guide to basic research in law.
National Directories Listing Agencies or Professional Personnel That May Provide Services for the Handicapped. The Library of National Easter Seal Society for Crippled Children and Adults Revised March, 1975. 2023 W. Ogden Avenue, Chicago, Illinois 60612.
Newsfront, Angele, Thomas M., Ed., Exceptional Children, Council of Exceptional Children: Reston, VA, March-May, 1976.
Opening Closed Doors: Deinstitutionalization of Disabled Individuals, Braddock, D., Council for Exceptional Children, 1920 Association Drive, Reston, VA. 22091 (1977).
Parliamentary Procedures: Tool of Leadership. Broadrick, King. *Phi Delta Kappan,* Eighth and Union, Box 789, Bloomington, Illinois 47401.
Past & Future Impact of Court Decisions in Special Education, Turnbull, H. Rutherford. *Phi Delta Kappan,* April, 1978.
Psychiatry of the Law. Hoch, Paul H. & Joseph Zubin, Grune & Stratton, New York, 1955.
Psychiatry for Lawyers: Revised Edition. Watson, Andrew S., International Universities Press, New York, 1978.

Public Law 94-142. Washington, D.C.: 94th Congress, November 29, 1975.

Public Policy and the Education of Exceptional Children, Weintraub, Abeson, Ballard, LaVor, Eds., Council for Exceptional Children, 1976.

Rights of Parents in the Education of Their Children. Published by National Committee for Citizens in Education, Suite 410, Wide Lake Village Green, Columbia, Maryland 21044.

The book is designed to "demystify" the laws affecting parents and their children, so they can assert their rights and bring violations to the attention of school officials.

School Psychology Role and Function, Professional Practice & Professional Concerns: Selected Bibliography 1970-1975, Fagan, T., Western Illinois University, 1975.

School Suspensions: Are They Helping Children? Children's Defense Fund, 1520 New Hampshire, N.W., Washington, D.C. 20036 (1975).

Service Directory of National Organizations Voluntary and Governmental. Issued biennially. $8.00. The National Assembly for Social Policy and Development, 345 E. 46th Street, New York, New York 10017.

Lists 121 Agencies, of which 77 are associated national organizations with the National Assembly. Reports the purposes of the organizations, kinds of services they give and the channels through which these services may be obtained by local communities.

Special Education: Past, Present and Future, Reynolds, Maynard C. and Rosen, Sylvia W., The Educational Forum, Kappa Delta Pi, Columbus, OH, May, 1976.

State Law and Education of Handicapped Children: Issues and Recommendations. Council for Exceptional Children, 1920 Association Drive, Reston, VA 22091.

Students' Right to Due Process: Professional Discretion & Liability Under Goss and Wood. Anson, Ronald J. & Peter J. Kuriloff, Eds., Educational Resources Division, 1975.

Teaching of Exceptional Children. Council for Exceptional Children, 1920 Association Drive, Reston, VA 22091.

Testing and Legal Stuff. Kamin, Leon, *Journal of School Psychology,* Vol. 13 (4), 1975.

The Complete Guide to Everyday Law, Kling, S., Pyramid Books, New York, NY, 1973.

The Constitution and American Education. Morris, Arval A., West Publishing Co., 1974 (American Casebook Series).

Thorough coverage of the law of public education in the United States.

The Legal Rights of Students. Flygare, Thomas, Phi Delta Kappa Educational Foundation, Eighth & Union, Box 789, Bloomington, IN., 47401.

The Legal Rights of Teachers. Flygare, Thomas, Phi Delta Kappa, Eighth & Union, Box 789, Bloomington, IN., 47401.

The Legalization for the School Psychologists World, Kirp and Kirp, Vol. 14 (1), 1976.

The Mentally Retarded Citizen and the Law, Kindred, N. et al., Eds., President's Committee on Mentally Retarded, Free Press, A Division of MacMillan Publishing Co., Inc., New York, 1976.

The Rights of Children (2 Vols), *Harvard Educational Review, Vol. 43,* No. 4, Nov. 1973 and *Vol. 44,* No. 1, Feb. 1974.

The Schools, the Courts, and the Public Interest. Hogan, John C. Lexington Books, 1974.

Thesaurus for Exceptional Child Education, 4th edition. Reston, VA: CEC Information Center on Exceptional Children, 1975.

Selected Newsletters and Periodicals

AMICUS. (Newsletter) National Center for Law and the Handicapped, 1235 North Eddy Stret, South Bend, Indiana. 46617.

ASHA. American Speech and Hearing Association. Subscriptions to: Editor, ASHA, 9030 Old Georgetown Road, Washington, D.C. 20014. $23.00/year ($31.00 foreign). $2.50 a copy ($2.75 foreign). Monthly.

American Journal of Mental Deficiency. American Association on Mental Deficiency. Publications Office, 49 Sheridan Avenue, Albany, New York. 12210. $20.00/year; $21.00 foreign. $4.00 a copy. Bi-monthly.

Child Development Abstracts and Bibliography. University of Chicago Press. Society for Research in Child Development. 5801 Ellis Avenue, Chicago, Illinois. 60637. $15.00/year. Three issues a year.

Childhood Education. Association for Childhood Education International. 3615 Wisconsin Avenue, N.W., Washington, D.C. 20016. $18.00/year. Monthly, October-May.

Children's Rights Report. (newsletter) American Civil Liberties Union, 22 East 40th Street, New York, New York. 10016. $15.00/year. Monthly.

Closer Look. (newsletter) National Information Center for the Handicapped. Box 1492, Washington, D.C. 20013.

Crusader. United Cerebral Palsy Association, 66 East 34th Street, New York, New York. 10016. Bimonthly. Apply to Public Relations Department.

Education of the Handicapped. (newsletter) Capitol Publications, Suite G-12, 2430 Pennsylvania Avenue, N.W., Washington, D.C. 20037. $75.00/year. Weekly.

Education of the Visually Handicapped. Association for the Education of the Visually Handicapped, 919 Walnut Street, 4th Floor, Philadelphia, PA. 19107. $6.00/year. Quarterly.

Educational Rights of Handicapped Children. Research Press, 2612 N. Mattis, Champaign, Illinois 61820. $15.00/year. Six issues a year.

Exceptional Child Education Abstracts. Council for Exceptional Children, 1920 Association Drive, Reston, Virginia 22091. Quarterly.

Exceptional Children. Council for Exceptional Children, 1920 Association Drive, Reston, Virginia 22091. $20.00/year. Eight issues a year.

Focus on Exceptional Children. Love Publishing Company, 6635 East Villanova Place, Denver, Colorado. 80222. $9.50/year. Nine issues a year.

Handy-Cap Horizons. 3250 E. Oretta Drive, Indianapolis, Indiana, 46227. $3.00/year—disabled; $6.00/year—non-disabled. Quarterly.

Hearing and Speech Action. National Association of Hearing and Speech Agencies, 814 Thayer Avenue, Silver Spring, Maryland, 20910. $5.00/year. Bi-monthly.

Journal of Learning Disabilities. Executive Office, 101 East Ontario Street, Chicago, Illinois, 60611. $12.00/year, ten issues a year.

Journal of Special Education. 3515 Woodhoven Road, Philadelphia, PA. 19154. $15.00/year. Quarterly.

Journal for Special Educators of the Mentally Retarded. 107-20 125th Street, Richmond Hill, New York, NY 11419. $9.00/year. Three issues a year.

Journal of Speech and Hearing Disorders. American Speech and Hearing Association, Kenneth O. Johnson, Business Manager, 9030 Old Georgetown Road, Washington, D.C. 20014. $28.00/year. Quarterly.

Law and Behavior. Research Press, 2612 N. Mattis, Champaign, Illinois 61820. $15.00/year. Quarterly.

Mental Disability Law Reporter. American Bar Association Commission on the Mentally Disabled. 1800 M. Street, N.W., Washington, D.C. 20036. $35.00/year. Bi-monthly.

Mental Health Law Project Report. Mental Health Law Project, 1220 19th Street, N.W., Washington, D.C. 20036. Quarterly.

MR/Mental Retardation. American Association on Mental Deficiency. AAMD Publications Office, 49 Sheridan Avenue, Albany, New York, NY 12210. $22.00/year to non-members. Bi-monthly.

Programs for the Handicapped. (newsletter) U.S. Department of Health, Education and Welfare, Office of Mental Retardation Coordination, Washington, D.C. 20201. Monthly or oftener.

Psychological Abstracts. American Psychological Association, 1200 17th Street, N.W., Washington, D.C. 20036. $190.00/year. Monthly.

Special Children. American Association for Special Educators, Box 168, Fryeburg, Maine 04037. $15.00/year. Quarterly.

Teaching Exceptional Children. Council for Exceptional Children, 1920 Association Drive, Reston, Virginia 22202. $12.50/year. Quarterly.

The Deaf American. National Association of the Deaf, 814 Thayer Avenue, Silver Spring, Maryland 20910. $5.00/year.

SELECTED LIST OF ORGANIZATIONS
SERVING THE HANDICAPPED

Alcohol, Drug Abuse, Mental Health Administration. HEW Public Health Service, 5600 Fishers Lane, Rockville, Maryland, 20852.

American Academy for Cerebral Palsy. Executive Office, 122 New Hampshire Avenue, N.W., Room 1030, Washington, D.C. 20036.

American Association for the Education of the Severely/Profoundly Handicapped. P.O. Box 15287, Seattle, Washington, 98115.

American Association on Mental Deficiency. 5101 Wisconsin Avenue, N.W. Washington, D.C. 20016.

American Association of Psychiatric Services for Children. 1701 Eighteenth Street, N.W., Washington, D.C. 20009.

American Bar Association Commission on Mentally Disabled. 1800 M. Street, N.W., Washington, D.C. 20036.

American Coalition of Citizens With Disabilities. 1346 Connecticut Avenue, N.W., Washington, D.C. 20036.

American Correctional Association. 4321 Hartwick Road, College Park, Maryland, 20740.

American Foundation for the Blind. 15 W. Sixteenth Street, New York, New York, 10011.

American Personnel & Guidance Association. 1607 New Hampshire Avenue, N.W., Washington, D.C. 20009.

American Psychiatric Association Joint Information Service. 1700 Eighteenth Street, N.W., Washington, D.C. 20009.

American Psychological Association. 1200 Seventeenth Street, N.W., Washington, D.C. 20036.

American Public Welfare Association. 1155 Sixteenth Street, N.W., Suite 201, Washington, D.C. 20036.

American Speech and Hearing Association. 9030 Old Georgetown Road, Washington, D.C. 20014.

Association for Children with Learning Disabilities. 5225 Grace Street, Pittsburgh, Pennsylvania, 15236.

Big Brothers of America. 220 Suburban Station Building, Philadelphia, Pennsylvania, 19103.

Boys' Clubs of America. 771 First Avenue, New York, New York 10017.

Bureau of Education for the Handicapped. Department of Education, 400 Maryland Avenue, S.W., Washington, D.C. 20202.

Center for Child Abuse Education. University of Virginia Medical Center, Box 275, Charlottesville, Virginia 22901.

Center for Law and Education, Harvard University Larsen Hall, 14 Appian Way, Cambridge, Massachusetts, 02138.

Center for Probation Studies. P.O. Box 109, Elmwood Park, New Jersey 07407.

Center for Studies in Criminal Justice. Law School, University of Chicago, 1111 E. 60th Street, Chicago, Illinois 60637.

Child Abuse Listening Mediation. P.O. Box 718, Santa Barbara, California, 93102.

Child Development Consortium. 7315 Wisconsin Avenue, Suite 601 East, Washington, D.C. 20014.

Child Welfare League of America, 67 Irving Place, New York, New York 10003.

Child Welfare League of America, 67 Irving Place, New York, New York 10003.

Children's Defense Fund. 1520 New Hampshire Avenue, N.W., Washington, D.C. 20036, and P.O. Box 1684, Jackson, Miss. 39205.

Citizen Action Group. 133 C. Street, S.E., Washington, D.C. 20003.

"Closer Look," Bureau of Education for the Handicapped, U.S. Dept. of Health, Education, and Welfare, Box 1492, Washington, D.C. 20013.

Commission on the Mentally Disabled. American Bar Association, 1800 M. Street, N.W., Washington, D.C. 20036.

Council for Exceptional Children. 1920 Reston, Virginia. 22091.

Council of Organizations Serving the Deaf. 4201 Connecticut Avenue, N.W., Washington, D.C. 20008.

Day Care & Child Development Council of America, 1012 14th St., N.W., Washington, D.C. 20005.

Developmental Disabilities Planning & Advisory Council of Virginia. Suite 400, Travelers Building, 1108 E. Main Street, Richmond, Virginia, 23219.

Easter Seal Society for Crippled Children & Adults of Virginia. 4841 Williamson Road, P.O. Box 5496, Roanoke, Virginia 24012.

Educational Law Center, Inc., 2100 Lewis Tower Bldg., 225 S. 15th Street, Philadelphia, Pennsylvania. 19102.

Family Location & Legal Service. 33 W. 60th Street, New York, New York, 10023.

Goodwill Industries of America. 9200 Wisconsin Avenue, Washington, D.C 20014.

Law Enforcement Assistance Administration. U.S. Department of Justice, Washington, D.C. 20531.

Legal Service for the Elderly Poor. 2095 Broadway, New York, New York, 10023.

Library of Congress. Division for the Blind & Physically Handicapped, Washington, D.C. 20542.

Maternal & Child Health Service. Public Health Service. HEW, Rockville, Maryland 20852.

Mental Health Association. 1800 N, Kent Street, Arlington, Virginia 22209.

Mental Health Law Project. 1220 19th Street, N.W., Suite 300, Washington, D.C. 20036.

Mental Health Materials Center. 419 Park Avenue, S., New York, New York, 10016.

Mideast Regional Resource Center. 1901 Pennsylvania Avenue, N.W., Washington, D.C. 20036.

National Association for Retarded Citizens. 2709 Avenue E. East, P.O. Box 6109, Arlington, Texas, 76011.

National Association for the Visually Handicapped. 305 E. 25th Street, New York, New York, 10010.

National Association of School Psychologists. 1511 K. Street, Suite 331, Washington, D.C. 20005.

National Association of Social Workers. Sociological Work Career Information Service, 1425 H. Street, N.W., Suite 600, Washington, D.C. 20036.

National Association of State Directors of Special Education. 1201 Sixteenth Street, N.W., Washington, D.C., 20036.

National Center on Educational Media and Materials for Handicapped. Ohio State University, Columbus, Ohio, 43210.

National Center for Law and the Handicapped, Inc. 1235 North Eddy Street, South Bend, Indiana. 46617.

National Clearinghouse for Mental Health Information. National Institute of Mental Health, Public Inquiries Section, 5600 Fishers Lane, Rockville, Maryland, 20852.

National Committee for Citizens in Education. Wilde Lake Village Green, Suite 410, Columbia, Maryland, 21044.

National Committee for the Prevention of Child Abuse. 111 E. Wacker, Suite 510, Chicago, Illinois 60601.

National Council of Community Mental Health Centers. 2233 Wisconsin Avenue, N.W., Washington, D.C. 20007.

National Council of Organizations for Children and Youth. 1910 K. Street, N.W., Washington D.C. 20006.

National Council on Crime & Delinquency. Continental Plaza, 411 Hackensack Avenue, Hackensack, New Jersey, 07601.

National Easter Seal Society for Crippled Children and Adults. 2023 West Ogden Avenue, Chicago, Illinois, 60612. and Washington Building, 1435 G. St., N.W., Suite 1031-32, Washington, D.C. 20005.

National Education Association. 1201 16th St., N.W., Washington, D.C. 20036.

National Information Center for the Handicapped. Box 1492, Washington, D.C. 20013.

National Institute for Community Mental Health. 2233 Wisconsin Avenue, N.W., Suite 322. Washington, D.C. 20007.

National Institute on Crime and Delinquency. 703 Market St., San Francisco, California, 94103.

National Organization of Legal Problems of Education. 825 Western Avenue, Topeka, Kansas, 66606.

National Rehabilitation Association. 1522 K. St., N.W., Washington, D.C. 20005.

National Rehabilitation Counseling Association. 1522 K. St., N.W., Suite 1100, Washington, D.C. 20005.

National Society for Autistic Children. 169 Tampa Avenue, Albany, New York, 12208.

National Welfare Rights Organization. Poverty Rights Action Center, 1420 N. St., N.W., Washington, D.C. 20005.

Office of Developmental Disabilities. U.S. Dept. Health, Ed. & Welfare, MES Memorial Bldg., 330 C. St., S.W., Washington, D.C. 20201.

President's Committee on Mental Retardation. 7th and D Sts., N.W., Washington, D.C. 20201.

Research for Better Schools, Inc., Suite 1700, 1700 Market St., Philadelphia, Pennsylvania.

Society for Research in Child Development. University of Chicago, 5801 Ellis Avenue, Chicago, Illinois, 60637.

United States Government Printing Office, Superintendent of Documents, Washington, D.C. 20402.

INDEX